T0300882

AFRICAN ISSUES

Land,
Investment
& Politics

AFRICAN ISSUES

AFRICAN ISSUES

Land, Investment & Politics

Edited by
Jeremy Lind,
Doris Okenwa
& Ian Scoones

Reconfiguring
Eastern Africa's
Pastoral Drylands

JAMES CURREY

James Currey
an imprint of
Boydell & Brewer Ltd
PO Box 9, Woodbridge
Suffolk IP12 3DF (GB)
www.jamescurrey.com
and of
Boydell & Brewer Inc.
668 Mt Hope Avenue
Rochester, NY 14620-2731 USA
www.boydellandbrewer.com

British Library Cataloguing in Publication Data
A catologue record for this book is available on request from the British Library

ISBN 978-1-84701-252-4 (James Currey hardback)
ISBN 978-1-84701-249-4 (James Currey paper)

The publisher has no responsibility for the continued existence or accuracy of URLs for
external or third-party internet websites referred to in this book, and does not guarantee
that any content on such websites is, or will remain, accurate or appropriate.

This publication is printed on acid-free paper

Typeset in 9/11 Melior with Optima display
by Kate Kirkwood Publishing Services

'Anyone with an interest in pastoral development – whether policy-maker, practitioner, pastoralist or investor – will find important lessons in this book. It shows how the institutional landscape shaping investment in Eastern Africa's drylands is becoming ever more complex – and that pastoralists themselves are key players in this. Investment strategies will only succeed if they are rooted in a thorough understanding of pastoral livelihoods and societies. This book is a welcome and timely addition to that body of knowledge.' – *Hon. Mohamed Elmi, former Minister of State for Development of Northern Kenya and other Arid Lands*

'This book convincingly puts to rest the idea that the pastoral drylands of Eastern Africa operate outside global circuits of finance, investment, security and politics. Indeed, through a series of carefully theorised and documented case studies, the volume shows that these lands represent a new frontier of global capitalism that brings together complex and con-tested alliances of private investors, state actors and local elites. The book will be of great interest to researchers, practitioners and students of development studies, political economy, African studies and a range of the social sciences.'
– *Peter D. Little, Director, Emory Program in Development Studies, Emory University*

'This is a brilliant book that stretches the boundary of what we know and how we think about the land rush, how it unfolds in various societies in the world, such as pastoralist communities, and its implications for various spheres of social life in Africa and more globally. Academics, policymakers and activists working in various fields and disciplines, in the Global South and North, must read this book.' – *Saturnino M. Borras Jr, International Institute of Social Studies (ISS), The Hague*

'In bringing the specificities of recent large-scale natural resource acquisi-tions of Africa's drylands to attention, this book is a timely and valuable reminder of how agro-ecological factors and climate change shape how smallholders and pastoralists experience and fight back against such life-changing disruptions.' – *Dzodzi Tsikata, Director, Institute of African Studies, University of Ghana*

CONTENTS

12

13

14

LIST OF MAPS, TABLES & FIGURES

NOTES ON CONTRIBUTORS

Gregory Akall completed his doctoral research in Geography at the University of Cambridge, UK. His research interests focus on the political ecology of irrigation development in drylands and farmer-led agricultural investments. His current work explores climate-induced displacements. He is a postgraduate member of the British Institute in Eastern Africa and an affiliate member of the Omo-Turkana Research Network (OTuRN).

Adriana Blache is a PhD researcher at Toulouse University, France. Her doctoral research examines the intersection of large-scale agricultural investments and environmental conservation in the Kilombero Valley of south-western Tanzania. With support from the French Institute for Research in Africa (IFRA), and the Rurban Africa ('African Rural-City Connections) research programme, she spent 13 months conducting fieldwork in Kilombero investigating changes in livelihoods and power relationships relating to processes of agricultural commercialisation that have accelerated as part of the Southern Agricultural Growth Corridor of Tanzania (SAGCOT) project.

Ngala Chome is a PhD candidate in African History at Durham University, UK. His research covers the politics of electoral participation, development and religion. Previously he was Graduate Attaché at the British Institute in Eastern Africa, Nairobi, and a Commonwealth Shared Scholar at the Centre of African Studies, University of Edinburgh, Scotland. He is guest-editor of a special issue of the Journal of Eastern African Studies that examines the political economy of growth corridors in Eastern Africa. His articles have appeared in *African Affairs*, *Afrique Contemporaine*, *Critical African Studies* and the *Journal of Eastern African Studies*.

James Drew teaches within the Departments of Geography, Anthropology and International Development at the University of Sussex. His doctoral research, entitled 'Pastoralism in the Shadow of a Windfarm: An Ethnography of People, Places and Belonging in Northern Kenya', was based on ethnographic fieldwork in northern Kenya between 2013 and 2015. During fieldwork he was a member of the British Institute in Eastern Africa.

Hannah Elliott is a social anthropologist and Postdoctoral Research Fellow at the Copenhagen Business School, Denmark, where she is undertaking research on the production of certified sustainable tea in Kenya as part of SUSTEIN, a project that is affiliated with the British Institute in Eastern Africa. She holds a PhD in African Studies from the University of Copenhagen for which she conducted research on anticipatory property making in Isiolo town in northern Kenya. Hannah has conducted research in Kenya since 2009, with a number of projects connected to and funded by the British Institute in Eastern Africa, including as part of the institute's graduate attachment programme.

Linda Engström is a researcher at the Department for Urban and Rural Development at the Swedish University for Agricultural Sciences, Uppsala, Sweden. Her research interests include development policy and agricultural commercialisation, finance and development, natural resource investment, poverty and rural property rights. Linda also works as an adviser to the Swedish Development Cooperation Agency, Sida.

Fana Gebresenbet is an Assistant Professor at the Institute for Peace and Security Studies of Addis Ababa University. His research interests focus on the politics of development and political economy of developmentalism, particularly in South Omo and Gambella, Ethiopia's pastoral margins. He has published articles in the *Review of African Political Economy* and *Africa Spectrum*, and has authored a chapter in *Trajectory of Land Reform in Post-Colonial African States* (A. Akinola and H. Wissink, eds, 2018).

Marie Ladekjær Gravesen is a cultural and social anthropologist, currently undertaking postdoctoral research at the Danish Institute for International Studies as part of the project Governing Climate Mobility. She has conducted research on the social-ecological dynamics and resilience of East African landscapes, focusing particularly on the highly contested character of land claims on Kenya's Laikipia plateau. Her findings demonstrate how these conflicts have emerged and shifted over time, offering insight on other similarly socially fragmented areas with contestations over land. Her PhD from the University of Cologne was carried out as part of the Resilience in East African Landscapes (REAL) programme in collaboration with the British Institute in Eastern Africa.

Clemens Greiner is a cultural and social anthropologist and currently the academic coordinator of the Global South Studies Center (GSSC) at the University of Cologne, Germany. He is member of the Future Rural Africa Consortium led by the Universities of Cologne and Bonn, in partnership with the British Institute in Eastern Africa. His research interests include political ecology, rural change, migration and translocality. He has done extensive fieldwork in Kenya and Namibia on land use and agrarian changes in pastoral environments. He has published articles in *African Affairs, Africa Spectrum, Development and Change* and the *Journal of Eastern African Studies.*

Jeremy Lind is Research Fellow at the Institute of Development Studies (IDS) at the University of Sussex, UK. He leads a research theme on livestock commercialisation for the Agricultural Policy Research in Africa programme. He works on livelihoods, pastoralism, extractionist development, and conflict, focusing on Kenya and Ethiopia. He co-edited *Pastoralism and Development in Africa* (2013) and has authored articles in *Development and Change, Political Geography, Environmental Management* and *Peacebuilding.*

Ahmed M. Musa is a PhD researcher in Dryland Resource Management at the Department of Land Resource Management and Agricultural Technology, University of Nairobi, Kenya. His doctoral research funded by the Governing Economic Hubs and Flows in Somali East Africa (GOVSEA) project focuses on post-1991 livestock trade in Somaliland's Berbera corridor. He is the co-author of 'State Formation and Economic Development in Post-war Somaliland: The Impact of the Private Sector in an Unrecognised State' (with Cindy Horst, *Conflict, Security & Development,* 2019).

Doris Okenwa completed her doctoral research in Anthropology at the London School of Economics (LSE), UK. Her PhD focuses on the generative potentials of uncertainty and how legacies of marginalisation and the discovery of oil combine to create new notions of 'rightful share'. The research is based on ethnographic fieldwork in Turkana County, the host community of Kenya's oil, and follows the various forms of negotiations around oil benefits. Doris is affiliated to the British Institute in Eastern Africa, the Omo-Turkana Research Network (OTuRN) and the Royal Africa Society in London.

Simone Rettberg holds a PhD in Geography from the University of Bayreuth, Germany. Simone is a senior lecturer in the Department of Geography at the University of Bonn and also a consultant in pastoral areas. Major past research projects have focused on issues of risk and vulnerability, conflict studies, and political ecology with a regional focus on Eastern Africa. Over the last 15 years, Simone has done extensive fieldwork on these topics in the pastoral drylands of Ethiopia and Djibouti.

Cory Rodgers is the Pedro Arrupe Research Fellow in the Refugee Studies Centre at the University of Oxford, UK. His doctoral research involved over two years of fieldwork in Turkana County, where he studied development-induced social differentiation between rural pastoralists and urban dwellers. His current work focuses on the relationships between herders and refugees living in the Kakuma camps, also in Turkana County.

Ian Scoones is a professorial Fellow at the Institute of Development Studies at the University of Sussex and is co-director of the ESRC STEPS (Social, Technological and Environmental Pathways to Sustainability) Centre. He currently leads the European Research Council-funded project, PASTRES (Pastoralism, Uncertainty and Resilience). He is a member of the editorial collective of *The Journal of Peasant Studies*. His recent books include *Africa's Land Rush: Rural Livelihoods and Agrarian Change, Sustainable Livelihoods and Rural Development* and *Zimbabwe's Land Reform: Myths and Realities*.

ACKNOWLEDGEMENTS

We met many people during the past few years to discuss the debates and themes covered in this book. We thank them for challenging our own thinking and in doing so to widen the perspectives shared in this book. The UK African Studies Association at the University of Birmingham offered an opportunity for debating early versions of many of the chapters during a series of panel discussions across several days in September 2018.

We gratefully acknowledge the UK Department for International Development who funded our work through the Agricultural Policy Research in Africa Consortium (www.future-agricultures.org/apra). We would also like to acknowledge support from the European Research Council through an Advanced Grant for the PASTRES (Pastoralism, Uncertainty, Resilience: Lessons from the Margins) project (www.pastres. org).

A few individuals provided critical support to complete the book, and we extend our immense gratitude to them: Monica Allen for accomplished copy-editing, John Hall for precise maps and Oliver Burch for tireless administrative assistance. We also thank two external peer reviewers for helpful comments. Finally, we thank Jaqueline Mitchell, our commissioning editor at James Currey and Lynn Taylor, managing editor, for their steady hands in seeing the book through to completion.

This volume follows, wherever possible, the Ethiopian naming system wherein the first name and the name of the father or grandfather are given in full in that order.

ABBREVIATIONS

BCP	biocultural community protocol
BRN	Big Results Now
CLO	community liaison officer
EPRDF	Ethiopian People's Revolutionary Democratic Front
FAO	Food and Agriculture Organization of the United Nations
FPIC	Free Prior Informed Consent
GDC	Geothermal Development Company
KISEDP	Kalobeyei Integrated Social and Economic Development Programme
KPL	Kilombero Plantation Ltd
LAPSSET	Lamu Port–South Sudan–Ethiopia Transport
LBC	land-buying companies
LTWP	Lake Turkana Wind Power
MCA	Member of the County Assembly
MoU	Memorandum of Understanding
NGO	non-governmental organisation
NIB	National Irrigation Board
NLC	National Land Commission
NORAD	Norwegian Agency for Development Cooperation
OECD	Organisation for Economic Co-operation and Development
RUBADA	Rufiji Basin Development Agency
SAGCOT	Southern Agricultural Growth Corridor of Tanzania
Sida	Swedish International Development Cooperation Agency
SRI	System of Rice Intensification
TAZARA	Tanzania Zambia Railway Authority
TISA	Turkwel Irrigation Scheme Association
TRDP	Turkana Rehabilitation Development Programme
UAE	United Arab Emirates
UNHCR	Office of the United Nations High Commissioner for Refugees
WFP	World Food Programme
WUA	water users association

1

Introduction   The Politics of Land,
Resources & Investment
in Eastern Africa's
Pastoral Drylands

JEREMY LIND, DORIS OKENWA
& IAN SCOONES

The rush for land and resources has featured prominently in recent studies of sub-Saharan Africa. Often happening alongside regional projects to upgrade and expand infrastructure, this urgency to unlock untapped economic potential has generated heated debate around the social and environmental impacts, as well as consequences for livelihoods, rights and benefit sharing.[1] More than ever before, the gaze of global investment has been directed to the pastoral drylands of Africa. This matters because of the varied land and natural resource uses, social organisation and the histories and legacies of development that are unique to these areas. Given ecological uncertainty and the patchy distribution of resources, adaptability and flexibility have been the basis for sustaining lives and livelihoods in the drylands (Catley et al. 2013b; Mortimore and Adams 1999; Scoones 1994).

The organisation of dryland societies emphasises decentralised decision-making, meaning that many voices count in deciding on land and resource uses. Tenure systems privilege the rights of groups to gain access to resources, as well as passage to move herds between key resource areas. Opportunism, such as in cultivating a riverbank after a seasonal flood, expanding the size of herds in good years or migrating further afield in search of alternative work and sustenance, defines livelihood strategies for many (Oba 2013; Little and Leslie 1999; Behnke et al. 1993). All these facets of dryland livelihoods suggest that the impacts and influences of large-scale investments in land, resources and infrastructure unfold in ways that are specific to dryland settings.

The unprecedented increase of investments in these areas also matters because, until recently, state planners and investors overlooked

---

[1] See for example, Enns et al. 2019; Stein and Kalina 2019; Enns 2019, 2018; Smalley 2017; World Bank 2017; Pedersen and Buur 2016; Ferguson 2015; Hall et al. 2015a, 2015c; Laurance et al. 2015; Cotula et al. 2014; Weng et al 2013; Mulenga 2013; Cotula 2013; Borras and Franco 2013; Edelman et al. 2013; White et al. 2013; Wolford et al. 2013; Fairhead et al. 2012; Mehta et al. 2012; Moyo et al. 2012; Borras et al. 2011, among many others focusing on the intersections of land, water and green grabbing and investment.

drylands. The assumption was that drylands were 'low potential' areas – unsuitable for farming – and thus were relegated as sites for investment. The prevailing notion was that pastoral land uses were destructive and inherently unproductive. Pastoralism as a way of life was and continues in many ways to be seen as outdated, backward and ill-fitting in a contemporary nation-state. The presence of central state power and corporate capital was previously minimal in such areas, but when state plans and capital investments arrived, new negotiations over rights and access unfolded.

The recent land and resource rush thus upends established patterns of state–society relations in the drylands. No longer seen as threatening borderlands in need of pacification, or low potential wastelands that can be ignored, in public and policy imaginations these areas are now seen as frontiers with abundant land and resources that can be exploited for national wealth (Greiner 2016; Mosley and Watson 2016; Browne 2015). The land rush marks a moment of repositioning for pastoralist frontiers in national development strategies and economic planning. The shift is all the more notable when considering that it follows decades of underinvestment and marginalisation by post-colonial governments. Ports, pipelines, roads, wind farms and plantations are all linked in the 'high modernist'[2] visions of states and private capital (Ferguson 2005; cf. Scott 1998).

Such large-scale investments are portrayed as part of wider commercialisation and growth imperatives, and even as a precursor to peacebuilding and the creation of 'resilient' livelihoods for pastoralists (Smalley 2017; Nicol 2015). Yet investments come up against the reality of existing intricacies of social and economic practices, and embedded regional systems of marketing and trade; they are always therefore tentative, provisional and in the process of becoming realised (Enns et al. 2019; Stein and Kalina 2019). The colonial depiction of these places on maps as 'uninhabited' or 'wilderness' is updated in new frontier visions as expanses of land that are cheap and for sale, while ignoring overlapping claims to land and resources, based on ancestral precedence, communal histories and practices of making use of these environments over generations.

Many influential actors are involved in the global investment push from international corporates to states and local elites, very often in interaction (Keene et al. 2015; Margulis et al. 2013; Wolford et al. 2013). But important questions are raised about who benefits and who loses out, and whether such large-scale projects do indeed deliver poverty-reducing development, as is often claimed.

---

[2] 'High modernism' refers to an unfaltering belief in the power of science, technology and expertise to transform nature and generate an ordered, legible, technology-driven modernity. Characteristic of the development plans of the 1960s and 70s, the features are replicated in the designs, for example, of investment corridors and grid-like plans for infrastructure development today.

As the chapters in this book show, this new emphasis on developing pastoralist areas through investment in resources, land, infrastructure and small towns is resulting in new forms of territorialisation, contentious politics and social difference. The chapters that follow address three related questions. First, what do investments look like and who frames their meaning, interpretation and pursuit? Second, how are investments generating wider impacts, and who wins and loses? Finally, what types of resistance, mobilisation, subversion and forms of contentious politics arise?

While states and investors continue to envision large investments as part of a wider vision of growth and transformation, seen from the dryland margins, struggles around the framing and meanings given to oil, wind, livestock, land and water are the crux of many contestations. By examining the ways in which large-scale investments enmesh with local political and social relations, the chapters show how, even the most elaborate plans of financiers, contractors and national governments, come unstuck and are re-made in the guise of not only states' high modernist visions, but also those of herders and small-town entrepreneurs in the pastoral drylands.

Changes in the drylands

The chapters offer local cases of investment from across Eastern Africa, stretching from the Gulf of Aden ports on Somaliland's coast in the north to the Kilombero rice developments in southern Tanzania (see Map 1.1). Dryland Eastern Africa – far from being at the periphery of regional integration and global economic change – sits at the centre of evolving systems of trade, investment and security that knit Africa ever more closely with Western Europe (Borras et al. 2019; Antonelli et al. 2015), Turkey (Donelli 2017), the Arabian Peninsula (Keulertz 2016; Woertz 2013b), Russia (Oğultürk 2017; Andreff 2016), India (Carmody 2013), Brazil (Cabral et al. 2013) and China (Brautigam and Zhang 2013), as well as other parts of the continent, notably South Africa (Hall and Cousins 2018). Many investments do not come from a single country, as commercial financing and development investments may involve multiple partners (Cousins et al. 2018; Keulertz and Woertz 2016; Scoones et al. 2016; Allan et al. 2012). A web of transnational relations is generated that links states and private capital through a complex mix of finance flows, including private companies, finance capital funds, public–private partnerships and development finance (Borras et al. 2019; also Clapp and Isakson 2018; Ouma 2016). Much is opaque, making it often very difficult to trace the origins of investment finance.

Many such networks have long existed (Bose 2009; Beaujard and Fee 2005), but the intensification and spread of capitalist relations and new investment in dryland Eastern Africa is changing social, economic

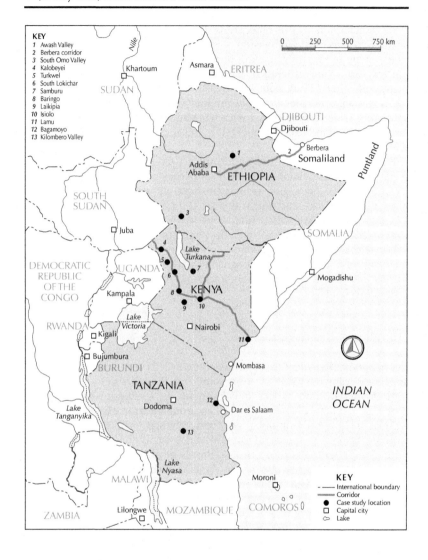

Map 1.1 Eastern Africa, showing case study sites

and political dynamics.[3] These perhaps have the greatest impact on the region's pastoral and agro-pastoral populations. Dryland Eastern Africa is home to the largest population in the world still active in pastoralism (Schlee and Shongolo 2012) – estimated at 12 million to 22 million people, accounting for more than 60 per cent of the world's total surface area supporting pastoral production systems (World Bank 2014).

Changes in the region's economic life bring into sharp focus the transformations in capitalism and capital that are reconfiguring political and social orders more widely. Droughts in the early 1980s devastated livestock herds throughout the region, precipitating migrations of destitute herders in search of new livelihoods and relief (Adepoju 1995). Combined with other demographic and social trends, many pastoralists began to settle. State, non-governmental organisation (NGO) and church efforts to provide services – schools, health centres and water points – encouraged wider sedentarisation and the growth of small towns (Homewood et al. 2009; Little et al. 2008; Fratkin and Roth 2006; Salih et al. 1995). As growing numbers of pastoralists settled, states and donors promoted irrigation as a way of turning pastoralists into full-time farmers. However, most schemes were capital intensive, technically complex and dependent on heavy machinery, which left the sustainability of the schemes ultimately dependent on external commitments and expertise (Sandford 2013; Unruh 1990; Adams and Anderson 1988; Hogg 1983).[4] This meant many ex-pastoralist farmers had to rely on food aid and loans of inputs to cobble together an existence. Unsurprisingly, many sought to reinvest in livestock-keeping as the surest way of making a living (Hogg 1987b), a trend that continues in the current regime of large-scale investments and advancement of global capital.

[3] The World Bank's *World Development Indicators* (https://databank.worldbank.org, accessed 6 November 2019) include 'Foreign direct investment, net inflows (BoP, current US$)'. The data below in million US$ for selected countries and dates show (outside Eritrea) the massive increase in FDI since 2000, although much variation. The data of course rely on reported inflows and government statistics, and do not include informal transfers, including remittances.

	1977	1993	2000	2005	2010	2015	2018
Ethiopia	5.85	3.50	134.64	265.11	288.27	2,626.52	3,310.30
Kenya	56.55	145.66	110.90	21.21	178.06	619.72	1,625.92
Eritrea			27.87	1.43	91.00	49.32	61.02
Somalia	7.78	2.00	0.27	24.00	112.00	303.00	409.00
Sudan	8.27	-0.16	392.20	1,561.69	2,063.73	1,728.37	1,135.79
Uganda	0.80	54.60	160.70	379.81	543.87	737.65	1,337.13
Tanzania	2.94	20.46	463.40	935.52	1813.20	1,604.58	1,104.80

[4] Data on total irrigated area across countries are scarce, but in Kenya the area under 'full control irrigation' increased from 73,000 ha in 1990 to 100,000 ha in 2003 to 140,200 ha in 2010, including investment in irrigation schemes in dryland areas (www.fao.org/aquastat, accessed 6 November 2019).

By the late 1990s, small towns had grown beyond their roots as sites of government offices, relief distribution centres and points for basic service delivery. In many areas, the settlement of refugees and internally displaced people from the region's conflicts added substantially to the population of such towns (Jacobsen 2002; De Montclos and Kagwanja 2000). Many were integrated into local economic life; sharing knowledge and business acumen (Alix-Garcia et al. 2018; Sanghi et al. 2016). Starting at first with small shops and vegetable stalls, often established by savvy refugees and migrants, business activities proliferated and diversified, as new entrepreneurs sought to emulate the success of pioneer shopkeepers and traders (Rawlence 2016; Fratkin 2013). This redefined the value of land and fuelled the growth of local capital as town dwellers and businesspeople took to fencing plots in anticipation of urban expansion. Local business elites anticipated opportunities to accumulate and diversify their wealth, investing in everything from rental housing in towns to transport services and fenced areas for private grazing (Caravani 2018; Korf et al. 2015). As Clemens Greiner shows in his chapter, recent trends in large-scale investments are not entirely responsible for changes in land-use patterns and social differentiation. Rather, they are occurring alongside long-term developments in Africa's drylands.

Beyond such towns and market centres, individuals fenced land to establish medium and small-scale ranches for hired grazing (Catley and Yacob Aklilu 2013; Tache 2013). As national government and aid investment in the drylands expanded in the early 2000s, more people invested in boreholes and leased grazing to herders (Flintan et al. 2011; Eriksen and Lind 2009). Small irrigation schemes established with private capital emerged across the region as local investors sought to supply valuable vegetables and fruits to local markets (Sandford 2013). Transport services, from motorbikes to public service vehicles and lorries, swelled in spite of poor infrastructure (Nunow 2013). This encouraged new marketing and trade activities in livestock, building materials, wild foods and charcoal (Devereux 2006).

While generating substantial wealth for some, processes of territorialisation have had profound consequences for livestock-keeping, social relations and conflict. The carving up of rangelands, through the establishment of private enclosures, water points and cisterns, agricultural and fodder plots, ranches and conservation areas, directly threatens adaptive processes in customary pastoralist systems (Reid et al. 2008). Movements become more difficult to make and key resource areas are fenced and set aside for non-livestock uses (Flintan et al. 2011). Resource claim-making by a new class of entrepreneurial pastoral capitalists has tested customary social relations based on resource sharing and reciprocal help within horizontal networks. Many local resource users deeply resent paying for grazing in fenced sites, or for water from a private borehole, in social settings where identity, belonging and kinship connections were the basis for determining rights to access and passage (Eriksen and Lind 2009).

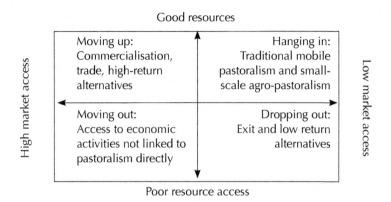

Figure 1.1 Pastoralist livelihood pathways in eastern Africa

Beyond the resultant resentment and tension, hostility has increased to pastoralists from other areas who pay to gain access to fenced enclosures and private boreholes. Conflicts in the drylands are transforming in other ways, as well, as the value of land increases (Cormack and Kurewa 2018). Traditional resource-based conflicts and livestock theft are driven by wider economic agendas and are becoming more difficult to resolve as relations fragment within groups, and between neighbouring societies (Lind 2018; Korf et al. 2015; Raeymaekers 2013; Hagmann and Alemmaya Mulugeta 2008).

Livelihood transformation and changes in this dynamic context are thus complex and contradictory. Rangeland fragmentation, sedentarisation, small-town growth, commercialisation and infrastructural investment, among others, are reshaping access to resources (to support herds) and markets (for livestock and other goods). This, in turn, is driving decisions about livelihood choices and creating new livelihood pathways for the region's dryland populations.

Catley et al. (2013) distinguish four different pathways for pastoral livelihoods depending on access to resources (a continuum of good to poor) and markets (a continuum of high to low) (see Figure 1.1, also Dorward et al. 2009). Areas and people with good natural resource access and access to markets are *moving up*, because they are able to maintain and sell livestock as a successful business enterprise, commercialising the milk and livestock trade, selling in high export zones, creating private abattoirs and finding lucrative opportunities along the livestock value chain. Areas and people with good access to natural resources, rangeland and water sources in particular, but who do not have a high level of market access are *hanging in*, practising customary forms of pastoralism based on high mobility, extended social ties for trade, and opportunistic use of key resource patches within the wider landscape. However, as already noted, rangeland fragmentation is constraining traditional mobile pastoralism because pastoralists are less able to gain access to the key resources that are needed to manage uncertainty.

When a livestock herd is no longer viable owing to lack of good resource access or inadequate markets, the household exits pastoralism, *dropping out*, at which point its members seek productive activities not directly linked to their own herds or flocks. Others elect to pursue economic activities that are not linked to pastoralism directly but make use of good market access, *moving out*. The opportunity to step out of pastoralism into 'value-added diversification' is limited to those able to take advantage of resources that add a high return to their activities. Still, small-town expansion, better connections with larger centres and the younger generation's acceptance of non-traditional livelihoods are enabling some to earn a living from activities in the pastoral economy that are not directly linked to pastoralism.

The global land rush, and the associated changes in land values, patterns of investment and changes in economic opportunity in the dry-lands, affects these four ideal-type pathways in different ways. Processes of inclusion and exclusion in new economic activity – whether the establishment of a wind farm or the carving out of a wildlife conservancy – result in opportunities for some but challenges for others. The 'traditional' extensive, mobile form of pastoralism is increasingly constrained though land fragmentation and competition. Yet new investments may offer business openings for others, whether a small-scale service supplier in a regional town or an emergent capitalist land speculator. All these processes are radically transforming pastoralism across Eastern Africa, and the chapters that follow illustrate how.

The global land rush and its aftermath

Debates around the global land rush provide both the framing and the context for discussions around investments and new territorialisation pro-cesses in pastoral areas. Land-based investments have multiplied around the world since 2008, as global capital sought to secure returns following the financial crash (Clapp and Isakson 2018; Ouma 2016; Visser et al. 2015; Fairbairn 2014; White et al. 2013). Galaty (2014: 83) outlines three factors driving the upsurge in land acquisitions: food shortfalls, and the resultant rise in food commodity prices in 2008, indicated that farmland could represent a lucrative investment; the relative decline of available land in both industrialised and middle-income countries – a condition heightened in wealthy yet farmland-poor nations such as the Gulf states; and the perception that in some developing countries abundant land with agricultural potential was underutilised, cheap and available.

On the last point, many governments present their drylands as vast tracts of empty, marginal, uncultivated or inefficiently used land that can be deployed more profitably towards commercial agriculture (Hall et al. 2015a; Nalepa and Bauer 2012). Thus, land deals are justified by narratives of scarcity and abundance on both local and global scales (Scoones et al. 2019b; Mehta 2001).

The recent land rush of course has important precedents; whether gold rushes in the 1850s in the USA, the South Sea Bubble in 1720 in the UK, or the sudden spike (then collapse) in demand for tulip bulbs in Holland in the mid-1630s (Li 2014b: 595). What is distinctive about land acquisitions over the past decade is its temporality and scope. The geography is also striking: more than 40 per cent of concluded agricultural deals globally since 2000 have been in Africa according to figures from the Land Matrix (Nolte et al. 2016: 16). Africa also leads the world in terms of the size of land acquired by investors: 10 million hectares out of 26.7 million hectares globally (ibid.).[5]

Rather than the process of land becoming a commodity, representing the outcome of a historical expansion of property rights and the rule of law, it in fact usually results in the abrogation of the rights of landholders by the state, in the interest of elites and investors (Galaty 2014: 85). Speculative land investments, as land becomes an asset class, do not result in increased productivity, but very often in land lying idle (Clapp 2014; Fairbairn 2014). That land is 'available' does not refer to whether those with legitimate land rights are willing to part with it. What is often taken into account is if a firm can make an arrangement with political elites to acquire land, usually in the absence of consent or awareness of those holding the land in question. Taking this further, Tania Li cautions that consent can become a means of dispossession, when a 'customary chief', who claims to have jurisdiction over communal land, signs off

---

[5] Land Matrix offers data on concluded, intended and failed deals. However, much caution has to be attached to such figures (Scoones et al. 2013). The focus is on land extent, which of course underplays the importance of focused, enclave investments for mining, oil and gas extraction, for example. The data show total hectares and numbers of deals (in brackets) for the greater Horn region (www.landmatrix.org, accessed 6 November 2019; there is no data for Somalia, Somaliland or Eritrea, however):

Area in hectares (number of deals)	Concluded	Intended	Failed
Ethiopia	1,447,101 ha (121)	520,550 ha (14)	380,829 ha (15)
Kenya	478,103 ha (55)	135,659 ha (8)	390,575 ha (11)
Tanzania	735,859 ha (77)	296,300 ha (12)	681,017 ha (13)
South Sudan	2,571,982 ha (15)	1,483,020 ha (9)	424,300 ha (12)
Sudan	762,208 ha (33)	3,427,578 ha (10)	588,000 ha (4)
Uganda	273,250 ha (49)	12,500 ha (4)	847,975 ha (5)

on a land deal without consulting the people affected (Li 2014b: 598).

In *Africa's Land Rush*, nine contributions assessed the early impacts and influences of the post-2008 land-based investments (Hall et al. 2015c). They found that, while land deals often entailed enclaved investments and the (re)creation of agrarian dualism, with large estates and small-scale farms sitting alongside each other, on closer inspection patterns of change were more varied. Not all investments involved dispossession, as critics feared they would, nor did they imply a simple incorporation into global capitalism from a pre-capitalist state. Instead, the fate of African smallholders rests on the terms of their incorporation in investment deals – something requiring attention to multiple, coinciding processes of both inclusion and exclusion in the spread of capitalist relations. This suggests a focus on labour, technology, expertise and markets, as well as land. Processes of 'accumulation by dispossession' (Harvey 2003), driven by the global forces of financialised, neoliberal capitalism and supported by states, are thus made more complex by the intersection of the agency of local actors, institutions mediating resource access and the dynamics of differentiation across class, gender, age and ethnicity (Hall 2012, 2013).

This book updates the story of Africa's land rush with a focus on the drylands of Eastern Africa, asking what has happened over the past ten years? The chapters show how, far from resisting and obstructing invest-ment, many have sought to position themselves to benefit from land investments. A major result is the heightened tensions across groups, between emergent local capitalists and those whose access to land is curtailed. Poorer pastoralists may gain employment to complement or replace their livestock-based livelihoods, while those with small-town businesses may profit from a boom in the economy, especially during establishment and construction phases. Speculative behaviour in anticipation of future development frequently characterises local responses to investment in many areas. Hannah Elliott's chapter in this book investigates investments in land by residents of Isiolo, an important hub in northern Kenya along the planned multi-billion dollar Lamu Port–South Sudan–Ethiopia Transport Corridor (LAPSSET). Anticipatory actions by residents such as fencing, building, occupying, purchasing, and acquiring legal documents of land are reshaping the social and spatial outcomes of LAPSSET. While the LAPSSET proposals induced a rush for land in Isiolo, Elliott explains that this is more than individuals and groups seeking simple profit. Rather, many see their actions as staking a claim on the future city.

In his chapter, Ngala Chome explains how diverse local stakeholders have redefined the state's modernist plans for a new deep-water port in Lamu on Kenya's coast. While the port's construction advances, the wider impacts of LAPSSET in Lamu are felt through local struggles over ownership and control of land, linked to potential future benefits and sub-national contestations over political power. These dynamics have transformed what appears to be 'top-down', large-scale investment driven by the state's 'tunnel vision' of generating and extracting wealth at source into something that is intimately networked with local visions of investment and future economic relations.

The chapters in this book highlight the often unpredictable and unexpected consequences of large-scale investments when they encounter local economies and societies. Linda Engström's chapter, for example, examines the consequences of delays in project implementation in a case from Tanzania. The project simplifications resulted in an unravelling of the investment plan, but with major material consequences for those living in the area. Also in Tanzania, Adriana Blache examines a rice investment scheme that has generated multiple conflicts through the creation of different categories of 'squatter' vs. original dwellers, fostering resentment and resistance among local populations.

The social and spatial outcomes of investments do not reflect merely the state's high modernist vision of 'development', or the interests of large global capital. Anna Tsing's notion of 'friction' (2011), drawing on the analogy of a tyre hitting the road, aptly focuses attention on the interaction between broader – global, national – forces and diverse forms of local agency. Anticipatory actions by local-level actors, be they investments in land, resources and property; new forms of social mobilisation or alliance-making; or the establishment of businesses in the hope of winning contracts and tenders, reimagine and restructure the grand plans of states and investors. This renders the distinction between global capitalist forces and local places and peoples less pointed than is often portrayed in discourses on investment. Such encounters produce the diverse impacts and influences of investment and responses to these in local settings observed across the chapters.

In short, the 'local community' is not singular, and the potential for enrolling villagers may be bigger than it first appears (Li 2014b: 600). Fana Gebresenbet's chapter on local responses to state-building in Ethiopia's South Omo Valley underscores the temporality of investments and the different reactions on the ground. The state coerced small-scale herders and agro-pastoralists into volunteering their labour for road-building in the Benna-Tsemay area of South Omo in the 1960s. In subsequent years, the state encouraged private land investments, resulting in the dispossession of Tsemay herders from rangelands, as well as the destruction of valued beehives. Workers brought in from other parts of Ethiopia bred hostility and conflict. Yet a longer trajectory of change in Benna-Tsemay has seen the growth of towns, services and marketing linked to better infrastructure and transport services in the region. Over time, the chapter shows, local attitudes to large-scale investment, even those involving the fencing of land and resources, have mellowed.

The outcomes of large investments are thus uncertain and contingent on a number of coinciding processes of enclosure, commercialisation, commodification and financialisation of land, resources and agriculture, as well as responses to these by residents of communities in investment areas.

Visions of the frontier and the making of resource value

This brief overview of debates on land deals sets up our exploration of investments in pastoral areas throughout the book. Not all of these are investments in land for agriculture – they also include exploration for oil and gas, efforts to harness green energy such as wind and geothermal, infrastructure such as roads and airports, and also abattoirs and other infrastructure for encouraging greater livestock marketing.

Common to both wider debates on the global land rush and narrower discussions around investments in pastoral areas is the notion of the frontier. Official justifications for large-scale investment in pastoralist areas often speak to frontier discourses – of growing economies and improving lives through the transformative power of large and capital-intensive projects. Previously 'untapped' regions become reimagined, revalued and re-made into new 'resource frontiers' of global capital. As Tsing (2011: 29) aptly notes, 'most descriptions of resource frontiers take for granted the existence of resources, they label and count the resources and tell us who owns what. The landscape itself appears inert: ready to be dismembered and packaged for export.' Thus, the frontier is not just 'a matter of political definition of a geographical space', as Kopytoff (1987a: 11) suggests, but a particular configuration of values and institutions related to the advancement of extraction and commodification, as defining features of capitalist development (Rasmussen and Lund 2018).

Imaginations of the frontier often reflect notions of civilisation and progress. As Clemens Greiner explains in his chapter, the idea of the frontier owes much to Frederick Jackson Turner's conceptualisation of the American westward expansion in the nineteenth and early twentieth centuries. While the American expansion was associated with rugged individualism and 'the wild west', the frontier of today's large-scale investment in pastoral areas has more in common with a penetration-type spread of capitalist relations and the reassertion of centralised state power. These are not the wagons and pioneer families moving west in search of a better life; these are the Learjets and executives of FTSE-listed oil, mining and biofuel companies in search of new resource wealth, with convoys of Land Cruisers ferrying ministers and presidential advisers from capital cities to sites where projects are imagined or unfolding.

In both cases, frontiers represent the discovery or invention of new resources (Rasmussen and Lund 2018) – land for commercial agricultural enterprises, hydrocarbon reservoirs beneath rangelands, other energy from subterranean steam and wind, and even pastoral populations themselves being drawn into wider markets for everything from pasteurised long-life milk to mobile phones and online betting. Thus, the dynamics that link space and resources are not a function of mere distance, but a particular configuration of values and institutions related to the advancement of extraction and commodification as defining features of capitalist development (Rasmussen and Lund 2018). Or, as Geiger (2008) explains, based on evidence from Latin America and Asia, the frontier is a zone of destruction of property systems, political structures, social relations and life worlds to make way for new ways of resource extraction.

In Africa, large-scale investments are inseparable from state visions of throwing off aid dependency and achieving rapid economic growth and national transformation (Mosley and Watson 2016). Thus, states are discovering resources in pastoral areas that can sustain national economic development and ambition for rapid industrialisation. Simone Rettberg's chapter shows how these dynamics have unfolded over a sixty-year period in the Awash Valley in Ethiopia's eastern lowlands. Successive regimes have sought to deepen and expand large-scale sugar plantations established on rangelands used by Afar herders. Increasingly, these have come to define the state's interest in the region, away from establishing a security buffer with neighbouring states and instead to asserting the state's claim to national resource wealth. Over time, far from resisting state-driven territorialisation, Afar elites have become complicit in seeking personal advantage from the state's agricultural investments.

The frontier is not a boundary between civilisation and wilderness, but rather a relational space that is characterised by interaction, connections and conflict (Goodhand 2018; Van Schendel 2005). Frontier dynamics emerge from the 'messiness' of competing spatial imaginations, and disputes over territorial claims, as existing institutional orders are unsettled, uprooted and ultimately reconfigured as new kinds of resources become subject to governance (Boone 2014; Lund and Boone 2013; Sassen 2008). Greiner's chapter describes the unfolding of these dynamics in Baringo in Kenya's northern Rift Valley. In the state's vision, Baringo is an unexploited frontier whose subterranean geothermal wealth can fuel Kenya's rapid national transformation. Yet this Turner-like imagination of Baringo as a frontier to be civilised in the interest of national development enmeshes with the frontier-making practices of the area's Pokot elites. These are akin to Igor Kopytoff's 'internal African frontier' (1987a): elites are at the forefront of land privatisation, involving the fencing of the most valuable land along new roads linking Baringo's geothermal sites with national infrastructure. Uncertainty in institutions and the threat of violence to stake claims are central to frontier-making.

Thus, this book argues, there are many ways of 'seeing' large-scale investment in the drylands. State actors at the national level see investments as engines for national transformation, which is inherently good for dryland areas with legacies of marginalisation and underinvestment. Invariably, investors promote the benefits of project activity to residents of nearby communities, through the construction of new infrastructure, easing transport difficulties and promoting marketing activity, providing opportunities for work, and creating corporate social investments in bursaries, classrooms and the provision of water, for example. State actors at the sub-national level may not see investments in the same way, however, depending on how power constitutes at the centre and the status of state–society relations in their area. The position of sub-national political administrations can waver between embrace and hostility. Mixed views of large-scale investments often hold among local capital, as well. Ultimately, investment is something to be welcomed, but the terms of inclusion in land deals, compensation, and contract and tendering opportunities dictate the nature of politics. The views of other dryland residents, small-scale pastoralists and dryland farmers, cover a spectrum, from opposition and resistance to the perceived loss of key grazing resources and farmland, to accommodation in anticipation of deriving personal benefit, to simple antipathy.

As argued in *Africa's Land Rush* (Hall et al. 2015c: 24), simple narratives of the 'state' and/or 'investor' versus 'local people' do not relay the more complex dynamics and assemblages of interests that mobilise behind, anticipate and pursue large-scale investments. In the following sections, we outline four ways of 'seeing', from different standpoints. Across these, it is the production and attainment of wealth and control that mediates relationships between actors, creating a complex politics of investment in the drylands. Of course, these actors overlap and intersect, with for example, global capital supported by states and local elites in the acquisition and governance of land and resources (Wolford et al. 2013). But, as a challenge to normative perspectives of mainstream development and investments, exploring competing ways of 'seeing' invites a robust debate on how these developments are unfolding at the margins.

The chapters that follow emphasise how winners and losers emerge from anticipation, contention and the multiple ways of seeing an investment. How states, global investors and non-state actors frame investments often diverges from local interpretations, as the cases in this book show.

Seeing like a state

The promotion of large-scale investment in dryland Eastern Africa is part of a wider vision of regional economic integration and transformation of the rural frontier, generating legible order for investment, thus 'seeing like a state' (Scott 1998; see below). From the perspective of states, large-scale infrastructure and resource developments are benign and even positive as they connect remote rural areas to larger markets and improve accessibility to outside investors, traders and service providers – be they government departments or other charitable and private agencies. Thus, integration, involving investment in trade and transport corridors to move goods, services and people between coasts and resource-rich hinterlands, is seen as central to development and economic growth, and even bringing peace to restive pastoral areas. However, the very idea of state-sanctioned investments as a type of new development that can bring about peace and stability stands in stark contrast with the experience of Eastern Africa's pastoralist societies in their encounters with state power over time. State violence against pastoralists is part of a long history of a 'civilising' mission to bring peace and impose a new social order, as the chapters by Fana Gebresenbet and Rettberg show.

Unsurprisingly, institutions of the state that were introduced – subnational political administration and other elements of the security apparatus – were mistrusted by dryland societies in many places where wide-scale violence against pastoralists was the official policy of colonial states and other central authorities (Vaughan 2013; Hagmann and Korf 2012; Lamphear 1992). The response of pastoralists in such areas was to seek an escape from the state's reach by resisting incorporation and other external imposition, avoiding taxation and maintaining an apparently war-like stance in relation to state attempts to impose its will (Catley et al. 2013).

Comparisons can be made between the experience of African pastoralist societies and the mobile swidden agriculturalists of the south-east Asian highlands that James Scott (2009) discusses in his book, *The Art of Not Being Governed*. As he explains, hill peoples operate outside the reaches of the state's authority when they can. State authority came not only through the threat of force, but also through the imposition of its vision of 'development'. Scott (1998: 88) likens state visions with 'high modernism', whose ideological variants incorporate 'a sweeping, rational engineering of all aspects of social life in order to improve the human condition'. Adding to this, Li (2007) contends that high modernist projects, like growth corridors, are framed by a so-called 'will to improve' by development donors and states, in line with a particular vision of progress. Central to Scott's (1998) thesis is the idea of legibility. His research on state efforts to settle or 'sedentarise' nomads, pastoralists, gypsies and people living outside mainstream society led him to the conclusion that making a society legible was an exercise in control and the establishment of state power. Understanding 'legibility' as a crucial problem in statecraft, he argues that

> the pre-modern state was, in many crucial respects, particularly blind; it knew precious little about its subjects, their wealth, their landholdings and yields, their location, their identity. It lacked anything like a detailed 'map' of its terrain and people. The state therefore views the complex, organic entities it governs as features that must be organized in order to yield optimal returns according to a centralized, narrow and strictly utilitarian logic. (Scott 1998: 2)

'Seeing like a state' assumes a particular form in the relationship between a highland-centric state (as in Kenya and Ethiopia) and peripheral pastoral areas, often by way of the civilising mission of settlement projects, irrigation schemes, road-building and the provision of basic services (see the chapters by Akall, Chome, Fana Gebresenbet, Rettberg and Elliott this book). Complementing other works on the region (cf. Asebe Regassa et al. 2019; Korf et al. 2015; Nunow 2015; Behnke and Kerven 2013), the chapters in this book show how state projects to 'develop' dryland areas have had a disciplining effect on pastoralist societies. Most projects have the intended or indirect consequence of sedentarising pastoralists, or at least minimising longer-distance movements, easing the burden of governing pastoral subjects through taxation, the delivery of basic services and other social assistance.

This style of development in turn generates a style of 'techno-politics' (cf. Mitchell 2002), where certain types of expertise and technological intervention are privileged, each with exclusionary characteristics. A homogenised, standardised, grid-like imposition emerges in the plans. Embedded within state plans in Eastern Africa is a heavy emphasis on the notion of 'unlocking potential' in particular pastoral and peripheral farming areas. This is the underpinning of Ethiopia's state-led approach to national growth and transformation (Mosley and Watson 2016). Over four decades, successive governments in Ethiopia have sought to expand large-scale cotton and sugar estates in the Awash Valley at the cost of restricting access to key grazing sites for Afar pastoralists, as Rettberg notes. Yet, this expansion happened despite evidence that the historical performance of plantations, especially cotton, was far less productive than pastoral use of valuable floodplains and river water to support livestock. Nonetheless, from the perspective of central state planners, the conversion of land use was profitable: this conversion to plantations 'has transformed a fiscally sterile grazing environment into a fiscally productive agricultural one, and displaced independent pastoral producers with tractable taxpayers' (Behnke and Kerven 2013: 69).

State-like visions and plans of tapping the economic potential of previously marginalised pastoral areas extend to humanitarian programming in the region, as well. As Cory Rodgers' chapter shows, populations long thought of as 'vulnerable' and requiring assistance, including pastoralists and refugees, become frontiers for international investments in humanitarian intervention. In 2015, the United Nations High Commissioner for Refugees (UNHCR) agreed plans with the Turkana County Government to establish a new type of 'integrated settlement' at a 15 km² site in Kalobeyei in Kenya's far north-west. This was conceived as a progressive model of refugee settlement and an alternative to the 'care and maintenance' approach inherent in refugee encampment. Planners envisioned a grid-like market town in which refugees and Turkana hosts lived side by side, accessing the same basic services and social assistance, and operating their own businesses. Even as Kalobeyei's population swelled to 40,000 in less than five years, the development has not gone to plan. An influx of newly displaced South Sudanese refugees, rather than longer-established refugees, has meant a population that is in greater need of social assistance. Turkana hosts themselves have rejected the idea of integration, preferring their own allocations of services and assistance and living outside the boundaries of the settlement.

Generating wealth for the state, whether by converting land uses to forms that can be captured to produce revenue for national treasuries or establishing new markets encompassing populations previously thought of as unproductive and a drain on state and donor finance, is the impetus of many plans for large-scale investment. The development of oil and coal reserves, alongside wind and geothermal power – mostly in rural drylands – are integral elements of state development visions in Eastern Africa. For example, Uganda's second National Development Plan aims to enable continued upstream capital investment by global companies in oil and gas exploration and appraisal in the Albertine Rift, which reached US$2.3 billion by 2013 (World Bank 2015: 41). Kenya is at the forefront of green energy development, ranking first in sub-Saharan Africa in investment in renewable energies. By one estimate, it receives a massive 38 per cent of the funds OECD countries put into developing renewable energy solutions in the region.[6] The Kenyan government is banking on further large-scale investment in renewable energy production and transmission to help it achieve middle-income, industrialising status by 2030. Already, the country hosts the largest geothermal and wind-power developments in Africa. Investment in the Ol Karia geothermal complex has expanded substantially in recent years, with construction underway on a network of pipelines, wells and plants to tap an estimated potential of 1,000 megawatts of energy. In Marsabit County in the country's north, the Lake Turkana Wind Power (LTWP) site – consisting of 365 turbines – was connected to the national grid in 2018.

As James Drew discusses in his chapter, the state's vision of green transformation has not translated into significant improvements in livelihoods for residents near the project site. As construction advanced on the wind farm in 2015, youth in neighbouring Samburu towns and settlements blockaded roads in protest against their alleged exclusion from investment benefits, including compensation for the extraction of sand and the felling of trees, as well as access to new LTWP jobs. Protestors directed their ire at local administrative officials as well as liaison officers employed by LTWP. They were accused of undertaking selective consultations on project plans, inequitably allocating work opportunities and keeping the community in the dark over leasing land to investors.

Beyond investing in big energy in the drylands, as part of plans for national economic growth and transformation, states in Eastern Africa are also upping their commitments to livestock sector improvements. These have a long history, involving the establishment of ranches and attempts to 'upgrade' marketing, aiming to encourage the commercialisation of

---

[6] www.thisdaylive.com/index.php/2018/11/13/report-nigeria-third-preferred-destination-for-green-economy-projects, accessed 20 November 2018.

livestock production. The history of interventions in 'modernising' pastoral production system based on models imported from elsewhere has been dismal (de Haan et al. 2001; Scoones 1995). Yet such projects are being revived in the context of wider investments in the drylands, and linked to efforts at reducing poverty and boosting livelihood resilience through market-oriented programmes.[7]

The formalisation of the livestock sector, including the expansion of corridor infrastructure, feedlots and processing facilities, feature in Ethiopia's second Growth and Transformation Plan. This builds on wider efforts by the state to promote the export and trade of livestock, most of which is supplied by pastoralists that have long been marginalised (Catley and Yacob Aklilu 2013). These efforts extend to investments in cross-border infrastructure to encourage further growth of the lucrative regional livestock trade. Ethiopia has a 19 per cent stake in the Berbera corridor, a US$440 million development encompassing a new 400m quay at the existing Berbera port in Somaliland, a 250,000m² yard and upgrades to the city's airport. This is matched with an additional US$100 million in financing from the United Arab Emirates to upgrade the 250km road connecting the port with Hargeisa – Somaliland's capital – and Togwajale, a town on the Somaliland–Ethiopia border. The corridor's proponents pronounce the anticipated increase in the flow of goods and associated impact this will have on the region's economic prospects. However, as Ahmed Musa explains in his chapter, the development has already given rise to other unexpected impacts, including new tensions that are upsetting Somaliland's complex clan politics.

Official narratives of development come up against critical discourses and contested political relations from below, themes explored in subsequent sections of the chapter. They constitute a new spatial politics of resource and infrastructural development – one that is unfolding well beyond the cases in Eastern Africa highlighted here.[8]

Seeing like a global investor

A different spatiality and way of 'seeing' large-scale projects emerges from the perspective of global capital investors. Although the types of invest-

---

[7] See for example, Cultivating New Frontiers in Agriculture (CNFA), www.cnfa-europe. org/program/agricultural-growth-program-livestock-market-development-2 and www. cnfa-europe.org/program/agricultural-growth-program-livestock-market-development-2 (accessed 29 July 2019).

[8] For example, in Angola (de Grassi and Ovadia 2017; Rodrigues 2017), Burkina Faso (Côte and Korf 2018), Congo (Hall et al. 2015c), Eastern Democratic Republic of Congo (Geenen and Verweijen 2017), Ghana (Nyantakyi-Frimpong and Bezner Kerr 2017; Adusah-Karikari 2015; Boamah 2014), Malawi (Chinsinga 2017), Mozambique (Milgroom 2015), Niger (Schritt 2018), Sudan (Verhoeven 2016; Hopma 2015; Sulieman 2015; Keulertz 2012) South Sudan (Deng 2011), Uganda (Carmody and Taylor 2016), Zambia (Manda et al. 2019; Nolte 2014), Zimbabwe (Mutopo and Chiweshe 2014) and elsewhere across Africa's marginal rural frontiers (Larmer and Laterza 2017; Schoneveld 2017; Hall et al. 2015c).

ments discussed in the book's chapters vary, as do the physical, social and political geographies of each focal site, the 'resource imaginations' of global economic actors (Ferry and Limbert 2008) is a significant influence in most of the cases. A range of global investors, from overseas private capital to foreign state investment agencies and global charitable organisations and foundations, are turning to drylands as destinations for accumulating wealth, often underpinned by a type of 'growth talk' that emphasises the presumed benefits of large outside investment for expanding markets and economic activities in marginal rural areas. Investors emphasise the value of outside capital and expert knowledge to unlock the potential of land, labour and resources in the drylands. In this way, these acquire a different value in relation to the interests and logics of global capital. Elizabeth Ferry and Mandana Limbert (2008: 4) remind us that 'nothing is essentially or self-evidently a resource. Resource-making is a social and political process, and resources are concepts as much as objects and substances.' It is not so much the resources and investments generated, but rather the process of appropriation and redeployment of these resources within the world economy that generates a new spatial politics and, with it, local social effects (Friedman 2011). This speaks to the incorporation of states and local communities into global networks (Duffy 2000): 'an economic order based on networks of actors linked in unstable hierarchies and partial dependencies which are loose at the level of interaction' (Friedman 2011: 35).

In 'Seeing Like an Oil Company', James Ferguson (2005) argues that multinational companies engaged in the extractives industry thrive on the establishment of resource enclaves, a political economic rationale that isolates resource-rich localities such that they do not only become 'sharply walled off from their own national societies' but also excluded from the benefits generated by the resources. This is because global capital does not flow in neat symmetry between its point of foreign origin and sites of extraction but 'hops, neatly skipping over most of what lies in between' (2005: 379). As capital 'hops' over its enclaves, repatriated back to its foreign point of origin, the model of 'seeing like a state' is up-ended in the neoliberal world where developmental states in Africa have less reach and traction. Contrary to the spatialised political order of standardised grids, the characteristic mode of 'seeing' by global extractive companies has not entailed homogenisation within a national grid, but the establishment of highly securitised pockets, often in areas with chronic violent insecurity and weakened central government authority. These have their own security and state-like features, as capital travels between disparate sites where rule, order and capitalist accumulation can be assured. Different ways of 'seeing', like a state or a global investor, entwine in these developments. As Mattias Rasmussen and Christian Lund (2018: 338) explain, territorialisation is a strategy of using bounded spaces for particular outcomes; a resource control strategy that involves classification of particular areas in order to regulate people and resources. Although states are often privileged as territorialising agents in the contemporary neoliberal regime, the spread of extractive, green energy, commercial agriculture, conservation projects and humanitarian operations in pastoral areas shows how non-state actors and organisations also have capabilities to define resources, as well as order and control land (Peluso and Lund 2011; Sikor and Lund 2009).

However, these processes of sorting sites into global capital-generating enclaves whether through resource extraction, large-scale agriculture and irrigation or market-oriented refugee settlements constructed on repurposed drylands, are not new. African countries and many of the localities in our case studies have a long history of these encounters (Ferguson 2005). It bears a remarkable parallel with colonial models of fragmentation and enclave economics reflected in the long-term implications of formerly colonised 'white highlands,' as Marie Gravesen's chapter shows, or similarities with the UN market expansion model of an integrated refugee settlement, as shown in Rodgers' chapter. Thus, territorialisation in this contemporary era of state sovereignty is only slightly disguised from the preceding colonial enclaves. It involves a series of operations that include establishing a territorial administration, instituting a legal system and with it the creation of rights subjects and laws of property, establishing boundaries and mapping space, and, critically, ensuring the capacity to enforce any and all of this by means of force if necessary.

Territorialisations associated with global investment across dryland Eastern Africa have a precedent in conservation efforts across the region. Contentious politics around land and resources in Laikipia, as Gravesen shows, and in the South Omo Valley, as Fana Gebresenbet demonstrates, relate in part to the influence of outside investors, as well as states in the region, to expand protected areas. As conflicts around conservation over recent decades show, neoliberal forms of territorialisation 'can be both a claim to control land and resources, as well as a claim to the authority to determine who controls those resources' (Corson 2011: 704). Catherine Corson, who documents the design and implementation of Madagascar's protected areas since the early 2000s, explores the critical role of a range of donor and private interests in defining the boundaries, rights and authorities associated with 125 new protected areas, covering 9.4 million hectares (ibid.). Observing this trend in Kenya, Peter Little (2014: 76) explains:

> What has surfaced as a twenty-first century conservation model in Kenya is a complex and often contradictory mix of private inves-tors, wealthy Western conservationists, private corporations, NGOs (international and local), local community groups, and an accom-modating state agency (KWS [Kenya Wildlife Services]). What also have emerged are new strategies of both local political resistance and strategic accommodation among local communities.

On the extractives front, as Doris Okenwa shows in her chapter on oil politics in Turkana, Kenya, these processes unfold with new forms of global economic integration, and coexist with 'specific – and equally "global" – forms of exclusion and marginalization' (Ferguson 2005: 380). Since 2010, an investor consortium led by the Anglo-Irish company Tullow Oil has established an infrastructure for oil exploration and appraisal across southern Turkana's rangelands. Viewed from the air, the fenced exploratory wells are mere pin-pricks in a huge landscape; the largest visible land-take is a 2 km by 1 km base by the village Kapese, including an airstrip, accommodation, offices and storage facilities for Tullow and other large oil sub-contracting firms. Land for the Kapese base was transferred following negotiations with local officials, including the area's Member of the County Assembly and the area chief, as well as elders and an influential seer. A deal was signed off, with a pledge to pay the Turkana County Government four million Kenyan shillings[9] a month in leasing fees. The Kapese deal spurred opposition and claims that the company bought the support of local leaders. Tullow has faced similar tensions in its efforts to acquire land for exploration wells. The company has negotiated land access on a case-by-case basis. Many have come to see both elders and seers, who were revered and highly respected individuals in Turkana custom, as self-interested because of their part in endorsing deals that deliver few wider public benefits from extractive activity (Lind 2017).

Thus, even where land takes by global investors are relatively circum-scribed, the impact on social relations, politics and cultural identity are significant. As Doris Okenwa explains, in a bid to localise global capital and counter corporate impunity, ethics and morality have become integral, and often contradictory, components of capitalism. Extractive companies aim in principle at promoting inclusivity in investments and economic growth beyond resource enclaves. These are pursued through various forms of 'community engagement' and corporate social responsibility programmes that bring together global investors, state actors at multiple levels of governance, other non-state actors (NGOs and local civil society groups), customary leaders and interest-based associations. Yet investor attempts to mediate the process of resource acquisition and extraction through elaborate consultation processes and related community engagement efforts often fail to engage effectively with the dynamic political context of operations. Investor efforts to establish consultative fora, provide work opportunities for local residents and fund social development projects often elevate the position of various local middlemen who seek to broker access to new spaces of local engagement and, by extension, the resources associated with these.

As a result, 'capital hops' are shifting within enclaves themselves, as local elites grab opportunity and wealth associated with investor efforts to cultivate closer ties with 'host communities', as many chapters show. What have also emerged are new strategies of inclusion that often take

---

[9]   US$1 = Ksh80.31 on 31 December 2010.

the form of subversion against established hierarchies. As later sections demonstrate, these draw on wider discourses of rights, belonging and inclusion. Thus, the spatial politics of resource and infrastructure investments at the dryland margins are characterised by alliance-making at multiple levels of governance. The book's chapters illustrate how investor visions entangle with other ways of 'seeing' by local capital, as well as smaller-scale pastoralists, dryland farmers and small-town dwellers, to influence the outcomes.

Seeing like local capital

While the optic of modernity and prosperity spreading outwards into underdeveloped peripheries is integral to state visions of development throughout the region and undergirds investor faith in securing social acceptance of operations, these projects often appear very different from the margins.

Large-scale investments in pastoral areas of Eastern Africa happen in parallel to the slow but steady rise of local capital among town-based entrepreneurs, transporters, livestock traders and political brokers. Local capital has become an important driver in territorialisation processes in pastoral areas. Benedikt Korf et al. (2015: 896) argue that 'the contemporary frontiersman in African drylands thus resembles less a state-backed settler than a post-pastoral capitalist who acts as a partly self-governing frontier entrepreneur'. They focus on Ethiopia's Somali Region, which they explain has experienced a kind of 'indigenisation' of sedentarisation since the late 1990s at the hands of Somali investors, traders and entrepreneurs. An economic rush in the region, incentivised by transnational marketing networks, has seen the rapid commodification of pastoral resources such as charcoal, water points and cash crops. These have combined with sovereign state claims to territory, such as the establishment of irrigation and commercial agriculture schemes, to produce new patterns of territorialisation. As pastoralist entrepreneurs covet monetised dryland resources, they thus become complicit in the state's project of territorialisation and vision of a sedentarised pastoralist society.

In some cases, frontier entrepreneurs invest capital in reviving infrastructure from earlier projects that fell into disuse. Gregory Akall's chapter documents the emergence of a new class of irrigation entrepreneurs in Turkana led by individuals with start-up capital, including retired civil servants and other Turkana who lived elsewhere in Kenya and returned in recent years. They have made use of a combination of their own investments and some external support to invest in entrepreneurial activities, often including fodder production to link to the wider pastoral economy. They have used old irrigation infrastructure but rehabilitated it in ways that can be sustained, often by linking it in innovative ways with elements of the flood cultivation system long used by Turkana pastoralist farmers along the Turkwel River. They have invested in pumps and other equipment and have begun to make profits from their businesses, which are a mix of individual and collective enterprises.

Improvements in roads and transport services are making markets and basic services more accessible for pastoral populations, helping to lift the position of local capital, while at the same time supporting the penetration of larger capital from outside, both domestic and foreign. As Musa explains in his chapter, the formally recognised Berbera corridor is contested locally by different pastoral groups who argue for alternative routes for new infrastructure, and in one case have themselves raised funds for an alternative investment in a road to improve marketing.

While certain investments in roads, transport and marketing infra-structure by states can represent a welcome injection of public resources in pastoral areas, and address historical marginalisation, the outcomes can be ambiguous. Drawing on longitudinal evidence from the Borana plateau in southern Ethiopia, John McPeak et al. (2011) observe that transport improvements can create new opportunities for livestock marketing and value-added processing. However, the benefits for the majority of dryland residents may not outweigh the costs, and such investments may result in accelerating the concentration of wealth among the better off.

Examples abound in pastoral areas of Eastern Africa of land and resource grabbing, or of pastoralists making ill-informed sales of individual land holdings. A land rush in Kenya's South Rift Valley, driven by speculators spurred by the area's proximity to Nairobi, has resulted in distress sales by local Maasai pastoralists. This has seen the rangelands become highly fragmented as the area becomes a peri-urban frontier. This has left many Maasai worse off through a process they explain as 'selling wealth to buy poverty', whereby Maasai sell their plots within group ranches to buyers, worsening fragmentation and further undermining the requirements for livestock-keeping in the area (Mwangi 2007; Rutten 1992).

Yet, the dynamics of land acquisition are context-specific across the drylands. It is not always the case that pastoralists are victims of the new push for land. Greiner's chapter shows how Pokot elites in Baringo in Kenya's northern Rift Valley acquire newly valuable plots along improved roads and other infrastructure developed to support geothermal exploration. Large livestock owners and other well-connected Pokot were also behind the push into new territories on the neighbouring Laikipia plateau. In turn, Laikipia shows the consequences of processes of land fragmentation over the longer term. Its landscape is divided into an array of enclosures, where smallholders settle according to shared ethnicity, and pastoralists negotiate access to grazing at the margins of other large-scale private conservancies, ranches and national parks. Gravesen's chapter shows how land-buying companies, established by Kenya's new political elite following independence to satisfy the demand for land, remain at the centre of land-use fragmentation, ambiguous ownership and disputes on the plateau. Many company shareholders (being smallholders from other areas of central Kenya) did not fence their land because of the dry conditions that made farming risky and unpredictable. This permitted livestock passage and settlement of some herders in a new pastoral frontier. The pastoralists saw the unfenced lands as an opportunity to make up for their exclusion from the redistribution of lands in the years following independence. Yet in 2017, ahead of Kenya's national and county elections, the expansionist potential of these lands once again became apparent in a wave of politically incited land invasions by other groups, including pastoralists from neighbouring Samburu and Baringo counties. In contrast to pastoralists who had already settled and crossed unfenced lands over many decades, incursions by Pokot and Samburu pastoralists in 2017 were encouraged by various elected officials and aspiring politicians as a way of influencing the election outcomes, as Gravesen explains in her chapter.

Thus, seeing like local capital in pastoral Eastern Africa entails seizing opportunities apparent in regional demands for rangeland resources, booming markets for livestock and livestock products, as well as state investment in infrastructure and land. As Greiner shows in his chapter, the advancing resource frontier, along with expectations of rising land values, accentuates the trend to privatise land. The rapid spread of dryland farming among the pastoral Pokot happens alongside and entwines with the early development of geothermal power. Capital investment in plots and rental property in Isiolo in anticipation of the Kenyan government's US$23 billion LAPSSET corridor development and future growth of Isiolo town in northern Kenya is fuelling the rise of an investor class, as well. While the LAPSSET project promises to make Isiolo into an economic hub along the corridor, Elliott shows in her chapter that it is the actions of ordinary people propelling the town's transformation thus far, as noted earlier.

Cases from elsewhere, including land and resource investments by local and transnational Somali merchants in Ethiopia's Somali Region (Korf et al. 2015), or the rapid growth of a rental market in Karamoja in north-east Uganda fuelled by well-off Karamojong constructing housing for recent migrants (Caravani 2018), show that these are not isolated examples. Rather, they illustrate broader trends that are reconfiguring access to and control over land and resources in the drylands. Further, they point to the likelihood of widening inequality, as an entrepreneurial class positions itself to benefit from investment, while the majority who are unable to acquire land, establish businesses or acquire training to gain employment are likely to fall further behind.

These developments are happening parallel to continued investment in livestock production by pastoralist elites. The regional trade in livestock and meat was US$1 billion in 2010 (Catley et al. 2013); exports of carcasses and live animals through the Gulf of Aden ports mean this has increased still further. Here too, the advancing resource frontier – in this instance, value in live animals and carcasses – intersects with the practices of local capital to accumulate greater wealth. As Musa (this book) shows, development of the Berbera corridor has intensified political competition along clan lines precisely because of the anticipated wealth it will generate. The dynamics of inclusion shift as the large-scale development of the port and associated infrastructure lead to uncertainty around who will benefit and who will miss out. Already, the burgeoning livestock trade through Berbera and other Gulf of Aden ports has concentrated wealth among frontier capitalists as many poorer pastoralists sell-up and exit livestock-keeping. Besides investments in livestock, land and rental properties in growing towns, indigenous capital has flowed into transport, ranging from lorries and private hire vehicles to motorbikes, petrol stations and mechanics' shops.

Commentators have often been too ready to assume that the kinds of transformations that large-scale capitalist development will generate will be 'top-down' and driven by the powerful. Jamie Cross's (2014) study of the economy of anticipation provoked by plans for special economic zones in Andhra Pradesh in India shows that it is not only the interests of big capital and powerful government elites that drive the reshaping of the local places where such projects are located, but also the anticipatory actions of ordinary people. In Isiolo, while the land rush undoubtedly relates to the rapidly rising value of land in the town and its environs, and thus residents' demands for economic inclusion, Elliott describes how laying exclusive claims, individually and collectively, is also a means through which residents seek to ensure political inclusion. Chome's chapter argues that, in Lamu, corridor-making creates a new local politics around a reconstructed indigeneity, with claim-making facilitated by Kenya's decentralised politics.

Seeing like local capital therefore suggests a different lens on investment and land politics, refracted through changing class relations at the local level and how the contested politics between local elites, government and investors are played out in particular places.

Seeing like a pastoralist

What about pastoralists themselves; how do they see investments in the drylands? As we have already discussed, rangelands have been carved up and fragmented through the establishment of new investments, and with this patterns of resource tenure and land control have changed. Pastoralism as a type of land use depends on access to key 'reserved' resources, such as riparian areas along rivers or hilltop forests, seasonally and during more serious droughts as well (Scoones 1995). Pastoralists also depend on mobility and access routes to track spatially and temporally distributed resources, gain access to markets and other services (Turner and Schlecht 2019).

From the perspective of pastoralists who depend on extensive resource use and the right of passage and movement between different parts of a highly variable and differentiated landscape, new processes of territorialisation, resulting from both large-scale and indigenous investments, are a considerable challenge. Rangeland fragmentation constrains traditional mobile pastoralism, as movements become more difficult to make and key resource areas are fenced and set aside for non-livestock uses.

As Li (2014b: 589) writes, although often treated as a thing and sometimes as a commodity, turning land into alternative productive uses requires a process of 'assemblage'. This generates regimes of exclusion that distinguish legitimate from illegitimate uses and users, inscribing boundaries through devices such as fences, title deeds and other legal documents, and regulations. In mobile pastoral systems, land is both passage and a seasonal resource. As we have seen, to the state, land is something investible through the use of technologies, and the selective application of law, to assign new exclusive rights. To a global investor, land may be nothing more than an operational space that needs to be secured from other uses for the unimpeded extraction of subterranean steam, oil and gas, or above-ground wind.

For local capitalists and entrepreneurs, many of whom are current or former pastoralists in these areas, land is something altogether different – something to claim for speculative reasons – anticipating future wealth creation as the value of land increases – and/or to stake claims to belonging and, thus, rights to future compensation, political representation or power. As Drew observes for the Samburu and Chome for Lamu in this book, the politics of belonging, linking to identity and new forms of citizenship are central to how claim-making is practised. Constructions of identity – through discourses of indigeneity, biocultural heritage and ethnic or clan belonging – become important in a 'politics of possession' (Sikor and Lund 2009), where land, property, territory and citizenship become intimately linked (Lund 2016, 2008).

For example, in Harshin in the Somali Region of Ethiopia, traditionally an important drought grazing reserve that lies on a strategic trekking route for livestock being exported from Ethiopia and Somaliland through Berbera, there has been a near total privatisation of grazing areas and water as the rangeland was carved up into household plots for farming and private grazing (Flintan et al. 2011). Based on experiences from Baringo County in Kenya, Greiner's chapter documents the rapid spread of dryland farming among the pastoral Pokot, on the one hand, and the early stages of large-scale investments in the exploitation of geothermal power, on the other hand. He shows how both processes increasingly converge and mutually reinforce each other in ways that lead to profound competition for and revaluation of land.

Seen from the margins, struggles around the framing and meanings given to resources – whether they are geothermal superheated steam, oil or land for agriculture, livestock-keeping or wildlife conservation – are the crux of many contestations in pastoral areas. Residents of areas where large projects are proposed or taking shape frame their claims variously, employing in particular discourses around ecology, ethnicity, heritage and social justice. Extraction channels resource claims into a 'rights talk' (Cornwall and Nyamu-Musembi 2004) that speaks to questions of local identity, territory, citizenship and the claims stemming from these (Lund 2011). Contestations around oil exploration activities, for example, connect to a social body beyond the enclave, underscoring the enmeshing of oil extraction with wider politics and governance. As shown for Turkana in Kenya, the operations of oil explorers, as well as the benefits of oil development and how these are shared, are mediated through a number of relationships at all levels from the global, regional and national, all the way down to the sub-national administrative unit (county or council), town, and village (Lind 2017).

Ultimately, given the divisions of class, age, gender and ethnicity, there is no uniform view among pastoralists on the impacts of large-scale projects; no simple view 'from below'. Social difference matters a great deal in terms of assessing both pastoralist perceptions and new investment and economic change. Men, women, older and younger pastoralists, for instance, see investments in very different ways. Investments may create jobs, which allow opportunities for accumulation for some and, in turn, a return to pastoralism. As pastoral systems transform through a variety of overlapping pathways (see Figure 1.1; Catley et al. 2013), diverse forms of accumulation emerge. This results in new patterns of social differentiation in pastoral areas, with implications for class, gender and generation (Caravani 2018; Hodgson 2000; Galaty and Bonte 1991; Rigby 1988). Impacts are non-linear and complex, and simplistic 'land grabbing' headlines usually never tell the whole story. This makes the processes of negotiation among different ways of 'seeing' an investment in the drylands highly contentious, as we discuss next.

Claim-making and contentious politics

Investments – be they in roads, pipelines, irrigation schemes, oil wells, geothermal plants or wind turbines – entail the increased presence of the state and the interests of centralised state power, alongside those of global finance and large companies involved in developing the frontier. As we have explored already, they have profound implications for governance, local politics, security and violence in the dryland margins. Yet, as we have seen, seeing like a state or a global investor is not the only way of seeing. Perspectives from indigenous, local capital or diverse pastoralists complicate the picture. Contestations over meanings and visions matter, and shape the nature of political contestation and conflict in these places.

In practice, as the chapters in this book show, neither a state-driven modernist plan nor enclave capitalism is the result. Ngala Chome et al. (2020) argue, in relation to corridor development along Africa's eastern seaboard, that local contexts and political negotiations result in many hybrids, as different visions compete and converge. State plans often fall apart as the realities of contexts at the pastoral margins impinge or morph into a new project more closely aligned with local capital interests, while enclaves can never fully isolate themselves and must articulate with other forms of local capitalism, politics and resistance on the ground.

The concept of contentious politics was first introduced by the historian and sociologist Charles Tilly during the 1970s. He observed that 'all forms of contention rest on performances' (Tilly 2008: 16). It is unsurprising that the various ways of seeing investments in Africa's drylands has set off a wave of contentious politics, created a range of claim-making factions and performances aimed at negotiating more favourable terms of incorporation into investment projects. As groups mobilise to make claims, particular modes of collective action are deployed, even though the interests of local actors differ.

Governments and investors may introduce local compensation schemes and use local gatekeepers to champion 'development', although often without fully grasping community experiences of and responses to new extractive development. Returning to Turkana in Kenya, the establishment of an infrastructure for oil extraction in Turkana has happened through ties that Tullow – the lead oil explorer in the region – has cultivated with county government officials, emergent local capital in Turkana and other community voices influencing public attitudes. Extractive activities have ignited debates around belonging, entitlements and inclusion, as the oil investors have sought to curry favour with communities and stem any potential resistance through 'participatory' and 'consultative' processes. Mirroring the behaviour of Kenya's national political elites to advance private wealth, county politicians and officials have used their positions to leverage local capital by insisting on more contracts for local companies. Like national officials, they have also sought to derive patronage by pressuring the company to create more work opportunities, social investments and funding infrastructure (Lind 2017).

Okenwa takes this up in her chapter in this book. On Turkana's oil development, she argues that these processes produce asymmetric power relations and the rise of brokerage. As a way to secure local support, or at least acceptance of extractive operations, the oil investors created casual work opportunities for local residents, financed social projects, such as building school dormitories and water points, and compensated residents directly affected by construction and drilling. However, the negotiation of these social investments inadvertently established community engagement as a place-making project and a relational process of soliciting cooperation based on particular performances of deservingness by emerging community factions and leaders seeking to lay claims to the resource benefits. As such, investor efforts to 'partner' with 'community' members takes on material forms as local residents assert their own understanding of what a community is, who should be included, and thus who has a right to benefit. As struggles have ensued to define what and who exactly is 'the community', oil development has fuelled new articulations of citizenship, inclusion and claim-making. As Okenwa explains, company efforts to encourage participation do not ensure equitable distribution or alter the social forces that perpetuate inequality and engender a kind of social relations that emphasise par— ticular knowledge systems and essentialist ideas of 'community'.

What we also find at the heart of these contentions and claims to benefits is part of what Ferguson (2015) considers the new politics of distribution in Africa – 'distributive claims grounded in ideas not of need or charity but of a "rightful share"' (2015: 24). In this light, the contention stems from a place of ownership and not mere subjects of state charity and arbitrary corporate interventions.

Conclusion

More than a decade on from the peak of Africa's land rush, the reality on the ground has panned out differently from what many expected. As the chapters in this book show, large-scale investments often have advanced in a piece-meal way as challenges of implementation have mounted. For instance, LAPSSET's high modernist vision has not materialised in a sudden multi-billion dollar boom, but rather emerged incrementally, such as through the completion of the Isiolo–Moyale highway in Kenya and the recent opening of Isiolo's airport. Mass expropriations to establish large-scale commercial farms in Ethiopia and Tanzania have by-and-large not happened, as only a small part of an agreed area is actually farmed.

Still, the reconfiguration of land ownership and use, while perhaps not as dramatic as the 'land grabbing' debate feared, has been profound, creating a new politics of land and investment in the pastoral regions. As the chapters in this book show, infrastructure and investments have ignited intense competition for and revaluation of land, as local elites, and other domestic and foreign investors, jostle to claim tracts of land. Development of oil, wind and geothermal reserves has fuelled further competition around 'local content' – the industry term for procuring goods and services from local suppliers and workers (Ovadia 2016). The footprint of these developments, and the arrival of workers and contractors from outside of local areas, sits uncomfortably with the reality of work opportunities that are thinly spread and temporary.

Box 1.1 lists some of the main impacts of resource and infrastructure investments in pastoral areas highlighted in the chapters that follow. These impacts emerge from the terms of incorporation in investment projects and the differential patterns of accumulation that emerge. They range from the consequences of speculation and the economies of anticipation to the

---

Box 1.1 Impacts of new resource and infrastructure investments

- **Restricting rights to land, water, other resources and passage.** Examples include fencing by new land buyers in Laikipia (Gravesen), pastoral exclusions and displacement in Kilombero (Blache), establishment of state-backed sugar estates in riparian grazing lands in the Awash and Omo valleys (Rettberg, Fana Gebresenbet) and geothermal development in Baringo intensifying existing internal processes of land commodification (Greiner).

- **Delays, uncertainties and lack of accountability in implementation.** Examples include the long process of delay in the implementation of the Bagamoyo sugar investment in Tanzania (Engström) and the long-running contestation of the KPL rice scheme in Tanzania (Blache). In both cases, responsibilities shifted between agribusiness companies, financiers and the state, with little accountability for negative consequences on local populations.

- **Land speculation.** Examples include land speculation in and around Isiolo town (Elliott) and around Lamu (Chome), both in anticipation of the major LAPSSET investment. An economics and politics of anticipation is created, even in the absence of the actual investment. A similar process occurs in Laikipia, also in Kenya, through land-buying companies (Gravesen).

- **Generating immigration.** Examples include the influx of South Sudanese refugees to new integrated settlement established on rangelands used by Turkana herders in Kenya (Rodgers), resettlement of Konso smallholders on borders of Boni rangelands in South Omo in Ethiopia (Fana Gebresenbet) and an influx of new settlers in Lamu in Kenya in anticipation of LAPSSET development (Chome).

- **Creating employment and contracts, which may privilege one group over another.** Examples include tensions concerning the allocation of work opportunities around oil exploration in Turkana (Okenwa) and construction of the LTWP site (Drew), which also stimulates various kinds of localism or separatism based on the expectation that a local monopoly on a specific resource will make possible more local political autonomy.

- **Initiating compensation mechanisms over which people then fight.** Examples include Banjuni pressure to formalise land titles in expectation of compensation from LAPSSET development (Chome), land-takes for establishing oil wells in Turkana (Okenwa), compensation to households displaced by wayleave for the LTWP transmission line (Drew) and Turkana resentment over inadequate social services provision as compensation for hosting refugee settlement (Rodgers).

- **Establishing new security arrangements involving increased state security/ policing presence and/or contracts with private firms and local militants.** Examples include increased state security presence around Awash (Rettberg) and Omo Valley (Fana Gebresenbet) commercial agriculture schemes, use of police to suppress protests by farmers opposing evictions in Kilombero (Blache), establishment of private security presence around oil installations in Turkana (Okenwa) and the LTWP site (Drew).

direct results of dislocation and dispossession, to the indirect effects on local economies, employment opportunities and service provision. This in turn has consequences for social differentiation, patterns of selective accumulation and class formation, as well as for local politics, identities and citizenship. Outcomes are not linear, nor are they always complex. Investment is neither necessarily 'good' nor 'bad'; it depends on context.

As noted earlier, this book asks three interlinked questions: first, what do investments look like, and who frames their meaning, interpretation and pursuit? Second, how are investments generating wider impacts, and who loses and wins? And third, what types of resistance, mobilisation, subversion and forms of contentious politics are evident? The case studies presented in the chapters that follow attempt to answer these questions in different ways. Overall, they show how the spread of large-scale investments in pastoral areas, the political and economic interests driving these, and the new valuing of land and resources they introduce, is reshaping the politics of resource contestations. These politics matter for the governance of security in pastoral margins, for whom, and in whose interests. Investments unfold in contexts that have experienced all sorts of dynamic change over recent decades, resulting in diverging trajectories for lives and livelihoods in the drylands. In different ways, investments are reconfiguring territory, as well as economies and politics, creating new forms of livelihood beyond conventional pastoralism, as pastoral settings transform along different pathways. This is significant for how pastoralists are seen and see themselves, with implications for the construction of citizenship and wider state–society relationships. Widespread sedentarisation of formerly mobile populations, the concentration of livestock wealth among elites, and the shift away from livestock-keeping for many are manifestations of significant structural changes that have accelerated with the rise of large-scale investments.

This book does not claim to have exhausted all the answers or the best possible interpretations of the emerging issues. What it does is to challenge existing assumptions about Africa's drylands, adding to the understanding of the future economic and livelihood trajectories of those moving up, moving out, hanging in and dropping out of the pastoral sector (see Figure 1.1). Those who *moved up* into commercialised systems, and participate in regional marketing and trade, are more likely to have the capital, social connections and business ties, and knowledge to take advantage of opportunities opened up by large-scale investment. The impacts of investment are more ambiguous for those who *moved out* into activities not dependent on owning livestock, such as irrigated farming or town-based trades and work. Opportunities for business and work around large developments are often restricted, as those with existing political and social connections capture the greatest share. Many opportunities are limited in time, as well, coinciding with a particular phase in project development, rather than something that will endure. For those who *hang in* traditional pastoralism and small-scale agro-pastoralism, improvements to roads can ease marketing barriers, but for most, new restrictions on passage and access to resources, as well as the disruptive influences of investments on the valuing of land and resources in drylands, may outweigh the marketing benefits. For the many who have *dropped out* of pastoralism, large-scale investments do not have the transformative effects that could lead to sustainable livelihood alternatives to livestock-keeping. Investment plans and implementation in most cases have little or no connection to local economies and livelihood activities. Meanwhile, the more imperceptible influences of investments on territory, as well as economy, politics, citizenship, will accentuate inequalities and social difference that increasingly characterise dryland margins.

Resistance, mobilisation and subversion are therefore something to anticipate as part of the ongoing development of infrastructure, land and resources across Africa's drylands. Central governments and investors often view any conflict in these places as localised disturbance to be overcome through the provision of more state or private security, corporate social investment and deals that incentivise local acceptance. In other words, the governance of investor operations can be largely contained in enclaves and made separate from wider political and social relations. However, state and global investor capital is unable to wall itself off – it has to navigate a spectrum of local interests. National government – the state – is unable to impose its will without striking deals and cultivating ties within political society at the margins. It is therefore the entwining of different ways of seeing – like a state, investor, local capitalist and pastoralist – and the logics and interests associated with them, which define the political topography of extractive landscapes and so the governance of contestations and struggles around these.

2

Local Transformations of LAPSSET

Evidence from Lamu, Kenya

NGALA CHOME

In Lamu County on Kenya's northern coast, several components of the ambitious Lamu Port–South Sudan–Ethiopia Transport (LAPSSET) corridor come together: a new modern port of thirty-two berths and a planned network of new transport infrastructure consisting of an airport, a series of highways, a standard-gauge railway and an oil pipeline (Atkins Acuity 2017) (see Map 2.1). In this grand vision, a planned oil refinery will sit adjacent to a Special Economic Zone, a 'growth area' and a new metropolis city with the capacity to accommodate approximately 1.1 million people – a significant increase on the 2009 recorded population of 112,252 people (Lamu County 2013: 1). To support this population, plans are also under way to create new sources of energy, initially through a coal-fired electricity generating plant – whose progress has been halted by a court order after local activists filed a petition – and a wind-power farm. There are also plans to construct new infrastructure for the supply of water, which will come from the yet-to-be-built Tana River Grand Falls dam (Kasuku 2013).

The LAPPSET project is part of a wider push across Africa by policy makers, development partners, and investors to promote corridors and growth poles, which all involve, or anticipate, major land-based investments in transport, mining and agricultural commercialisation (Smalley 2017). Since LAPSSET was first mooted in 2009, the project has been marketed as a way of transforming northern Kenya – not just Lamu – by opening up the region for investment and economic development, as Elliott explains in Chapter 3 on plans to remake Isiolo as an economic hub of northern Kenya. The LAPSSET project has also been marketed to potential investors around the world as part of a larger, continent-wide Great Equatorial Land Bridge via Juba and Bangui to Douala on Cameroon's Atlantic coast. It consists of new highways, railroads, dams, pipelines and ports (Browne 2015). Visions for LAPSSET connect with plans to position Kenya as a key player in north-east Africa's oil and gas sector – details also presented by Okenwa in Chapter 4. In May 2018,

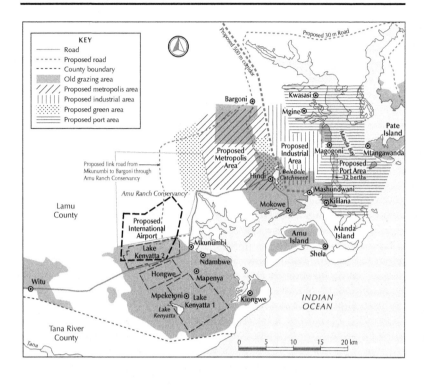

Map 2.1 Kenya, showing Lamu's future under LAPSSET

Wood Group, a British firm, won a US$2 billion bid to construct an 800 km pipeline connecting oil fields in Kenya's Turkana County with Lamu.

Senior bureaucrats and national politicians have presented these high-modernist visions (see Scott 1998) in slick artistic impressions depicting Lamu's imagined future as an infrastructure-heavy prosperous dream. These are to be realised through state-capital alliances or public–private partnerships. Financiers including the African Development Bank, the United Kingdom's Department for International Development (DFID), and Chinese private firms, especially Exim Bank, among others, are named in project documents. Such imaginaries of a frontier that is newly ripe for global investment are also part of a wider securitisation agenda in Lamu and northern Kenya, a region that until recently was seen as lawless and ridden with conflict (Mosley and Watson 2016). In sum, LAPSSET's framing of Lamu and northern Kenya as empty (of 'civilised' people and modernity) but full (of resources, especially land and minerals), legitimates the appropriation of 'underutilised' land, while 'casting the state and its elites as heroes who will make these regions anew' (Asebe Regassa and Korf 2018: 614). (The location of the LAPSSET corridor within Kenya is shown in Map 3.1 in the next chapter).

Despite the rhetoric, these discursive frameworks are generating material and social consequences on the ground in advance of any serious investments. Through varied economies of anticipation (see, for example, Cross 2014), LAPSSET's future direction is currently being negotiated and renegotiated by a set of diverse actors, through different local processes, which promise more hybrid, unpredictable outcomes as a result. In particular, the establishment of new structures of local government since 2013 following the promulgation of a new constitution in 2010, and a wider legal language of communal rights, consultation and local participation, has provided local actors with opportunities for engagement and for contestation of the LAPSSET agenda. This has allowed local dynamics to transform what appears on paper to be an exclusivist tunnel vision into one that may be more responsive to local interests in the future (Chome et al. 2020).

This chapter examines how these local transformations of LAPSSET are spurring complex economies of anticipation through which networks of patronage, alliance and mobilisation are entrenched in advance of major investments. These local 'contentious politics' (Elliott 2016; Greiner 2016; Mosley and Watson 2016) are not only determining the current progress of LAPSSET – as targets shift, priorities are reset and outcomes renegotiated – but will also influence its future political direction, including who will get what, when, where and how.

Contending meanings of land and belonging

In Lamu, renewed meanings of land as property, driven by the anticipations of LAPSSET, are conflicting with meanings of land as a cultural resource, or as ethnic territory (see Chome 2020). Ethnic territoriality is a widespread ideology in Kenya, where land is inexorably linked with ethnic identity (Jenkins 2012; Lynch 2006). Conflicting meanings of land, identity and belonging are also projected through ideas of vulnerability and marginality, which have not only been deployed to make moral, legal and sometimes exclusive claims but are also giving prominence to autochthonous discourses of belonging and citizenship. Commonplace terms such as *wageni* ('guests' or 'migrant' communities) and *wenyeji* ('hosts' or 'indigenous' communities) are being cast in a new light, as individuals and groups anticipate LAPSSET's promised prosperous future (Elliott 2016; and see Elliott in Chapter 3, this book). As this happens, LAPSSET is also intersecting with pre-existing territorial restructuring processes, especially increased sedentarisation and intensification of land use, alongside other claims of community-based land ownership (Greiner 2016; and see Greiner in Chapter 8, this book).

Various actors in Lamu are thus remaking and shaping the present around a diverse, uncertain and changing future. In particular, the politics of Lamu have been influenced by the migration and settlement of people from elsewhere in Kenya in recent years, especially in the mainland areas of the county. While human settlement on the archipelago of over sixty-five islands spans centuries, people have settled on the mainland areas at least since the 1960s; before that time most of the land had been covered by forests following the abandonment of slave-run plantations since the abolishment of slavery in 1907 (Romero 1986).

It was in the late 1960s that Kenya's post-colonial government initiated plans to establish commercial agricultural enterprises (and later settlements) on the mainland areas and some parts of the archipelago (see Chome 2020). Between 1973 and 1975, the government issued 14,212 ha of land on the mainland through the Lake Kenyatta Settlement Scheme Phase 1 to mostly Kikuyu families with origins in Kenya's central highlands (Ngilu 2014). While the government has, since the 1990s, issued a further 23,910 ha of land to 2,991 households, the majority of the beneficiaries have remained Kikuyu, a predominantly Christian and politically dominant group in Lamu and elsewhere in Kenya (Lonsdale 2008). This has influenced local narratives of exclusion and perceptions of favouritism of Kikuyu interests at the expense of the interests of the predominantly Muslim Bajuni community, who trace their settlement in Lamu over hundreds of years. By 2014, only 6,372 ha of land had been allocated to 4,123 households on the Bajuni-dominated islands (Ngilu 2014).

In addition to the Kikuyu community on the mainland areas, since the early 2000s principally, there has been a migration of smallholders from elsewhere in Kenya, most of whom have no title to their plots, and who have been in competition with other claimants of land, especially pastoralists, ranch owners and conservationists (Mosley and Watson 2016). Through cultivation and settlement, these recent inhabitants of Lamu have 'opened up' parts of the mainland that have remained largely uninhabited since the early 1900s (see Chome 2020). This recent pattern of migration has not only led to increasing disagreements over land ownership, boundaries and access to valuable land-based resources, but it is also reshaping the meaning of land and belonging.

The result has been a widespread demand for the formalisation of claims to land, especially by those, such as the Bajuni, who see themselves as the most landless, despite being 'indigenous' to Lamu. This is also part of a local mechanism to seek benefits from LAPSSET's future – including immediate benefits such as financial compensation for land in private use that will be claimed by LAPSSET activities. As a result, questions of land have featured in local discussions regarding LAPSSET since the project's inception and featured prominently during the official launch of LAPSSET at the village of Kililana on 2 March 2012. Initially, fears were informed by widely circulating rumours of a 'land grab' in neighbouring Tana River County, where proposals to establish sugar-cane plantations and oil-seed crops were accentuating pre-existing communal tensions, leading to intercommunal conflict in 2012 when more than 160 lives were lost (Goldsmith 2012). At this time, media reports were awash with rumours of a 'Lamu land grab', where people – acutely aware of the possibilities for wealth creation through land ownership – wanted to own a piece of the modernised port-city of the future (Kihara 2013). As a result, Lamu was reframed in national and local discursive frameworks as a county of anticipated economic potential. Enclosures and informal demarcations emerged in cleared and forested areas, and advertisements for 'plots for sale' were widely shared through text messages and social media platforms. Revolving around the defunct Lamu County Council, these anticipations created multiple networks, cutting across familiar fault lines of class, ethnicity, gender, religion and race, as petty land-brokers, bureaucrats, local farmers, traders, politicians, international investors and others all came together to create an economy of land speculation that was steeped in the promise of a lucrative future (Bocha 2014).

Matters came to a head in June–July 2014, when the mainland town of Mpeketoni and its environs were brutally attacked by a contingent of Al-Shabaab Islamist militants who had set up camp in the vast Boni forest that runs from Lamu into Southern Somalia (Anderson 2014; Mwakimako and Willis 2014). The majority of the victims were Christian and male, and were residents of the Kikuyu-dominated mainland areas. The attack deepened existing social and political divisions, which had been accentuated by the LAPSSET land debates (Anderson 2014). The fact that some of the victims had been embroiled in legal tussles over land ownership with powerful local land claimants fed a narrative – subsequently picked up by the president, Uhuru Kenyatta – that the attack may have been motivated by more local factors (Mosley and Watson 2016; Mwakimako and Willis 2014).

The government responded by revoking formal titles that were allegedly issued to a total of twenty-two companies between 2011 and 2012, and that covered 202,343 ha of land, or 70 per cent of all land in Lamu available for settlement (Ilado 2014: 2). After compensating occupants of land claimed by LAPSSET in 2015, the government issued some of the land it reclaimed after the 2014 mass revocation of titles to 4,073 individuals, the majority of whom were Bajuni smallholders, with promises of more adjudication and titling in the future (*Standard Digital* 2016). The issuing of formal titles may partly have been a response to rising Bajuni discontent regarding insecure land rights, but it was also meant to deny groups such as Al-Shabaab an array of local grievances to exploit. Despite this, invocations of ethnic territoriality and autochthonous discourses around land and resources have continued. In sum, contending meanings of land are part of local struggles through which the residents of Lamu are negotiating the future distribution of costs and benefits under LAPSSET in advance of any major investments, as the next section shows.

Debating the future distribution of costs and benefits

The fear of loss of land notwithstanding, LAPSSET promises a number of benefits, in particular opportunities for employment and for industrial, logistics and tourism development. However, a history of minimal investment in local infrastructure, public education and agricultural development is informing a nervous politics of belonging, and fears of potential exclusion, especially among groups who see themselves as 'indigenous' to Lamu, most of whom lag behind in formal educational attainment (see Kenya National Bureau of Statistics 2018). The main fear is that it is people from elsewhere in Kenya and beyond, and with better education and the skills required in a modernised industrial and business environment, who will benefit.

In response, the local leadership has not only been demanding the preservation of pre-existing livelihoods and cultures, but also of strategic public investment in education. Two features in Lamu have lent such discourses prominence: its long history of settlement (especially on the archipelago), combined with years of government neglect that have left people dependent on traditional knowledge systems. In particular, Lamu's status as a UNESCO world heritage site since 2001 and multiple conservation efforts protecting endangered marine species have given such concerns prominence. A local civil society group, Save Lamu, has been at the forefront of demands for a comprehensive environmental and social impact assessment study, communal safeguards and communal consultation in the implementation of LAPSSET. In addition, the group has developed a biocultural community protocol (BCP) with the help of the South African non-governmental organisation (NGO) Natural Justice and of the United Nations Environment Programme, which details traditional knowledge systems regarding the conservation of the ecological diversity of Lamu (Chome 2020).

A biocultural community protocol is usually a tool that is used by self-defined local communities to engage with governments, NGOs and researchers working in their localities, but in Lamu – and in the context of LAPSSET – it can also be viewed as part of local efforts to push back against a Nairobi-led process. For instance, during the hearing of a petition in the High Court of Kenya that challenged the constitutionality of LAPSSET, especially its alignment (or lack thereof) with Kenya's expanded bill of rights, actors associated with Save Lamu spoke authoritatively about LAPSSET by deploying multidimensional traditional knowledge systems that they claimed had been transmitted culturally through generations. (For details on proceedings during the hearing of the petition, see Republic of Kenya 2018.) Such alternative knowledge systems, the speakers claimed, offered a better understanding of local and interconnected patterns and processes over large spatial and temporal scales – including better insights into the effects of port dredging on turbidity, cycles of resource availability within forests and shifts in climate or ecosystem structure and function (Chome 2020). Deploying such 'indigenous' knowledge is a way for local actors to speak out against LAPSSET, and in this case, it resulted in a successful judgement, with a ruling in favour of some 4,700 fishermen who claimed they had been displaced from fishing grounds at the site of port construction (Kazungu 2018). While the ruling was rescinded after a successful petition, discourses of traditional knowledge, 'indigeneity' and global conservation (Lynch 2011) have continued to feature as part of local strategies adopted by a section of Lamu's residents in their struggles for ownership and control of the LAPSSET agenda, as was the case during the revocation by the High Court of Kenya of a license for the construction of a coal-fired electricity generating plant.

In multiple petitions, court cases, street demonstrations and stakeholder engagement fora concerning the future direction of LAPSSET, it is such pre-existing local concerns and debates that dominate, leading to delays in project implementation, resetting of priorities and renegotiation of targets. In addition to such local strategies, which have been amplified by a post-2010 constitutional landscape that promotes a language of public consultation and rights, local residents have also turned to the offices of the newly established county governments to advance their multiple claims, aiming to make the proposed corridor more responsive to local interests in the future. The chapter will now turn to the nature of political mobilisation in Lamu and how this has recently been influenced by the anticipations of LAPSSET's future.

Political mobilisation and narratives of exclusion and inclusion

Politics in Lamu took an interesting turn in 2013, with the coming into power of the first county government, consisting of its own executive and legislative arm (county assembly). Before 2013, local politics had revolved around the defunct (and poorly funded) Lamu County Council, including the personal political machines that centred on a number of individuals, with links to other elites based especially in Mombasa and Nairobi. Such individuals dominated local patronage networks and sponsored the candidatures of parliamentarians who represented Lamu's two constituencies: Lamu West and Lamu East (Willis and Chome 2014). Through their alliances, local elites have benefited from access to land and other valuable resources in the county. In exchange for their electoral support during elections, MPs have responded to a series of local demands for clientelistic goods, such as distribution of bursaries, help with funeral costs or settling of outstanding hospital bills, building of schools and sinking of wells (ibid.).

Operation of these patronage networks and competition between local political bosses have continued to influence the direction of LAPSSET in Lamu. For example, in 2014, the first County Governor of Lamu, Issa Timamy, used his previous position as the Chairperson of the National Museums of Kenya to initiate investigations of irregular allocations of sand dunes and water catchment areas (Beja 2010). Locally, this was understood as an attack on a long-serving MP for Lamu West, Fahim Twaha, against whom Timamy contested the seat of County Governor in 2013. News about the investigations re-emerged in February 2017, a few months before the next elections, with the National Land Commission (NLC) threatening to revoke titles to land owned by Fahim Twaha and other members of his local network (Kenya News Agency 2017; Nema 2017). Individuals seen to have been part of Twaha's networks (such as his wealthy and influential father-in-law, the late Tahir Sheikh Said) had been implicated in the land speculation activities in 2011–12 that revolved around the defunct Lamu County Council. From 2013 onwards – when the LAPSSET agenda was taking shape in Lamu – such local politics would become central in debates over land rights and access to land.

During this time, Issa Timamy also sought greater political control of the LAPSSET agenda (as his successor, Fahim Twaha, has continued to do since 2017). For instance, Timamy's county administration approved the allocation of 4,492 ha of public land at Kiongwe village on the mainland to an American energy company, Cordisons Limited, for the establishment of a wind-power generating project, without consulting the NLC, which is legally mandated to allocate public land (Lwanga 2018). After the NLC issued a separate lease for 1,297 ha of land to another company in the same area for a similar project, Cordisons, supported by Timamy's administration, sued the NLC but lost the case (Oketch 2018). Despite this, Timamy's tussle with the NLC ensued, and in early 2016, he rejected the NLC's allocation of 11,331 ha of land in Lamu for LAPSSET, accusing the NLC of failing to consult his county administration while making the allocation (Beja 2018). The struggles over the fate of land in Lamu between the County Governor and the NLC continued, and Timamy – to the chagrin of the NLC – went ahead to involve his county administration in matters of monetary compensation for land earmarked for LAPSSET activities that the NLC was mandated to undertake (Praxides 2014). The resulting fragmentation of authority, associated with competing multiple interests, not only led to the creation of three different lists of names of project-affected people before a final list was agreed upon but also created opportunities for those aligned with networks of influence to benefit from the monetary compensation that would eventually be paid by the national government (Swazuri et al. 2018).

Meanwhile, Timamy's struggles with the NLC and other departments of the national government were generating considerable local hostility against his county administration, especially among those that had long benefited from the networks that Timamy had excluded from local influence (Chome 2020). There were claims that his county government was excluding Lamu's residents on the mainland areas and that his actions were causing delays to LAPSSET projects that required land, denying people access to monetary compensation (Praxides 2017; Nema 2016). Claims of local exclusion, especially of non-Bajuni interests, and failures to meet popular expectations regarding LAPSSET, constituted the central discursive thread within local politics in the run-up to the 2017 general elections.

Fahim Twaha, who had campaigned aggressively in the mainland areas where such feelings of exclusion were felt most acutely, won the elections with a narrow margin, defeating Timamy. However, just like his predecessor, and probably due to local pressures, Fahim Twaha has adopted a hard-line stance when it comes to matters of compensation of land and sea earmarked for LAPSSET activities. The county leadership also seeks a greater share of control over the LAPSSET agenda, debating, among other things, the future political direction of the project. In sum, these negotiations and economies of 'knowing about', 'imagining' and 'living towards' the future (see Cross 2014), are underpinning the contemporary political economy of Lamu and, as the chapter has shown, are shaping relationships of power and consent at different levels.

Conclusion

Economies of anticipation, as shown in this chapter, underscore the complex nature of responses 'from below' that arise when capital (and the state) are extended into rural and marginal areas (see Hall et al. 2015a; Borras and Franco 2013). Yet much of the literature emphasises the domination, expulsion or resistance of 'local communities' that results from rural development programmes or large-scale infrastructural projects (e.g. Asebe Regassa and Korf 2018; Buffavand 2016; Chinigo 2014; Planel 2014). This chapter, however, has shown how, when such projects hit the ground, they interact in complex ways with social groups within the local state and society, in ways 'that are differentiated along lines of class, gender, generation, ethnicity and nationality, and that have historically specific expectations, aspirations and traditions of struggle' (Hall et al. 2015a: 468). In Lamu, these dynamics produce diverse responses involving multiple actors, with different consequences.

Specifically, the chapter has shown how a high modernist vision such as LAPSSET can be transformed by local struggles over ownership and control of land, future benefits and local political power. In the process, the realities on the ground impinge on LAPSSET's exclusionary designs, and as a result, targets are shifted, priorities are reset and outcomes renegotiated. In short, a grand government vision such as LAPSSET might seem like 'a mountain at the national level ... but shrinks to the size of a leaf at the county level'; it does not really turn to 'ash at the grassroots' (Emmenegger et al. 2011: 748) but, rather, the high modernist vision is transformed to fit more local realities.

3

Town Making at the Gateway to Kenya's 'New Frontier'

HANNAH ELLIOTT

The anticipation of large-scale infrastructural development in northern Kenya sparked collective land investments among residents of Isiolo. Despite its geographical positioning at the centre of the country, Isiolo has long been popularly imagined as a dusty frontier town: the 'end of the tarmac' (*mwisho wa lami*) marking the boundary between Kenya 'proper' and its neglected north. Yet in recent years, Isiolo has been reimagined as a future industrial capital. This reimagining has been majorly facilitated by the town's positioning along the Lamu Port–South Sudan–Ethiopia Transport (LAPSSET) corridor, with Isiolo as the gateway into a 'new frontier' for economic growth in northern Kenya (see Map 3.1 and Chome, Chapter 2 this book). Isiolo features as a meeting point for LAPSSET's highways, while the oil pipeline and railway are expected to pass through the vicinity of the town. The scheme also promises Isiolo a number of additional projects: an international airport, a modern abattoir and a mega-dam to serve one of LAPSSET's three 'resort cities', currently planned for a site 70km outside the town.

Cross (2014) notes that scholars often readily assume that the transformations generated by large-scale capitalist development will be 'top-down' and driven by the powerful. His study of the economy of anticipation provoked by plans for special economic zones in India counters this notion, and shows how the anticipatory actions of ordinary people also contribute to reshaping the social and spatial outcomes of these investments. Similarly, while LAPSSET promises to make Isiolo town into an economic hub, it has thus far largely been the actions of ordinary people that have propelled the town's transformation. With the exception of the airport, the majority of the LAPSSET projects have yet to be completed or remain entirely unmaterialised in Isiolo, as national partners' commitments waiver, the Kenyan government struggles to secure private investment, and disputes by local governments and communities along the corridor disrupt and delay the project's ambitious timeline (Browne 2015). Yet, as with residents and political leaders in

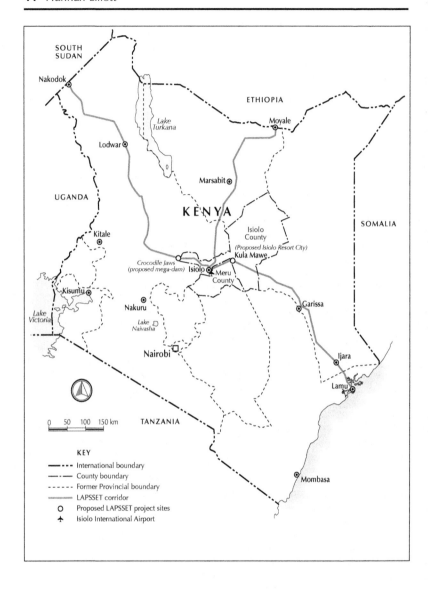

Map 3.1 Kenya, showing the LAPSSET corridor with the locations of Isiolo and Meru

Lamu County, LAPSSET has set in motion an economy of anticipation in and around Isiolo town as people prepare for a LAPSSET future. Most prominently and strikingly, these future preparations are related to land. Whether by 'cutting', fencing, building upon, occupying, purchasing or seeking documentation stating ownership, diverse actors are individually and collectively investing in land in Isiolo, the monetary value of which has risen dramatically, a trend evident in other northern Kenya contexts detailed in this book including Lamu as well as in towns near Turkana's oil wells (see Okenwa, Chapter 4) and geothermal fields in Baringo (see Greiner, Chapter 8). By doing so, Isiolo residents, as well as investors from elsewhere, seek to secure a stake in the city of the future.

Based on twelve months of ethnographic fieldwork in Isiolo in 2014 and 2015, this chapter focuses on collective claims to land at the edges of Isiolo town by residents who typically organised themselves along ethnic lines. Isiolo has an ethnically diverse population dominated by Borana, Turkana, Somali, Samburu and Meru groups, each with historical and contemporary claims to 'owning' the town and belonging to it (Boye and Kaarhus 2011). Collective land claims, I show, are a continuation of longer-standing efforts by different groups to secure this belonging and to ensure rights to the town. These investments are efforts at what I call 'town making' at Isiolo's edges: the production of constituencies, led by patron pioneer settlers, through which ordinary people seek to connect up to, make claims on and ultimately 'break in' to the government. Town making in a time of LAPSSET is amplified and rendered more fraught by the rising monetary value of land and heightened anxieties about exclusion from the future city.

Cutting land at Isiolo's edges

Early into my research, Isiolo residents were quick to inform me of their concerns about LAPSSET. Suspicion was rife as to whom LAPSSET, a project driven by Kenya's national government, was really 'for'. Elected politicians and appointed civil servants working for the new Isiolo County Government[1] criticised the lack of consultation. They were of the opinion that local representation was scant at the national government's planning and negotiation table, echoing widespread misgivings that the projects might only serve the interests of so-called non-locals. A major bone of contention was that a number of the LAPSSET projects were to be constructed on land claimed by both Isiolo and neighbouring Meru County. This dispute over boundaries can be traced back to 1930, the year after Isiolo's establishment as the headquarters of the Northern Frontier

---

[1] Forty-two county governments were established across Kenya following the 2013 elections as part of a national project of political devolution. Kenya's most significant political reform since independence, devolution is a key facet of Kenya's current constitution, voted in by two-thirds of the population during a referendum in 2010.

District, when the British realised that the town in fact lay within what was then Meru District. Although the British sought to rectify this mistake by redrawing the NFD's boundary to encompass the town, the boundary's exact position has remained contested since independence (Boye 2007; Hjort 1979).

Isiolo town continues to lie precariously at the edge of the central part of Isiolo County, hemmed in to the north, east and south by the Meru border, creating a palpable sense among Isiolo locals of an encroaching neighbouring boundary. The LAPSSET highway, oil pipeline and railway are all expected to pass through contested land between the counties to the north and north-east of Isiolo town, while the Isiolo International Airport, now complete, is positioned so that its terminal building and control towers are situated in Isiolo County while its runway extends into Meru. This raised questions of control and who would benefit from the LAPSSET projects (Elliott 2016). Non-Meru Isiolo residents pointed out that, as part of a group of central Kenyan ethnic groups known under the acronym GEMA (Gikuyu, Embu, Meru, Akamba), Meru people have been privileged *vis-à-vis* successive national governments as an important voting group, with Meru political representatives holding key positions of power. The national government was thus assumed to favour Meru County in any judgements it made on the boundary, including via the Independent Electoral and Boundaries Commission. There was also ambivalence around the assigning of the roles of chairman of the LAPSSET Development Authority and the Minister for Land to prominent Meru politicians (ibid.).

Beyond the question of whom the projects would be 'for', LAPSSET provoked anxieties in Isiolo around the ethnic make-up of an expanding population. The secretariat for Vision 2030, the overarching national development blueprint that includes projects such as LAPSSET, projected that Isiolo County's population would increase dramatically from around 143,000 to 1.5 million by 2017. In a 'sensitisation' workshop on LAPSSET I attended, a non-governmental organisation (NGO) programme coordinator rhetorically asked participants 'those one million people, where will they come from? Will they come from Isiolo or from other parts?' (27 February 2014, Isiolo town). The question reflected apprehensions over ethnic domination. Should the town come to be dominated by ethnic others, Isiolo's core ethnic groups would be outnumbered and at risk of losing political power; ethnic others could not be expected to vote for 'local' political representatives.

Anxieties about population were closely connected to uncertainties about land. Residents knew all too well that land in other parts of Kenya, and particularly in neighbouring central Kenya, was congested and expensive and that many people there perceived northern land as abundant and 'up for grabs'. At the time of my research, the majority of land in northern Kenya continued to be classified as 'trust land', though this was set to change with the impending Community Land Bill that sought to render land rights in pastoralist areas more secure. Trust land was supposed to be held 'in trust' by the local authority (now the Isiolo County Government and, prior to devolution, the County Council) on behalf of 'the community', a framework that has historically been abused, rendering community rights to secure land ownership precarious (Ministry of Lands 2009: 11–12, 15). Locals feared that, as the Community Land Bill was being worked out in the Kenya Parliament, 'trust land' on the town's fringes and beyond, which was becoming increasingly valuable and desirable since the announcement of the LAPSSET plans, remained insecurely owned and vulnerable to 'land grabs'.

Fears of grabs by 'others' propelled a rush on land acquisitions among Isiolo residents themselves. The Trust Land Act was designed to preserve 'customary' land-use practices and protect pastoralist land from alienation and speculation, but in and around Isiolo town, where the majority of residents pursue livelihoods outside of pastoralism (combining, for example, the rearing of small numbers of sheep and goats with casual labour or small enterprises), privatisation of land has long been taking place. Aside from formal plot allocations issued by the local government to a privileged few, private ownership has tended to be consolidated through collective acquisitions and informal settlement projects (whereby pioneer settlers 'gift' plots to settlers in return for small payments in money or livestock) or through individual purchase, with residents typically seeking formal land documents retrospectively, if at all (Elliott 2018). The anticipation of LAPSSET catalysed moves to privatise land ownership. Groups of Isiolo residents rushed to collectively participate in 'cutting' land, demarcating plot boundaries with beacons and fences and by building wooden structures, suspecting that otherwise 'others' would get there first.

As a means of reckoning with uncertainty for survival as well as for profit (Bear et al. 2015), speculative land acquisitions are, thus, not only the preserve of the elite but also a strategy deployed by ordinary Isiolo residents who consider themselves most vulnerable to exclusion from a LAPSSET future. This was made clear to me during encounters with Isiolo residents Guyo and Regina. Guyo, a Borana man, was in his early thirties and a father of four when I met him. He had casual work as a night watchman at a hotel, while his wife sold basic food items from a small shop in the corner of their plot in a predominantly Borana village some few kilometres north of the town centre. Guyo was keen to gain additional plots in the hope of preserving them for his children's future or to sell, based on the popular assumption that land prices would only continue to rise. Together with members of a youth group from his village, Guyo had cut and claimed a large piece of land on the village's periphery that residents claimed as village property for livestock grazing and farming projects. Concerned that the land could be perceived by 'outsiders' as 'up for grabs', the group divided the land into individual plots. Those who could afford poles and wires fenced their newly acquired property, while others made do with freely available stones and thorny shrub. On one occasion, I bumped into Guyo in the town centre and he told me of another plot acquisition that he had made further out of town on the disputed Isiolo–Meru boundary. There, he had been part of a much larger group of about a hundred Borana participants who had collectively seized the land and divided it into plots. Probably thinking that I might pay a good price, Guyo asked if I might be interested in one of these plots. 'Don't you want land here?' he asked. 'In five years' time Isiolo will be a city, and there will be no such thing as a *kiwanja* [livestock compound]' (6 October 2014).

While acquisitions such as Guyo's sought to pre-empt the acquisition of the same land by 'outsiders', including residents across the Meru County border, other groups local to Isiolo were keenly engaging in collective acquisitions to prevent procurements by groups such as Guyo's. Borana dominate numerically as well as politically in Isiolo. At the time of my fieldwork, the Isiolo County Government was perceived by non-Borana residents as Borana-controlled; the position of county governor was held by a Borana lawyer, and several key positions in the county government, including the office dealing with land issues, were held by Borana civil servants. Other ethnic groups were afraid that collective Borana acquisitions could lead to their disenfranchisement and exclusion from the town. In October 2014, acting upon these concerns, hundreds of Turkana from central Isiolo descended on an area 5 km north of Isiolo town, also on the disputed border with Meru County. The land was already claimed by Isiolo's Turkana community (including those living further out of the town who were more dependent on livestock) as a grazing area, but fears of its appropriation by others pushed residents to 'cut' the land into individual plots. Regina, a Turkana woman in her sixties, participated in the acquisition. She lived in a dilapidated mud house in a settlement known as a 'Turkana' village where rising prices of plots sparked fears of future displacement. Regina and her husband owned some fifteen goats, which they grazed on vacant neighbouring plots already bought by investors and speculators, while their children sought casual labour as construction workers or pursued small businesses selling tea and alcohol. When describing the collective acquisition on the outskirts of the town, Regina, like Guyo, explained that Isiolo would become a 'city': 'Isiolo will be Nairobi', she said, and 'Borana want to make Isiolo theirs'. She listed neighbourhoods of the town that Borana already 'owned' (2 November 2014). As she saw it, the Turkana land acquisition would ensure that that place, at least, would be 'for the Turkana'.

Connecting up and breaking in

As I learned from my encounters with Guyo and Regina, while collective land acquisitions anticipated the rising monetary value of pastoral land at the town's fringes, they also sought to secure rights to belonging in Isiolo town through building ethnic urban constituencies. While rapidly rising land value is a relatively recent phenomenon in Isiolo and correlates with the announcement of LAPSSET in the mid- to late 2000s, collective land acquisitions have a much longer history. Towns in northern Kenya and other colonial frontiers in this region have long been deemed 'places of the government' (Leonardi 2013) – sites of state power and resources – and have thus long been centres to which people have sought to forge belonging. Isiolo, like many of these towns, started out as an administrative station or *boma*, a Swahili word meaning 'compound' appropriated by the British. The colonial governance objective in northern Kenya was to maintain the region as a buffer zone, protecting the colony both from the expansion of Menelik's Ethiopia and Italian imperial ambitions in the region, while taxing local populations to generate the funds by which to rule (Whittaker 2014). *Boma*s were the bases from which this governance took place, typically via chiefs and headmen (Dahl 1979), rendering them major points of articulation between the region's predominantly pastoralist communities and the government (Waweru 2002).

Towns were, however, not considered places for pastoralists. Colonial policies sought to keep those classified as 'natives' out of towns and to restrict them to their 'proper places' in the rural areas, while chiefs and headmen would shuttle between the towns and 'their people' in the countryside (Waweru 2002: 91; Dahl 1979). 'Clean-ups' and 'repatriations' sought to keep 'natives' out and return them to their designated areas (Elliott 2018; Broch-Due 2000). Those with connections to the administration tended to be better able to negotiate rights to Isiolo town, reinforcing the association between 'town' and 'government'. While rural areas were seen as the proper place for the 'native', northern *boma*s were associated with the 'non-native' who had privileged access to trade and employment in government service (cf. Taylor 2013): Arabs, Asians and so-called 'alien Somalis' whom the British had recruited as interpreters, clerks and as soldiers in the colonial military. To differentiate the latter from 'native' Kenyan Somalis, the British required applicants for residence in the town to demonstrate their connections to the government, including through written requests to the local administration. This meant that it was largely those who could 'speak' the colonial language of English, Kiswahili and bureaucracy (or had access to someone who could) who were able to negotiate rights to Isiolo town (Elliott 2018).

During and after the Second World War, permission to reside in towns as traders was extended to sections of 'native' pastoralist ethnic groups in line with a policy to open up the north's economy (Dahl 1979). Those who managed to forge connections to towns via shop ownership once again tended to be those who could forge connections to the government: trading licences were typically granted to those who had been employed by the colonial administration as chiefs and headmen or in the native police service. Towns became increasingly popular with these figures, who began to invest their government salaries in livestock in the rural areas and shops in the towns (ibid.). Once again, the connection between 'town' and 'government' was reinforced.

After independence in 1963 and the lifting of colonial restrictions on African mobility and residence across Kenya, a number of dramatic changes struck the north and saw large swathes of its pastoralist population seeking out towns such as Isiolo. While wealthy pastoralists not employed by the government had generally steered clear of towns during the colonial period (Waweru 2002), the secessionist war that followed independence impoverished many of their livestock and displaced them out of the pastoralist economy, a situation exacerbated by periods of severe drought and famine that followed. Many sought out Isiolo and other towns as places of survival, famine relief and waged labour (Hogg 1986).

During these hard years, some such migrants in Isiolo sought to secure their claims to residence in the town through patrons who were seen to have connections to the government. Some of these patrons tried to build constituencies of support through fashioning themselves as pioneer settlers, recruiting migrants to settle on unoccupied land at the town's edges. These figures had typically been employed by the government (often the police, army, paramilitary or other forms of security services) and were deemed able to speak its language of Kiswahili, English and 'paper',[2] thus giving them the authority to settle migrants and ensure their rights to residence and resources. As Regina, whom we met earlier, put it when she described the pioneer settler of the village she resided in: 'He was together with the government because he worked in the police' (Interview, 6 September 2014, Isiolo town). For migrants such as Regina, accessing secure residence in Isiolo through direct negotiation with the local government and its bureaucracy was virtually impossible given their lack of connections and money. Participating in settlement projects was thus a means of accessing land and more secure rights to reside in Isiolo town (Elliott 2018).

Settlement under the authority of pioneer settlers also became a means through which poor residents could begin to form connections 'up' a hierarchy of authority. This was possible through building constituencies of (typically ethnic) support and votes. One pioneer settler, Jarso, a retired security guard who had been employed by the Magadi Soda Company (a former enterprise closely connected to the colonial government), explained how he had built a career as a self-described 'small president' through forming a 'Borana' village to the north of Isiolo town during the 1990s:

> Finally we reached six houses. Then I went to the DC [District Commissioner] and explained I want a chief here. We were given … an

---

[2] Cf. Leonardi (2013) on chiefs in South Sudanese towns.

assistant chief. When we got the assistant chief we started to publicise and market the place. We told people there is free land here. We went around with the chief recruiting people. We became eighty houses. The assistant chief was promoted to chief and we got a new assistant chief. The whole place became settlement and I asked for even a councillor. (Interview, 1 March 2014, Isiolo town)

Jarso's account shows that forming settlements was a way of trying to connect up to the government and, ultimately, to break into it. Once a village was significant enough to have a councillor, the people residing there had the power to determine who would represent them in the County Council, effectively producing their own politicians. Through the possibility of their affiliation to another candidate, a village could hope to wield some influence over their political representative: in return for their votes, the councillor would, ideally at least, provide them with protection and 'bring development', for example in the form of a school, food aid or formal recognition of their land rights through providing documents (cf. Willis et al. 2017). By forming constituencies through settlement, ordinary people could effectively break into and shape the government, influencing and directing its powers and resources.

This 'breaking in' was, as one friend and civil society activist, Adan, explained to me, a direct logic behind 'making a town'. Adan was telling me about a contemporary example of town making in a small rural centre called Gotu along the 'corridor' of Isiolo North that links the central Isiolo area to the larger part of the county to the east. Gotu is an important centre in local pastoralist geographies as a watering point for livestock because of its location on the Euaso Nyiro River but, as a place used and inhabited by both Borana and Garre groups, its 'ownership' has been contested. At the time of my fieldwork, there was suspicion among Isiolo's Borana community that the county government was influenced by a wealthy Garre businessman who had been a major contributor to his electoral campaign. Borana were complaining that the governor had been favouring Garre over his 'own people' by giving Garre and Garre-owned companies a disproportionate number of jobs and contracts, and were concerned that, as a result of this empowerment, Garre would come to claim Gotu as 'theirs', excluding Borana from the area. Gotu had a Borana chief, however, and Adan explained that the chief was calling Borana to come and settle there in order to 'make Gotu into a town'. I asked what 'making a town' meant. 'They start by calling chiefs, and then you can get a councillor', Adan explained. 'And once you have a councillor, you can impeach governors' (11 August 2014). In the context of Kenya's devolved political system (and a trend across the country during 2014 of efforts to impeach governors who were not seen to be doing their jobs properly), 'having' a councillor was a way in which ordinary people could command that the government work for them, which might include deposing one governor in favour of another who promised to protect them and 'bring development'. Pioneer settlers' making of villages at Isiolo's edges followed similar 'town making' logics and can be seen as part of a bigger project of securing belonging to Isiolo town, itself contested by different ethnic groups.

Town making at Isiolo's peripheries became particularly fervent during the 1990s with Kenya's return to multi-partyism and growing political competition, amplifying ethnic claims to 'owning' the town. Poor residents descended on unsettled land under the authority of pioneer settlers, often backed by politicians as senior as the area member of parliament for Isiolo North as they sought to build their voter bases and exclude those of rival candidates (Elliott 2016; cf. Schlee and Shongolo 2012). These acquisitions also sought to prevent rival elements in the county council from reorganising land ownership through town planning and plot allocation processes (Elliott 2016). Once again, town making was a means through which ordinary people sought to demand political inclusion and belonging.

Town making in a time of LAPSSET

The time of LAPSSET marked a season of speculation and town making through collective land investments in Isiolo. Residents in their varied ethnic constellations anticipated future exclusion from the town with the arrival of further ethnic 'newcomers' possibly backed by national government interests. Without sufficient ethnic votes, residents feared being no longer able to produce the politicians who could secure their rights to town. Some spoke of creating arrangements 'as in Dubai' whereby only those considered 'locals' could be elected into political power. Others suggested alliances between local ethnic groups in order to ensure their continued political power. However, who counts as 'local' in Isiolo (and indeed elsewhere in Kenya) remains a highly contested subject (Boye and Kaarhus 2011). Concretely, it was once again through efforts at town making that residents sought to preclude exclusion from the city of the future. In some places along the disputed boundary between Isiolo and Meru counties, town making was being consolidated through, for example, the establishment of chiefs' camps and taxation points by both the Isiolo and Meru administrations as they sought to exert their sovereignty over these places. On occasion, competing efforts at town making between ethnic groups from within Isiolo County and across the border sparked outbreaks of violence.

As happened during the decades following independence, town making in the time of LAPSSET demanded political inclusion and belonging. But it also became a means of demanding inclusion in the speculative real estate economy that had emerged since the announcement of the mega-projects. Isiolo residents sought to firmly locate themselves in this economy and ensure their profit from it, so that collective acquisitions also became a means of procuring a valuable commodity 'for free'.

This double logic to town making could prove contradictory. During interviews, pioneer settlers complained that those they had settled and granted plots to as part of political projects of ethnic constituency building had come to undermine these projects when they sold their land to wealthy 'outsiders'. As villages' ethnic homogeneity began to unravel through such sales, leaders saw collective land acquisitions at Isiolo's edges as opportunities to recreate ethnic constituencies (Elliott 2016). Yet leaders were wary that the same processes could play out through these new investments. Regina, when telling me about the Turkana land acquisition described above, reported that Turkana leaders instructed participants to invest in their plots by fencing and building on them to secure their claims. They were warned not to sell their land to ethnic others (2 November 2014). Borana participants in collective investments faced similar instructions, whereby they were particularly discouraged from selling to wealthy Somali from neighbouring counties who were rumoured to show up in cars filled with cash with the intention of buying plots from locals.

For Borana, however, selling land to ethnic 'kin' was more possible than for Turkana, as wealthy Borana from neighbouring Marsabit County who were interested in Isiolo's future prospects and possibilities of political careers in the Borana-led county government were migrating to Isiolo and keen to buy land. Comparatively, Turkana lacked wealthy ethnic affiliates to whom they could sell. As an Isiolo group with particularly low socio-economic status, Turkana were seen as vulnerable to what was often referred to as 'displacement by money' (*kuondolewa na pesa*) in a time of LAPSSET: forced to move out of the area having sold all their land to others (Elliott 2016). This had major implications for Turkana political reproduction. As one Turkana councillor lamented: 'The Turkana community will be extinct! I fear the Turkana name will be history!' (Interview, 27 November 2014, Isiolo town). By 'extinction', the councillor implicitly referred to the ways in which ethnic groups across northern Kenya have historically shifted identity and affiliated with 'stronger' ethnic groups (who have, for example, superior access to grazing and water sources) for purposes of survival, in the process losing their former ethnic names and identities (Schlee 1989). The councillor envisaged that loss of fellow urban constituents through 'displacement by money' would force Isiolo Turkana to affiliate politically with another group, potentially weakening their rights to the town (Elliott 2018).

Conclusion

The LAPSSET corridor effects have yet to fully materialise in Isiolo, but the announcement of development plans have propelled residents into strategic practices of town making at the town's peripheries, especially among those who anticipate exclusion from the imagined city of the future. As this chapter has shown, these collective land acquisitions build on longer-term investments by poor communities seeking to secure political inclusion and belonging in Isiolo town. Collective acquisitions under the authority of pioneer settlers who speak the language of the government have allowed ordinary people to connect up to power, presenting themselves as ethnic constituencies and, ideally at least, producing political representatives who can ensure their belonging in the town.

In a time of LAPSSET, town making is amplified and accelerated, as Isiolo groups perceive their future exclusion as imminent and local political leaders strive to secure their own political continuity in the face of a changing ethnic population and encroaching Meru County boundary. Yet while collective acquisitions are a continuation of the kinds of town making efforts that took place during the decades that followed independence, contemporary town making is also driven by demands for economic inclusion as the monetary value of pastoral land continues to rise. As land becomes an increasingly valuable resource in monetary as well as political terms, participants in collective land acquisitions fantasise about the profits that can be reaped from their newly acquired plots in the future and see them as important forms of security in uncertain times (Elliott 2018).

Despite these apparently contradictory interests, it is clear that ordinary residents continue to be at the forefront of the transformations taking place in Isiolo. As is shown in other cases in this book, including Lamu (Chome, Chapter 2), Turkana (Okenwa, Chapter 4), South Omo (Fana Gebresenbet, Chapter 10), Samburu (Drew, Chapter 5), and Baringo (Greiner, Chapter 8), 'new frontiers' are shaped not so much (or not only) by the interests of the powerful behind the proponents of large-scale development as by the anticipatory actions of a multitude of actors. This includes those deemed the most vulnerable to disenfranchisement and dispossession, whose actions are propelled by their fears of exclusion and demands for inclusion.

4

Contentious Benefits
& Subversive Oil Politics
in Kenya
DORIS OKENWA

In an era of so-called ethical capitalism, global codes of conduct have proliferated to regulate the operations of investors and companies involved in the extractives sector. Local consent and the participation of host communities, combined with transparency and accountability mandates for multinationals and national governments, now constitute benchmarks to measure corporate social performance. While this has increased the prominence given to indigenous communities in the last couple of decades, as many have gained traction in mobilising for resource rights by drawing on these global templates of ethical extraction, the politics of participation and inclusion are not without limits. This chapter explores the inadvertent outcomes of local-level struggles in Turkana County around power, inclusion and voice: contentions that belie any notion of a unified way of 'seeing' extractive development, let alone a homogeneous agreement on who should benefit and on what grounds. Whose voice counts? Whose knowledge matters? Who is the 'community'?

Such questions are at the forefront of debates around oil finds in Turkana County, a historically marginalised hinterland in Kenya's far north-west now being promoted as one of Kenya's new 'dream zones' (Cross 2014) of economic progress. Since the discovery of oil beneath the sprawling rangelands of the South Lokichar Basin in southern Turkana in 2012, state and investor efforts to win over local opinion in the host community have included promises of lucrative benefits, the transformation of livelihoods and economic prospects for the area's predominantly pastoral inhabitants. Consultations have been held in public and private with a cross-section of local 'stakeholders' complemented by corporate-funded 'development' projects in a move to obtain a 'social license to operate' (Dolan and Rajak 2016; Prno and Slocombe 2012; Rajak 2011). Local politicians continue to demand 'a rightful share' (*Star* 2017b; Ferguson 2015) for their constituents while civil society groups mobilise to scrutinise investor operations and sensitise local residents to their rights. Yet the manifold ways that investors have sought to engage with 'community stakeholders', and social audits carried out by non-state actors, have not allayed local concerns of being 'cheated' of the benefits from resource extraction in Turkana. For, as Barry notes, consultations do not particularly guarantee the total incorporation of local concerns. Rather, 'consultation may be treated by an oil company or an international institution as a technical practice of qualification' (Barry 2006: 247). One of such mandates is Free Prior Informed Consent (FPIC), a United Nations initiative to protect the rights of indigenous people and ensure they give consent to any extractives or investment processes in their area whether forest logging, conservation or mineral extraction. This 'bottom-up' approach to local participation, however, has had ambivalent results.

Consequently, the notion of oil politics as a cloak-and-dagger operation, involving networks in the shadows that funnel benefits to select groups and deals that transfer rights to communal rangelands to outside companies and investors, has gained purchase in the minds of many in Turkana. Seen from the perspective of residents living in the area of extractive operations, the oil finds heighten a sense of an impending disaster or 'resource curse' (Auty 1993) that needs to be averted through micro politics of vigilance and subversive tactics. Thus, local contentions rather than global extractive ethics or government interventions, have done more to shape the configuration of oil benefits and its beneficiaries. Who benefits and how, is determined by whose voice and might prevails.

Conceptualised here as 'inclusion by subversion' (Okenwa 2020), subversion in this sense highlights particular strategies of resistance and manoeuvres not just for resistance to extractive operations in a normative sense but as a means of engagement and inclusion in the distribution of benefits. Thus, protests and contentions can be understood as a bridge to forge connections and not only as a way to sever them. It is not so much what happens during protests, demonstrations and blockades but what emerges from these acts of seeming resistance that puts into relief the contrast between the public enactment of consultation and participation, and the 'backstage' of deal-making and pursuit of opportunities that involve various stakeholders, intermediaries and investors themselves. It moves beyond reductive critiques of community participation towards practice and performance. This way of 'seeing' extends our attention from the investor to the internal dynamics among people within the community, with the state and, more importantly, how 'community' becomes re-enacted by new social borders created via resources.

The chapter draws on ethnographic fieldwork carried out at different times between 2014 and 2019. This included interviews with a range of residents and officials, participation in negotiation meetings between investors, subcontractors and various local interest groups, as well as observations of everyday life gathered from living in town and through accompanying and moving with pastoralists.

Locating oil and enacting the host community

Exploration in the South Lokichar Basin, an area that lies in the south and east of Turkana County, dates to the early 1990s. In 2010, plans were announced to expand exploration activities through a joint venture between the Anglo-Irish investor Tullow Oil and Vancouver-based Africa Oil Corporation. Nevertheless, it still came as a surprise to many Kenyans, especially residents of Turkana, when in 2012 Kenya's Minister of Energy announced commercially viable deposits of up to 300 million barrels of crude oil in the basin. The Ngamia-1 well in Turkana East marked the first viable exploration well pad and more have since followed. Many Turkana saw oil as a divine intervention if not poetic justice of sorts. 'God has remembered us', I was often told. Having been overlooked by the state for the perceived lack of 'productive' resources and more contemporary forms of livelihoods than subsistence pastoralism, Turkana has come to be reimagined as a frontier awash with oil riches.

At the onset of Tullow's advancement in Turkana, corporate–community relations were fraught with the crises of community representation, a low level of awareness and spatially dispersed benefits, to mention but a few. As one of Tullow's Community Liaison Officers explained to me, 'the real problem we are facing now is who should be engaged first?' (Interview with Tullow Community Liaison Officer, Lokichar, April 2016). The conventional practice of exploration in the host community begins with gaining access to land through public *barazas* (meetings), dialogue with groups and leaders, and an agreement over what will be exchanged for the land. Though Free Prior Informed Consent was not deployed at the start of Tullow's operations, the company published a human rights report in 2016 reflecting a commitment to establish the mandate in their operations in line with the funding stipulations of the International Finance Corporation (Oxfam 2017). Beyond the public *baraza*, Tullow deployed other forms of community engagement such as seeking counsel from elders, women's groups, local associations and working with civil society. Commendable as these are, the emergence of an extractives governance juggernaut fuelled the larger dynamics of local suspicion that this was a selective engagement with the more influential and literate sections of the population.

The discovery of oil is unfolding at a time when pastoralism is under pressure from a range of crucial factors that have not only influenced the state and investor framing of the resource potential but also shaped local expectations (often deemed unrealistic). These factors range from historical marginalisation and a lack of investment in the livestock economy to low-intensity conflict, destitution, slow recovery from intense seasonal droughts, and new territorialisations associated with the rise of local capital and external speculators. Pastoralism remains the backbone of livelihoods in Turkana, though in recent years Turkana's economy has evolved with emerging opportunities in livestock trading and casual labour, the growth of small and medium enterprises and the mushrooming of administrative and technical positions in the new county government, giving rise to a class of civil servants based mostly in towns. But the pace of change is glacial when seen from the perspective of many residents who struggle to make ends meet. To quote some young men, everyday life is about 'pushing time' by engaging in whatever opportunity that comes along 'in pursuit of permanence' (Okenwa 2020) and stable livelihoods. These have all combined to influence corporate interventions and blur the boundaries of responsibility to the extent that much of Tullow's social investments have been geared towards the provision of basic amenities that fall within the domains of government responsibility (Soni and Essex 2019). More so, oil discovery coincides with the establishment of sub-national government and the proliferation of aid and civil society advocacy efforts on 'extractives'. With devolution, the rise of a new political class and an increasing number of school leavers marks a shift in generational relationships and customary forms of leadership towards more contemporary and contentious forms of politics. Thus, to understand the emerging contentious politics around inclusion and distribution, a closer look is needed at the ways in which benefits and beneficiaries (or stakeholders) are constituted but also influenced by historical antecedents. Given that oil is a spatial project and wells do not line up in a linear pattern, part of what has emerged is a kind of distributive politics that creates communities of interests and social boundaries within the host community.

Turkana County is administratively divided into seven sub-counties with settlements organised mostly around livelihood patterns based on the resource potentials in a location: fishing along Lake Turkana, agro-pastoralists in the riverine areas (the rivers Turkwel and Kerio), mobile pastoralists in the drier parts of the north, south and east, and small trade and business activities in towns and villages close to major roads. Oil exploration activities have been carried out in varied capacities across the county; however, it is the southern and eastern sub-counties that constitute primary 'areas of influence' (Tullow 2017). It then follows that, while in principle the host community of Kenya's oil deposits is the entire Turkana County, proximity to the resource is what qualifies the primary beneficiaries, as clearly articulated in Tullow's *Stakeholder Engagement Framework* (Tullow 2017: 78), thereby confining operational distinctions largely between the directly and indirectly impacted communities (Map 4.1).

A key development from this has been the rise of 'hyper' indigeneity in Turkana – a hierarchy of localness, as it were. When discussing a rightful share of benefits, many Turkana imply a hierarchy of 'localness' that seeks to differentiate between Kenyans in general, the broader Turkana community and those in settlements having direct proximity to oil exploration sites (Okenwa 2020). While Turkana is regarded as the 'host community' of Kenya's oil development, exploration and appraisal operations are synonymous with a border-making project in which

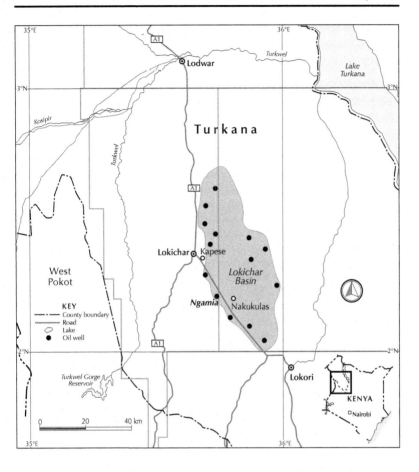

Map 4.1 Kenya, showing location of oil exploration sites in the South Lokichar Basin, Turkana

various discrete stakeholders are identified and accorded a relevance in ensuring social acceptance and, ultimately, security of oil operations. These include residents directly affected by construction activities or the need for land for operations, customary authorities, sub-national political administration, civil society, businesspeople and local contractors. Thus, while claims to resource benefits draw on a Turkana identity, that identity also fosters nuclear notions of 'community' in terms of those in direct proximity as well as those with the ability to disrupt the company's operations and need to be won over.

Lokichar town and Nakukulas village are two of the most prominent sites in the South Lokichar Basin where Tullow's oil exploration activities are based. Smaller affected settlements are often submerged within these two prominent locations making consultations and consensus building more challenging. It requires negotiation on a case-by-case basis, as one solution for an affected town might not work for a pastoral settlement. Each of these affected communities differs in demography, livelihood, land-use patterns and lifestyle. Communal aspirations for dividends from oil development obscure a highly individualised, heterogeneous society – one that is very different from the 'egalitarian' ethos of pastoral societies feted in early ethnographies (Goldschmidt 1971).

Processes of community engagement inadvertently produce new forms of exclusion and social differentiation. Ballard and Banks (2003: 297) note that, in the context of natural resource exploitation, host communities 'are only summoned into being or defined as such by the presence or the potential of a mining project'. Watts (2004: 199) takes this further to posit that 'each community is imagined ... through and with oil – the communities are "naturalised" in relation to the effects, social, environmental, political, of oil exploration and production – but produces forms of rule and identity that are often fragmented, unruly and violent.' In Turkana, the process of mapping the boundaries of oil and its beneficiaries has produced multiple forms and representations of community. To borrow from Comaroff and Comaroff (2009), these are akin to a performance – the contradictions of ethnic identities refashioned and repositioned to fit the requirements of global investors. Here, questions of authenticity or falsehood are moot. What is at stake is how communities or groups mobilise to negotiate access to benefits. Critically, distribution skews to those with might, information and, above all, an understanding of the industry lexicon. But, as the next section will show, subversion becomes the way to assert inclusion and disrupt established hierarchies.

Inclusion by subversion: burning tyres by day, building bridges at night

On a September morning in 2016, residents of Lokichar, the administrative and commercial centre of southern Turkana, woke to news of burning tyres on the main A1 road that bisects the town. A group of protestors, mostly young and middle-aged men, were blocking trucks carrying oil from leaving town. These were the first shipments planned as part of the Early Oil Pilot Scheme, a gambit of the ruling Jubilee governing coalition ahead of Kenya's 2017 elections to boost investor confidence and convince a wary public that it was delivering on plans for the country's economic transformation. Resentment in Turkana against the Early Oil Pilot Scheme simmered long before it was formally announced in 2016. As early as 2015, some residents alleged that oil was being 'sneaked out' of Turkana disguised in water tankers. The notion that 'our oil is secretly moving at night' (Interview with resident, Lokichar, December 2015) rankled local opinion on the oil development. The demonstration was spearheaded by an association of drivers and backed by local businesspeople and some unemployed youths. 'We were monitoring them [Tullow] since night', a protestor described. 'We were phoning them [residents around the Ngamia-1 oil field where the trucks departed from] and asking them what is happening and when the trucks will start moving so that we can block them from this side' (Interview with protestor, Lokichar, September 2016). He spoke excitedly of the intricacy of planning, collaboration across communities and the tactics that led to the stand-off.

Threats of military intervention were bandied about by government representatives as the trucks were grounded while Tullow and its contractor resorted to dialogue. The bone of contention, as put before Tullow when all parties were invited for a discussion, was that Turkana locals had been side-lined from the oil transportation process in favour of better-connected Kenyans as represented by Oil Movers Limited (OML), a company contracted for the task. The drivers' association wanted to be given the opportunity of both driving the trucks and possibly supplying them via a collective registered company and some assistance with raising the capital. It also reflected disaffection with the mainly menial work opportunities that have been made available to Turkana people, such as security guards or 'road marshals' to prevent accidents involving company vehicles and construction equipment. An instructive point was that the contractor, and not Tullow, spearheaded the negotiation, defending his contract though he is a Kenyan citizen and *de facto* beneficiary of the nation's wealth. Later, one of the ringleaders with the drivers' association explained the situation to me: 'They are looking at us like we have no brain. Can we not work? Like other Kenyans down country?' (Interview with protestor, Lokichar, September 2016).

The blockade was not only an act of disobedience by a disgruntled group of stakeholders but a show of power from below. Besides demonstrating resistance, protests can be productive forms of engagement. In this respect, there was a marked difference between this demonstration and a protest in 2013 led by politicians that halted Tullow's operations. The 2013 protests resulted in a non-binding agreement that made provisions for labour and contract opportunities for the host community, which largely favoured local politicians in the end as few people could afford to register companies to access contracts. Such experience of 'elite capture' fuels both tacit and overt subversion when benefits appear to have ended up in the hands of those supposedly representing the community, *ad hoc* groups as new alliances are forged to stage direct engagements without go-betweens. The struggle becomes how to channel benefits directly, as various communities of interest emerge to speak for themselves either through blockades, disruptions or dialogue.

Local opinion of the blockade was mixed. 'They burn tyres in the morning and get work at night', an unimpressed resident opined to denounce the protestors as attention seekers who, like the politicians or 'representatives' before them, would eventually resort to shadow negotiations to secure some advantages over others. 'What happens at night?' is a question many residents ask in the context of the local conversations on who benefits and who misses out. As a young man put it, 'I was together with my friend fighting for work in the morning and we all went home after. But by the next day morning, he was chosen, and I was still without work. So, what happened at night?' (Conversation with Lokichar resident, September 2016). His ire was not only for the companies that employ local casual labourers, but also for his friend who sought to negotiate in the shadows.

This is a kind of nuanced contentious politics that opposes the worst of an investment but also seeks to secure new terms of local incorporation by stretching the mandate. It is precisely these kinds of moves that shift the balance of power in ways that spread benefits more widely to those who agitate and otherwise subvert the norms of participation, dialogue and inclusion valorised in front-of-stage community engagement practices. The outcry from the drivers' association representative was about challenging the stereotypes of Turkana as a 'backward' region and the corporate defence that area residents lacked the technical skills required in oil exploration operations. 'At least we can drive! We can do many things even without paper [certificates]' (Interview with protestor, Lokichar, September 2016). Statements along these lines – demands for work opportunities – were even made by livestock-keepers outside town in search of their own engagements with investors.

The question of who benefits, or even more fundamentally whether Tullow's operations are 'good' or 'bad', is contingent. Opinions differ. Beyond accusations and counter-accusations, this points to the ephemeral nature of emerging benefits and the need for long-term plans. The nature of oil extraction is that work opportunities dry up as exploration and appraisal, involving extensive construction operations, moves to production, which requires only minimal technical expertise and security to guard installations. The diminishing opportunities lead to souring relations between the oil company and communities but also within the wider community when the scale of benefits is weighed between one person or group and another. The situation with the demonstrators was partially resolved after talks that promised more inclusion mollified aggrieved parties – 'partially' because those roadblocks continued and eventually stalled the oil export trucks – up to June 2018. Nonetheless, if the perception persists that such is the kind of engagement that generates results, then it is one way to guarantee otherwise potential losers a win and diminish the established authorities Tullow depends on for its smooth operations.

Conclusion: expelling 'bad' politics and redirecting benefits

'Everything is politics' is a common refrain in the towns and settlements in the oil basin. It goes to show how shifting power relations are also at the core of tensions that have arisen around oil development in Turkana. Other scholars have observed similar trends in their studies of natural resource host communities where corporate claims of local partnerships and community engagement schemes rely heavily on existing social hierarchies (Gardner 2012). Yet power also resides in small and unassuming places. Spheres of influence extend well beyond constituted authority. If a representative or broker appears to be 'selling out' (real or imagined), what emerges are new forms of dispute and interest groups to contravene the dominance of so-called opinion shapers that have dominated negotiations (Lind 2017). As noted earlier, changes in demography (an increasing non-pastoralist population) and contemporary politics complicate attempts at consensus building.

Developments in Nakukulas bring these tensions into focus. Nakukulas is the largest settlement around a cluster of oil fields including Ngamia-1, the first well where commercially viable oil was discovered. Both sedentary and mobile pastoralists call it home. In 2014, two years after the discovery was announced and construction operations were ramping up for oil exploration, there were occasional meetings between Tullow Oil and residents. Yet much of the business of operational activity was discussed in Lokichar, 20 km to the west. For amenities or information, residents had to walk for several hours to Lokichar if they were unable to afford or hitch a ride. Barely three years later, by 2017 Tullow had opened a liaison office in Nakukulas, had enlisted many young men in casual work, and was financing a variety of social projects in the area. Some in Lokichar noted that 'Nakukulas is now where it is happening because those people know how to fight!' Residents of Lokichar saw power shift to Nakukulas, a small settlement that nonetheless was able to wield substantial power owing to its proximity to the exploration wells. Nakukulas residents had barricaded wells and roads leading to oil installations on several occasions, pushing Tullow to widen its engagement. It was a type of resistance that created some measure of direct benefits for those living closest to the wells. Indeed, at a negotiation meeting with Tullow over land access for more oil wells, I witnessed this defiance as both elders and youths ensured the agreement was signed in the absence of their local Member of Parliament. 'Let him stay away, he has eaten enough' (Conversation with Nakukulas resident, December 2016), my host noted with glee.

Part of what inspired the clamour for direct benefits was also an earlier encounter that foreshadowed the potential for subverting existing hierarchies early in Tullow's operations: the acquisition of a large swathe of land in Kapese on the outskirts of Lokichar by a Kenyan company African Camp Solutions. The company is still referenced as a symbol of exploitation aided by complicit representatives such as elders and politicians who negotiated on behalf of the community. African Camp Solutions was introduced, in principle, as an employment-generation enterprise to be fully equipped with lodgings, wildlife and an airstrip. The 'community' represented by the elders and local politicians negotiated the lease. Shortly after, the site was leased to Tullow and remains the company's main operational base in Turkana. Some jobs, projects and scholarships were awarded to the community in addition to monetary payments to the county. Having observed these events in nearby Lokichar over a period of time and the widespread dissatisfaction with seemingly isolated negotiations, other settlements like Nakukulas began to push for direct monetary compensation, which eventually led Tullow to benchmark 7 million Kenyan shillings to any affected community for each oil well established in the area.

Some acknowledge that the fractured nature of local politics and treachery by community representatives were to blame for the disputes with Tullow around benefits. These views are often directed at local politicians, civil society activists and, most especially, Tullow's Community Liaison officers. The recruitment of local people as community mediators resulted in mistrust as they were deemed company pawns and not community envoys (see Drew, Chapter 5 this book). Tacit and overt forms of subversion are then deployed to ensure benefits are not sabotaged by these middlemen and women. It is unsurprising, then, that rumours abound in the oil basin of secret participation and underhand dealings. Misinformation circulates and deceit is practised despite public consultations and various other investor-supported 'participatory' engagements with community groups. These include the posting of work opportunities in shopfronts and public buildings, support to local theatre groups to promote awareness, and efforts to identify and raise the voices of elders and other respected customary figures. Attendance at public meetings varies. Many come to air their grievances in the hope of directing attention to their interests or reading between the lines of the public transcript for later mobilisation efforts. In short, vigilance is the watchword, such that obtaining information becomes an object in itself – a resource that facilitates other networks of benefit sharing. In 'The Return of the Broker', James (2011) directs our attention to the ways in which rapid transitions bring about community brokers, a nuanced approach to what has been banally termed 'elite capture', in the wake of Kenya's discovery of oil. Transparency and participation have front and back stages with different dynamics of how people, communities, the state and corporations represent themselves. Contrary to public transcripts, inclusion is not guaranteed, nor is it an open process. It requires skill, tactical manoeuvres and, as the case of what happens at night shows, the ability to fight for the collective good but also negotiate one's own opportunity away from the public space.

This chapter concludes that other domains of contestations in Turkana and the wider stage of Kenyan politics have inadvertently shaped the current struggles around oil benefits. It would be remiss to assume that oil exploration has brought on divisions and conflict in an erstwhile united and egalitarian Turkana without reflecting on the prevalence of conflict over scarce resources and the scant opportunities for social mobility among its hybrid population. Further, everyday politics in Kenya is often perceived by laypeople as a game of shadows that places a burden of responsibility on individuals to forge alliances and networks that keep them in the loop. Thus, what has emerged as counter-logic among Turkana to the public transcript of economic inclusion from large-scale investments such as oil is that, if previous national development and revenue allocation processes have institutionally excluded the region, and political representatives sought clandestine connections to enrich themselves, the odds are that oil politics will be no different 'unless the people fight for it' and build their own channels. As some research participants articulated, this kind of subversive engagement demands assertiveness and vigilance: 'if you sit down, you will eat nothing' (Okenwa 2020; Hetherington 2011). Engagement is therefore conceptualised as a stage for public show, but power lies beneath the stage. Li aptly summarises this: 'complexity, collaboration, creative engagement in both local and global arenas, rather than simple deceit, imposition, or reactive opportunism, best describe these processes and relationships' (Li 2000: 173). For some, organising along shared interests has proven to be productive. For others, mobilising by disruption invites negotiations that lead to more immediate and meaningful results.

5

Meanings of Place & Struggles for Inclusion in the Lake Turkana Wind Power Project

JAMES DREW

Relationships between place, belonging and identity are at the core of many local-level struggles around large resource investments in the drylands of Kenya. Focusing on the Lake Turkana Wind Power (LTWP) project in northern Kenya, this chapter explores how these relationships become visible through a Samburu pastoralist community's struggle for inclusion, including the key roles played by local intermediaries. It also discusses the divisions and alliances that emerged within and between the Samburu community and other communities. It is based on ethnographic data collected during fieldwork between 2014 and 2015 when the LTWP project was under construction.

In the drylands of Kenya, community-level struggles for inclusion in recent large-scale investments, including the LTWP project (Cormack and Kurewa 2018), in terms of access to information, compensation, jobs and other benefits, have led to increasingly contested exclusive (ethnic) claims of different groups to place. These claims are often based upon selectively remembered communal histories. This amplification of territorialised ethnicity (Schlee 2010) is affecting social relationships.

This chapter adds complexity to discussions of territorialised identities and investments. It shows how attachments to place for members of one Samburu community underpin, emerge and are negotiated through their struggles for inclusion in the LTWP project and other investments. Meanings of place and belonging are understood through the concept of 'our place' (nkop ang'), which derives salience from the way it is a part of lives through ancestry, herding, defending land and ceremonies. Nkop ang' involves inclusive, exclusive, territorial and non-territorial notions of place.

The chapter discusses the central role played by intermediaries in the community's struggle for investment benefits. Embodied notions of place and belonging, and a perceived breaching of moral codes, are key to understanding community members' feelings of exclusion from investments and the anger many felt over the role of local intermediaries

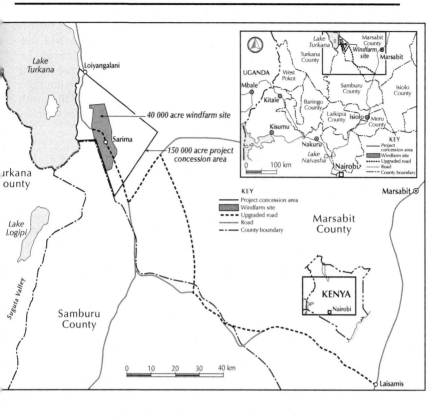

Map 5.1 Kenya, showing location of Lake Turkana Wind Power project

in facilitating this exclusion. Perceived inequitable distribution of investment benefits caused divisions between communities. Anger and discontent surrounding these divisions were focused on intermediaries.

The chapter details the ways that intermediaries tried to subdue protest
against them by dividing, and forming alliances within, the community;
while some Samburu County politicians strategically supported the youth
protest and inflamed certain portrayals of nkop ang' for political gain.

Investments, exclusion and protest

LTWP is Africa's largest wind farm and the largest public–private investment in Kenya's history (see Map 5.1). Many communities in the area
feel excluded from the investment project in terms of consultation and
benefits (Cormack and Kurewa 2018; Drew 2018; Voller et al. 2016).
In 2015, the youth of one Samburu community[1] organised themselves
to protest against LTWP Community Liaison Officers (CLOs), the CLO
boss and local chiefs for excluding them from the project benefits. The
CLO boss was a local businessman who was seen as the face of LTWP
– the main intermediary between the company and communities and
the main protagonist of exclusion. The youth group alleged that the said
individual, in collaboration with the chiefs allocated jobs inequitably by
favouring people from their communities and families, or in exchange
for money. To this end, the youth organised two roadblocks to voice their
concerns. They were also hoping to convince the CLO boss (and the CLOs
and chiefs under his control) to include them in the investment project
through access to information and economic benefits. They requested jobs
from LTWP subcontractors, compensation for building sand unearthed
from a riverbed, and compensation for trees cut for the electricity pylon
wayleave in 'their area' (*nkop ang'*). Most elders[2] and women from the
community supported the protest.

A middle manager for one LTWP subcontractor revealed to the youth
group that their community had been left out of LTWP job allocation
because their main settlement was in Samburu County and LTWP was a
project for Marsabit County. Such a revelation questioned and challenged
the livelihoods and identities of this community, who consider this area
to be theirs.

People's reactions towards the CLO boss and the chiefs, and the depth
of feelings of exclusion relating to the LTWP project, were part of wider
disenfranchisement felt by those protesting over exclusion from other
investments in the area. Resentment arose in 2014 when it emerged that

---

[1] The youth included males of *Lmeoli* and *Lmetili* (or *Lkishami*) Samburu age-sets. *Lmeoli*
are the Samburu age-set whose initiation started in 1990. *Lmetili* are the Samburu age-set
whose initiation started in 2005.
[2] Elders included men belonging to *Lkiroro*, *Lkishili* and *Lkimaniki* Samburu age-sets, whose
initiations started in 1976, 1962 and 1948, respectively.

the Samburu County government agreed a concession with an investor for a further renewable energy project nearby. As with the LTWP investment, anger was directed at local intermediaries, in this case a Member of the Samburu County Assembly (MCA) and businessmen, for allegedly excluding them from consultations and dividing the community in the process. Suspicion and anger also focused on their sublocation chief[3] and a few community members for allegedly assisting the MCA (Interviews with residents of the Samburu community 2015).

Feelings of exclusion from investments in the area were further compounded by the suspicious way that another piece of land (known here by the fictitious name 'Salty Place'), located in Marsabit County and claimed by some residents of the Samburu community as their place, was given to an outside investor. People from the Samburu community and wider area accused the CLO boss and his brother, chief of the location within Marsabit County where Salty Place is located, of facilitating the deal, without consulting the wider population. The accused location chief denied any wrongdoing. According to him, the piece of land was in Marsabit County and the correct residents, those of Marsabit County, had been consulted. Such selective consultation and inequitable LTWP job allocation divided the Samburu community who were excluded from their 'brothers' residing in Marsabit County who were included.

Suspicions and anger surrounding this land deal and exclusion from investments by the LTWP CLO boss, LTWP CLOs, chiefs and politicians reached a crisis point in 2015 after the alleged land lease to a renewable energy investor was revealed and subcontractors began work related to LTWP, including the upgrading of the access road to the wind farm site. At the core of Samburu community members' anger was the lack of recognition of their authority in the area, their area – *nkop ang'*. People of the community expressed disbelief that land could be sold; away from towns there was no precedence of private land titles in the area.

Meanings of 'our place'

Our place (*nkop ang'*) is a relational concept, involving connections between people, livestock, place and *Nkai* (divinity). A key aspect of *nkop ang'* is current and past access to resources through custodianship and the authority this affords. For many people, young and old, living in the Samburu community, their identity as Samburu pastoralists and their status within the society is connected to their lineage's past custodianship over sections of the mountain next to their settlement.

Nowadays, people talk of a 'Samburu community *nkop ang'*' in which the whole community are the custodians of grazing and watering at

---

[3] Locations are administrative areas; they are subdivided into sublocations. Each location and sublocation has a chief, appointed by the state. Sublocation chiefs are assistants to a location chief.

wells. The area, which includes parts of Samburu and Marsabit counties, is vast and incorporates highlands and lowlands and all lineage places claimed by the community, such as Salty Place. No one can be excluded from accessing resources and everyone should respect the wishes of the custodians. Lack of emphasis on mountain lineage land and a fixed representation of a large 'Samburu community territory' reflects the coming together of families to live in a permanent settlement in the late 1990s and 2000s, when piped water was installed, and people increasingly lived together to send their children to school and access food aid, and for security due to increased conflict with pastoralists of Turkana ethnicity. Prior to this, families lived more dispersed lifestyles and often migrated away from the mountain; today only livestock camps are mobile. Since the 1990s, increasing sedentarisation of pastoralists has occurred across Samburu and Marsabit counties (districts until 2013) (Fratkin and Roth 2005); development resources such as famine relief are unavailable to people in perpetual motion (Galaty 2005).

Samburu community members sometimes conflate a whole Samburu territory and/or their Samburu community territory with the upland and lowland areas required to fulfil their livestock's needs. This area (*nkop ang'*) is a part of, and a product of, relationships between people, livestock, places and *Nkai*. People, livestock and *Nkai* are co-agents in influencing the goodness of a place, including the presence of water points and the fertility of land. A moral framework rooted in the concept of *lkereti* is central for many in these world-making practices. *Lkereti* is a correct and propitious way to act during certain situations, such as ceremonies and blessings. People's claims to *nkop ang'* depend upon their and their ancestors' relational engagement and familiarity with these places through living, herding and performing ceremonies, among other things.

Salty Place is claimed by people of one lineage living in the Samburu community. Their claim to Salty Place, which is located on a mountain in Marsabit County, is based on ancestral custodianship rights over a well and grazing. Meaning associated with such an ancestral claim emerges from the way it is a part of people's lives and their identities as herders and members of a certain lineage. A Samburu elder has spent his life migrating with livestock to Salty Place, his ancestral place, because of the goodness it brings his livestock. But this is now in jeopardy because, '[p]eople are saying [the CLO boss] has closed our route to [the mountain in Marsabit County] by bringing [the investor] to settle' (Interview with an elder from the Samburu community, September 2015).

An elder related to the CLO boss and his brother (the location chief) insisted that Salty Place, along with the rest of the mountain in Marsabit County, was his clan's ancestral land. He legitimised this claim by telling his clan's origin story, which is based in the mountain. The meaning of this ancestral claim and his clan and family's seniority and custodianship is enacted today through playing a lead role in ceremonies on the mountain.

A member of the lineage from the Samburu community who see Salty Place as theirs dismissed the claims of this elder as lies – an attempt to enhance his lineage's societal status by seeking positions and places not 'rightfully' theirs. In an unequal world of lineage, seniority and associated places determined by birth (the order of which is determined by *Nkai*), 'truths' are up for negotiation; a negotiation that is underlain by people's embodied conceptions of *nkop ang'* and lineage seniority through their own experiences and/or recollections of their ancestors' experiences. Lynch (2006) and Schlee and Shongolo (2012) remind us that pastoralists' identities are continually renegotiated based on selectively remembered communal histories, and that the territorial nature of these identities emerged in colonial times through networks of patronage.

The chief (brother to the CLO boss) of the location in which Salty Place is located dismissed Samburu community claims about their right to be involved in its annexation. Rather, he emphasised that pastoralists can herd their livestock anywhere, but rights over land correspond to current residence and the county and location a person resides in. This resonates with the revelation that rights to benefit from LTWP correspond with county residency, the alleged reason for the Samburu community's exclusion.

A few elders from the Samburu community were chosen by the CLO boss and taken to Salty Place to give their consent for the investor to use the land. However, many Samburu community members claimed that those elders did not represent the interests of the community and were unaware that their actions would lead to the investor securing a land title. The community members expressed anger at the CLO boss for using a few of their elders to give Salty Place to the investor instead of including the whole community in open discussions and for ignoring the lineage authority of those who claim custodianship of Salty Place. Through these alleged actions, the CLO boss was denying this Samburu community lineage their past and present custodianship roles in managing goodness for the place and those who use it. Such roles are often grounded in the concept of *Ikereti*. Excluding others and assuming seniority that is not rightfully theirs is immoral and goes against *nkanyit* (a sense of respect and honour), and 'badness' will follow the culprits. An elder exclaimed: 'If you claim land then the land/*Nkai* will claim you ... That place will never be good for that person ... His family will get "badness" and disappear' (Interview with an elder from the Samburu community, August 2015).

Widespread Samburu community anger against the CLO boss, for his role in the lack of openness surrounding investments and for aligning people's rights to inclusion in investments (leasing Salty Place and LTWP benefits) with county residency, stems from the disregard for the community's authority and agency relating to Samburu community *nkop ang'*. Moreover, an elder supporting the youth protest emphasised the inclusive nature of Samburu community *nkop ang'* or any form of *nkop ang'* for all Samburu – and anyone else, if they are peaceful. They are free to move their livestock everywhere without the question of which county they are in. 'No Samburu can be excluded from this land; we do not say that this place belongs (exclusively) to such and such.' The elder questioned me rhetorically: 'Why now, when there are jobs, should [the CLO boss and location chief] bring all this talk about Marsabit and Samburu counties … that [specific places] belong to Marsabit?' (Interview with an elder from the Samburu community, 7 September 2015).

For many in the Samburu community, that their community *nkop ang'* consists of a bounded territory is not new – rather, this fact mirrors their and their pre-colonial ancestors' scope of custodianship and authority. Their community *nkop ang'* is within a 'Greater Samburu' bounded territory, which, as legend has it, was demarcated as the 'original' Samburu District by the British administration under the guidance of a Samburu man. Although no evidence of such an original district could be traced in archival documents, this widely held claim shows how inclusive relationships with place are not seen as separate from more exclusive ways of experiencing place through administrative territories.

Recent talk of the Marsabit–Samburu county boundary being located close to the Samburu Community, and this being reason for the community's exclusion from investments, not only goes against the inclusionary basis of nkop ang' but also confirmed many elders' fears that the district boundary changed during the colonial period. Accordingly, part of Samburu District was 'grabbed' by a colonial Rendille chief, in collusion with a colonial Samburu chief (grandfather of the CLO boss and current location chief). As with the recent investments, the authority of the Samburu community as custodians was ignored by the Rendille and Samburu colonial chiefs. They knew that they were contravening 'truths' of Samburu nkop ang', and so kept those duped Samburu in the dark to avoid protest. Samburu were divided from their Rendille brothers and sisters (dwelling in Marsabit District) in the same way that the sons of the colonial Samburu chief were dividing current Samburu brothers and sisters (those included in recent investment benefits from those not included).

For many Samburu community members, their anger at intermediaries for allegedly excluding them from investments hinged on a notion of *nkop ang'* in which current and past ideas of ancestral land merge with administrative territories. This merging and the depth of betrayal felt is due in part to the ways *nkop ang'* is a part of people's everyday lives and identities through herding and ceremonies.

Defending 'our place'

Perceptions and experiences of *nkop ang'* as a place for family, lineage and Samburu – as a delineated territory, and inclusive of all – are imbued with the universally accepted notion that it is not for people of Turkana ethnicity; rather it is something that needs to be protected from them.

During peaceful periods in the past, Turkana lived and herded with the Samburu community. Episodes of increased livestock raids between Samburu and Turkana of the area caused the friends to separate, but they always came back to live together. Samburu agree that this changed in the 1990s, when Turkana united around political support to try and chase all Samburu from their land; conflict was no longer just about stealing livestock. The aggressive and expansionist behaviour of Turkana has forced Samburu to defend and exclude Turkana from 'their land'.

Many Turkana from the north of Samburu County disagree with the Samburu assessment of changing conflict dynamics. Turkana have been marginalised politically and in terms of development since colonial times. Political networks of patronage have become increasingly dependent upon territorialised notions of identity and belonging since the beginning of multi-party politics in 1992 (Schlee and Shongolo 2012; Schlee 2010) and again since devolution (D'Arcy and Cornell 2016; Carrier and Kochore 2014). Marginalisation of Turkana in Samburu County has heightened since devolved governance in 2013; Samburu politicians have increasingly propagated anti-Turkana sentiment to gain popularity. Samburu attack and kill Turkana with impunity; it is they who have changed the rules of conflict and no longer just want to steal livestock – Samburu are trying to exclude Turkana from Samburu County.

Relations between the Samburu community and their Turkana neighbours reached breaking point in the 2000s. Their ties were severed, and Turkana no longer live and graze among the Samburu community. Such segregation is not uncommon across much of the area. Ongoing tensions and fear of Turkana attacks are part of everyday lives and routines for the Samburu community. For example, in the past people's main homesteads were separate and dispersed; today members of the Samburu community have one large settlement for safety. The possibility of attack within livestock camps influences everything from camp location to grazing patterns and watering of livestock.

Injustices voiced by the Samburu community youth and some elders at being excluded from investment benefits by intermediaries centre on a conception of *nkop ang´* that owes its existence to their bravery in defending it from Turkana. The daily reality of this exclusive conception of place and the centrality of it to people's identities combines with more inclusive and non-territorial aspects of *nkop ang'* and the ways in which they are a part of people's lives and identities. This complex amalgamation and the associated seniority and custodianship rights, were mobilised to claim due benefits from the recent investments.

These insights into how and why notions of belonging are malleable and (ethnically) territorialised add detail and complexity to suggestions that struggles for inclusion in recent large-scale investments – based on selectively remembered communal histories – lead to increasingly contested exclusive ethnic claims of different groups to place (e.g. Cormack and Kurewa 2018). The insights show the embodied, more-than-discursive ways that the territorial nature of identity is continually negotiated in the context of networks of patronage (Schlee and Shongolo 2012; Lynch 2006).

Divisions and alliances within the Samburu community

The unity and consensus among the Samburu community youth protesting against the CLO boss, CLOs and chiefs for the alleged intentional exclusion of their community from investments, including sand and tree compensation and LTWP jobs, and for keeping the community in the dark over leasing land to investors, reached its peak during their first roadblock in 2015. Underlying the anger at their exclusion and the division this created between them and their Marsabit County 'brothers' was the way that these leaders had violated 'sacred truths' about *nkop ang'* and not included the rightful custodians who have defended this land from Turkana enemies.

After the first roadblock, the CLO boss and the Samburu community's sublocation chief worked hard to quash the protest and suppress the allegations against them of excluding the community from investment consultation and information, and inequitable distribution of investment benefits. It was clear to protestors that these actions were a desperate attempt by the CLO boss and sublocation chief to cover up their immoral behaviour and blasphemous disregard for *nkop ang'*. The area MCA also used spies living within the community to try to quash rumours about the other renewable energy land lease.

The CLO boss and the sublocation chief tried to accomplish this by spreading doubt about the validity of protestors' accusations and by stopping people from speaking out or supporting those who did. Their approach involved splitting the community along old and new divides to try to reduce the protest. To achieve this, the CLO boss and the chief influenced and manipulated people using a variety of methods, including exploiting people's moral obligations aligned with *lkereti* that inform relationship dynamics, and by taking advantage of their own positions within community relationships.

The sublocation chief relied on his loyal inner circle of elders within the Samburu community to spread doubt among their own community as to the validity of the protestors' claims, by discrediting the lead protestors and their patrons. The inner circle contained elders who were influential among their peers. Elders' loyalty to the sublocation chief is ensured through gifts, kinship and life-long ceremonial bonds he shares with them. The power such social bonds have rests in the ways they are embedded in relationships between people, place and *Nkai*. To disrespect such bonds would be to question *Nkai*, *Ikereti* and identities of oneself and place, which would go against *nkanyit* and invite badness. Elders found themselves in difficult positions, torn between supporting their protesting sons against the chief and not going against their age-mates aligned with the chief, which would go against *nkanyit*. This caused some elders to remain silent and/or to pressure their sons to stop protesting. Youth also found themselves in a moral quandary, because it is disrespectful for sons to disobey their fathers.

The youth of the Samburu community lost faith in their elders, especially those loyal to the sublocation chief who they felt had deceived the community. However, many elders, including some of his 'loyal' inner circle, were unhappy at the chief for trying to divide them from their sons whom they supported; and they were angry or ashamed of their peers for trying to deceive the community. Some of these elders attended the protests.

In the months that followed the first roadblock, the CLO boss and sublocation chief used various ways to divide the youth to quell the continuing protests. They befriended and gave jobs to the brothers of key protestors to coax them into pressuring their brothers to cease protesting. They used money or jobs to secure the allegiance of influential youth able to persuade their peers not to protest. The CLO boss also used his status as a member of the *Lmeoli* age-set to suppress protests from his peers across the area and gain their support by securing their blessing at a ceremony.

Incumbent politicians within Samburu County government and political candidates for the 2017 elections used and inflamed the Samburu community's protests against intermediaries and politicians, and associated divides and alliances, for political gain. Some people allied to the CLO boss accused 'elite' sons of the Samburu community and Samburu County politicians of instigating the youthful protest as part of their power struggle against the governor within the newly devolved county government. The governor allegedly sanctioned the land lease for the other renewable investment rumoured in the community's sub-location. A candidate running for office in the 2017 election publicly supported the Samburu community's claims for investment benefits and allegations of land theft by tapping into the emotive concept of *nkop ang'*.

Despite encouragement from elites and political patrons, the youth protest fragmented as appetite for protest waned. The tactics of the CLO boss, sublocation chief, MCA and their allies – to supress the revelations, arguments and support for the protesting youth – caused much confusion and suspicion surrounding the alleged investments, land leases, the actions of chiefs, CLOs, intermediaries, patrons and protestors.

Those people who chose to remain silent, succumbed to enticements from the CLO boss and chief and/or ceased protesting did so for various reasons. Some were compelled to remain silent and loyal by moral obligations (*Ikereti* and *nkanyit*) associated with kin, ceremonial and generational relationships. Others valued money and jobs, or the promise of these, over protest. Whatever the reason, people manage current relationships in ways that do not jeopardise potential future goodness associated with *Ikereti* or future patronage ties that depend upon kinship, peer group, chiefs, intermediaries or political patrons.

Conclusion

The chapter has shown how meanings of place and belonging underpin and emerge through one community's struggle for inclusion in recent large-scale investments, including the LTWP project, and how these struggles were manifested through protest and divisions within and between the community and other communities.

Anger at being excluded from investments, including the inequitable distribution of benefits and the divisions this created between those communities included and those not included, was expressed by youth in protests towards key local LTWP intermediaries. Anger and suspicion towards the main intermediary (the CLO boss) were contextualised within accusations against his family's history as community leaders of inequitable state and non-state resource distribution.

Underlying the anger of the youth was the way their perceived rights to be included in investments, based upon their versions of *nkop ang'*, were violated by intermediaries when annexing land and allocating benefits. Anger intensified after the CLO boss and other intermediaries tried to supress protests by splitting the community along old and new divisions using a variety of means, including manipulating their position within relationships with community members. These community divides, the protest and associated claims of *nkop ang'* were used and inflamed by incumbent politicians within the newly devolved Samburu County government and political candidates for political gain.

It was abhorrent to the Samburu community that rights to LTWP jobs and consultation in the leasing of Salty Place lay with residents of Marsabit County because it went against their idea of *nkop ang'* and associated authority, custodianship and rights to benefit from development. These rights are based upon ancestry, herding, ceremonies, defending land, administrative areas, inclusion and exclusion. The salience and 'truth' of *nkop ang'*, and the anger felt by people at the way intermediaries ignored this, lies in the way that it is embedded within people's identities and biographies and a moral code rooted in the concept of *Ikereti*. Ancestral precedence in an area takes meaning from the way this is a part of current lives, such as through herding or ceremonies.

The insights gained through careful consideration of meanings of *nkop ang'* reveal the complexity involved in negotiation of territorially based identities and belonging, which are becoming more commonplace in Kenya's drylands through recent large-scale investments. Exclusive notions of place and belonging associated with administrative areas blend with more inclusive relationships with place. This connection emerges through *nkop ang'* as a part of people's everyday lives and identities.

6

Conflict & Resistance around a Rice Development Scheme in the SAGCOT Area of Tanzania

ADRIANA BLACHE

The Southern Agricultural Growth Corridor of Tanzania (SAGCOT) is a public–private partnership that promotes 'green agricultural growth' (SAGCOT 2013: 1) by linking small-scale farmers to the global market through a nucleus–outgrower model (Maganga et al. 2016; Sulle and Smalley 2015; Bergius 2014). Within SAGCOT, the Kilombero cluster, one of six planned clusters comprising an area of 126 villages, is focused on sugar cane and rice production. The government plans to transform 182,198 ha of village land into large industrial plantations (SAGCOT 2012: 12), even though to date no new investment has emerged in this cluster.

The Mngeta farm, located in the centre of the Kilombero cluster, is an example of how foreign private large-scale investment can have significant consequences on the local economy and villagers' livelihoods. This arises in particular through the generation of land conflicts (Greco 2015; Hall et al. 2015c; Locher 2015). This chapter asks: what lessons can be learned from the Mngeta farm case, which was originally promoted as a 'showcase' for future large-scale investments in Tanzania?

In 2006, Agrica Ltd (previously InfEnergy) acquired the 5,818 ha Mngeta farm from the parastatal Rufiji Basin Development Agency (RUBADA). Together, they formed a public–private partnership, Kilombero Plantation Ltd (KPL). The project was financed by a number of international public and private institutions, including US-based Capricorn and USAID, Norway-based Norfund and UK-based AgDevCo. The project was promoted as a success story and a project website proclaimed: 'KPL has increased the income of local people employed by 60%'.[1] Despite these claims, things were not so idyllic, as discussed below.

The land transaction involved a participatory mapping survey, a Resettlement Action Plan and an environmental and social impact assessment report (Coleman 2015). Despite such efforts, the investment

---

[1] AgDevCo, www.agdevco.com/our-investments/by-investment/Kilombero-Plantations-Limited-KPL, accessed 15 April 2016.

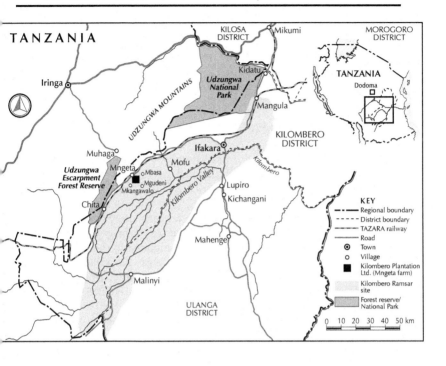

Map 6.1 Tanzania, showing location of the Kilombero Plantation in the Kilombero Valley and surrounding villages

has been dubbed 'irresponsible' (Oakland Institute et al. 2015: 1), causing a 'crisis of eviction' (Chachage 2010: 12). In 2019, KPL was declared bankrupt after defaulting on loans from several donors. After such positive expectations, what contributed to such dramatic failure over the thirteen years since the original investment?

The investment context

Located on the western side of the Kilombero wetlands (see Map 6.1), the Mngeta farm was historically farmed by the Ndamba people. On the Udzungwa hills the Hehe historically used the forests for rubber production, canoe-building and farming. The villages in this area were registered during the Ujamaa[2] period in the early 1970s and some were created around the TAZARA (Tanzania Zambia Railway Authority) railway stations. At this time, many people immigrated to the area. In 1977, Maasai from the Namyaki clan came to Mkangawalo village to ask for land and registered a ranch area in Mgudeni hamlet (Interview with Maasai elder from the Namyaki clan, Mgudeni, 27 July 2015).

During an earlier investment by the Korean government between 1986 and 1995, Maasai pastoralists and farmers were still using the land, as only 300 ha were farmed by the company. Immigration increased in the late 1990s and early 2000s, especially with the arrival of the Sukuma people from Shinyanga and Mbeya regions. The Sukuma were allocated land where they produce rice, maize and also keep livestock.

With 117 per cent demographic growth since the 1980s (URT 2013), the Kilombero Valley is experiencing a huge transformation in the uses of its natural resources. Furthermore, the Mngeta farm is located within a Ramsar[3] site and is surrounded by a Game Controlled Area, the Udzungwa Escarpment Forest Reserve and the Mngeta wildlife corridor that is still being developed. All of these conservation areas restrict access to land. The arrival of the new investment in 2006 therefore occurred in an already densely populated and farmed area.

Resettlement Action Plan: who are the squatters?

Kilombero Plantation Ltd started to clear the land in December 2007 and planted rice on 641 ha in early 2008 (Mung'ong'o and Kayonko 2009: 2). However, in 2008 many villagers were still occupying the land. In April 2008, a land surveyor from RUBADA and the KPL administrative

---

[2] A rural socialist economic policy aimed at promoting cooperative production by clustering people into villages. For details, see Nyerere 1966.

[3] The Ramsar Convention on Wetlands of International Importance was signed in 2011 and aims at protecting the 'wise use' of wetlands (www.ramsar.org/about/the-wise-use-of-wetlands, accessed 10 May 2017).

manager organised a village meeting in Mngeta, saying the villagers 'must vacate the land in dispute and those who will not oblige, a coercive mode will be used'.[4] In October 2009, the Prime Minister, Mizengo Pinda, 'directed the regional and district authorities to relocate the villagers to other places where they would be helped to settle' (*Citizen* 2009). In early 2009, the company aimed to farm 3,000 ha but found that farmers were still occupying 25 per cent of the land (Mung'ong'o and Kayonko 2009: 1).

A Resettlement Action Plan commissioned by KPL (2010) distinguished 'true' squatters, who had moved to the farm from other areas, and 'local' squatters, who had moved to the area before the original farm was established in 1986 or who had been allocated land since. Surprisingly, Maasai herders were not included, despite the fact that they used the farm from 1974 to 2008 to graze their cattle. They were not considered as active land users because no crops were planted. The research concluded that 'approximately 2,238 people continue to live or farm on about 25% of the titled area, some who have been there since 1999. They have no legal right to occupy the farm but they are resisting relocation' (ENATA and Diaz-Chavez 2009: 81).

The Resettlement Action Plan recognised 230 households as affected by land loss. Out of these, eighty were deemed to have lost their homes and the remaining 150 had lost their farms. Some families received compensation of 10,000 Tanzanian shillings (US$4.35 in 2009) per acre (0.405ha) cultivated (compared to the 15,000 Tanzanian shillings promised), and KPL constructed eighty houses in Mbasa and Kichangani resettlement sites. However, the majority of people who used or lived on the land received no compensation, partly owing to the non-recognition of their customary land rights, but also because they were not on their land on the day of the assessment.

In the villages bordering KPL, inhabitants described the bulldozers that destroyed their houses, crops and fruit trees in the middle of the night:

> I didn't want to leave, I was born here, my family is here, I built my life here. When the police arrived, I stayed at home. They threatened to destroy the house even if I stayed there! They threw away the chickens, chairs, and everything that was in my house! (Interview with a farmer in Isago hamlet, 25 August 2016)

These expulsions have led to long-term migration. Without land, people had to diversify their livelihood activities, adopting precarious strategies, including employment in neighbours' fields, occasional employment on the plantation and the development of small businesses in the valley.

---

[4] Letter from Beatha Fabian, Executive Director of the Land Rights and Resources Institute (Haki Ardhi), to Executive Director, Legal and Human Rights Center, 16 September 2010, headed 'R.E: Legal Aid Mr. Msafiri Mbibo and Mr. Boniface Venance', Haki Ardhi, Dar es Salaam, Ref No. HL 10/1/143, http://hakiardhi.org

Those who had been allocated a house and land after eviction complained that it is too small to engage in any crop production:

KPL promised farmland and a house. But what we have now is just a small garden behind the house. The house as well as toilets collapse because of their poor construction. And during the raining season, this is a river here! We even have water inside the house. We borrow money to neighbours in order to rent a land, or we buy milk from the pastoralists to sell it in the market, but it is hard to survive. (Interview with a farmer resettled in Kichangani resettlement, 26 August 2016)

Some villagers reported that KPL offered them land that is located on the Ramsar wetlands[5] site to the east, and so they are not allowed to grow any crops or graze cattle:

When they told us to leave, they told us they had reserved land for us near the wetlands, but in 2012, the district came with guards saying the Ramsar boundaries had changed and we had to quit this land too! Now the only activity I can do is to go and find medicinal herbs in the forest to get money to survive. (Interview with a farmer from Mbasa hamlet, 18 July 2015)

From evictions to failed promises of new available land: the animosity towards KPL increased among the villagers.

A development fund and employment disputes

In order to cool the tensions, KPL committed to giving development funds to the affected villages as part of a 'corporate social responsibility' initiative. The Agrica Business Plan (2011: 30) states that 50 million Tanzanian shillings (US$21,745, which represents 1 per cent of the annual development cost of the farm) would be spent for 'annual community development funds for the construction of school classrooms and wells'. However, the development funds were conditional. The chair of KPL, Carter Coleman, in his letter to the four village chairs insisted: 'The company shall keep a record of all seed, diesel and fertilizer that has been stolen from the farm each year, and these costs shall be deducted from the community development fund. If the villages are vigilant then a few bad people will not cost everyone development.'[6]

The company claimed to have built schools, but while roofs have been supplied, the schools were still in a poor state of repair in 2015.[7] The promise of electricity and water supplies also failed to materialise in

[5] Villagers and district officers speak about the Ramsar site, while it is actually the Game Controlled Area boundaries that have been reinforced.

[6] Letter from Carter Coleman, 11 February 2009 headed 'RE; Mngeta Farm Community Development Fund', quoted in Mung'ong'o and Kayonko 2009: 54.

[7] Field visit, Mkangawalo village, 12 July 2016.

2017.[8] Conflicts arose between and within villages around the allocation of development funds, with accusations of misappropriation and failure to deliver. By 2015 the funds were stopped. Graham Anderson, the general manager of KPL, explained: 'we stopped the funds two years ago; there is endless conflict with surrounding villagers. And actually, we are not an NGO, we do business here' (Interview with Graham Anderson in KPL offices, Mngeta village, 1 March 2017).

The corporate claims of community development via discourses and practices of corporate social responsibility reverberate through studies of investment projects in marginal areas (Dolan and Rajak 2016; Gardner 2012; Rajak 2011). The ambiguity of corporate social responsibility continues to raise questions over the ways in which patchy community development projects, often arbitrary, are a smokescreen (Benson and Kirsch 2010) for entrenched corporate impunity. Furthermore, the 'impermanent development' (Okenwa 2019) that characterise these corporate interventions speak more to immediate superficial solutions to local disturbances rather than long-term solutions to the livelihood precarity experienced in these investment areas, as the villagers also remarked.

The generation of employment for poor villagers was one of the claims that the company made at the outset. The majority of villagers interviewed said they were not employed permanently by the company.[9] Some gained employment as casual workers, gaining employment for one or two days per month and were paid 3,800 Tanzanian shillings a day (US$1.64 in 2015), but with no job security. The casual work consisted of weeding, clearing the irrigation canals and mixing chemicals. A few gained employment working with the milling machines and could get up to 150,000 Tanzanian shillings a month for working eight hours a day, six days a week, plus an allowance for children's schooling. Those interviewed noted the difficulty of working conditions in the plantation, especially those working with pesticides or in the processing of the rice.

Access to permanent employment was influenced by clientelism, with employment opportunities given preferentially to those from the home areas of senior managers. Such migrant workers – for example from Tanga – were provided with houses in the company buildings. Skilled workers such as technicians received a salary up to 300,000 Tanzanian shillings a month (US$130 in 2016), with free accommodation, water and electricity. Some migrant workers also invested in land for cultivation as well as in small businesses in the nearby area, such as guesthouses and restaurants.

Outgrowers and socio-economic differentiations

One of the reasons KPL was promoted as a 'showcase' in the SAGCOT

---

[8] Field visit, Mkangawalo and Mgudeni villages, 23 March 2017.
[9] Focus group in Mkangawalo village, 13 July 2015; focus group in Mgudeni village, 15 July 2015; interview with Maasai pastoralist in Mngeta village, 27 July 2016.

programme was its outgrower scheme. When the then prime minister visited the Mngeta farm in 2009, he stated that even if relocated from the farm, 'the peasants could still be useful to the commercial farmers as out-growers and contract farmers' (*Citizen* 2009) and 'the move would enable the farmers acquire farming skills and access to rice farming infrastructures' (*Guardian* 19 October 2009, cited in Swahilitime 2009).

To support outgrowing as a focus for development, KPL received US$650 million in support from USAID, directed especially at training and technical assistance for the rice outgrower scheme, and a US$12 million investment from AgDevCo, supported by the UK Department for International Development and Norfund for the microfinance programme for the outgrower scheme. Grants were also received by KPL from Norfund in December 2010 to expand the System of Rice Intensification programme to 250 smallholders (Agrica 2011: 35). In May 2011, another grant of US$750,000 from the African Enterprise Challenge Fund was awarded in order to expand the programme (De Lapérouse 2012: 13). A study recorded up to 7,403 farmers from ten villages within 65 km of the KPL rice scheme who had been trained in the use of glyphosate and good farming practices between 2009 and 2016 (Lahr et al. 2016: 51).

As noted by Sulle and Smalley (2015: 125), referring to the Kilombero sugar-cane plantation in the north of Kilombero Valley, 'incomes from out-growing and auxiliary businesses have raised the living standards of many villagers ... but the distribution of wealth is uneven and some people have not been included, leading to social differentiation.' The outgrower scheme around Mngeta farm also led to socio-economic differentiation, a pattern seen elsewhere in Africa (Adams et al. 2018; Hall et al. 2017).

The outgrower scheme was centred on the new System of Rice Intensification (SRI), which is an agro-ecological methodology for increasing the productivity of irrigated rice by changing the management of plants, soil, water and nutrients, including through labour-intensive transplantation techniques.[10] The company has offered training to the farmers and most of them are happy to have gained this new knowledge. Indeed, the yield with the SRI technology is around 40 bags per acre (7 tonnes/ha) compared to the previous 25 bags (4.3 tonnes/ha) (Kilave and Mlay 2019). Some farmers, though, complained that the company did not allow them to use herbicides or pesticides, and that SRI was too labour-intensive. Furthermore, the scheme introduced new hybrid seeds (Sarro 5) and the taste and quality were not appreciated.

The outgrower scheme was accompanied by a system of loan-based microfinance supported by the National Microfinance Bank and the Youth Self Employment Foundation; 849 farmers received a loan of 360,000 Tanzanian shillings with which they had to buy 12 kg of hybrid Sarro 5 seeds (30,000 Tanzanian shillings), chemical fertiliser (100,000 Tanzanian

---

[10] SRI International Network and Resource Center website, http://sri.ciifad.cornell.edu/aboutsri/methods/index.html, accessed 14 May 2019.

shillings of Yara fertiliser), plus a weeder (70,000 Tanzanian shillings). They had to pay back 10 per cent of the loan every two weeks before harvesting. At the end of the agricultural season, they also had to pay back ten sacks of rice (worth 50,000–70,000 Tanzanian shillings a sack). The loans were difficult to repay and some had to work elsewhere or sell some of their assets – including beds, cooking equipment or livestock – to be able to pay back the loan. Many have quit the scheme, and those who stay have other sources of capital elsewhere or other income-earning activities.

Renting farm blocks

As KPL could not farm the whole area allocated to it, it proposed that villagers organise themselves into groups so they could rent a block of land in order to grow rice. Commenting on the sugar plantation further north, Sulle and Smalley (2015: 129) asked whether 'block farms will offer a solution to these problems or simply present more opportunities for elite capture'. The same question arose around the Mngeta farm investment. The renting programme initially targeted medium- and large-scale farmers. The price of land rentals from the company varied according to the location and the presence of irrigation channels, but interviews revealed the villagers' discontent regarding the price and the amount of land proposed.

In Mkangawalo village, village leaders explained that 'if you want to rent a land, you have to organise a group of people and for each acre rented you have to give one bag of 100 kg to the company' (Interview with Mkangawalo village representatives, 1 March 2017). By 2016, only one block had been rented to the villagers. Instead, external investors from nearby areas had seized the opportunity. A Mkangawalo village council member explained:

> Investors from outside of the district come and rent 50 to 100 ha. They come with tractors from Morogoro, Dar es Salaam or Arusha. They grow rice and sell it to KPL. A KPL manager also owns a lot of blocks, apart from the other investments he made in guesthouses in Mngeta. (Interview with Mkangawalo village representatives, 1 March 2017)

The capture of land through rentals has therefore fostered feelings of neglect and disempowerment among residents of the poorest villagers around the farm.

Environmental issues

Mngeta farm is squeezed in between a number of conservation areas (Map 6.1). The reinforcement of Ramsar boundaries between 2012 and

2014 led to the eviction of more than 5,000 pastoralists and their 486,736 cattle (IGIWA 2013: 3–4). The killing of pastoralists and the violence of the arrests are still part of local memories. One Maasai youth in Mgudeni explained: 'Police patrols came to the village; they had trucks and they asked us to go to Ifakara with our cattle. They forced us to walk up to Ifakara and were beating us on the way with long sticks! They took our cattle and sold them' (Discussion with Maasai pastoralists in Mugdeni, 23 August 2016).

Kilombero Plantation Ltd is promoted as an environmentally friendly company, and it has implemented a full environment impact assessment and signed an agreement for payment for ecosystem services in the Kabisara swamp (Agrica 2011). It has also invested in the implementation of the Mngeta wildlife corridor and local biodiversity conservation (Tanzania Forest Conservation Group 2018). Nevertheless, many conflicts with villagers concern environmental and health problems. This includes the spraying of herbicide from the air, the use of pesticides and fertilisers that affect local water supplies, and the depletion of water resources (Interview with Ndamba fisherman, Fibwe hamlet, 27 August 2016). Large plantations have impacts beyond their boundaries and affect surrounding resources and people; a wider spatial socio-politics needs to be considered, linking the investment to wider networks of economy and ecology (Blache 2018).

Growing conflict and resistance

Over time, conflicts over land access have grown and with this, resistance to the farm investment. The early much-hailed successes began to unravel, as different groups competed over land and with the company. The KPL farm investment, combined with the reinforcement of boundaries around conservation areas and the inward migration of local investors, had generated local scarcities and exacerbated tensions between local farmers, pastoralists and investors. This resulted sometimes in violent conflicts and growing discontent in an increasingly divided community.

Farmers and pastoralists from villages near the farm adopted different kinds of resistance strategies. From the beginning, villagers resisted eviction by staying on their farms, while being threatened by the police and bulldozers. In Mngeta and Lukolongo, villagers launched a collective land case at the High Court of Tanzania to reclaim their rights to the land.[11] When KPL cut the road linking Mkangawalo to Mngeta, villagers organised strikes on the main road, which were severely repressed by the police.

---

[11] Letter from Beatha Fabian, Executive Director of the Land Rights and Resources Institute (Haki Ardhi), to Executive Director, Legal and Human Rights Center, 16 September 2010, headed 'R.E: Legal Aid Mr. Msafiri Mbibo and Mr. Boniface Venance', Haki Ardhi, Dar es Salaam, Ref No. HL 10/1/143, http://hakiardhi.org

In Mkangawalo, villagers complained several times to KPL, asking them to stop using aeroplanes for the spraying of glyphosate herbicide. In 2010 the loss of 360 acres of villagers' crops had been compensated by KPL at 72,000 Tanzanian shillings per acre (Interview, Mkangawalo village council members, 27 August 2016). Mkangawalo village representatives explained how the tensions escalated:

> KPL caught six youths suspected of having stolen fertilisers from the Company. KPL guards came here and took them to the police station. When news spread in the village, around twenty villagers locked two KPL guards inside the village office. Police officers arrested everyone who was in the office and released the guards. That is when villagers went on the plantation. Villagers organised an occupation of the plantation and cut three acres of maize grown by KPL. They were caught by the police. (Interview, Mkangawalo village council members, 1 March 2017)

Villagers from Mkangawalo undertook legal action, demanding that the company compensate for the loss of production. On 23 February 2016, they received a letter from the Tropical Pesticide Research Institute (TPRI) saying that the institute had received village leaders' request to engage in a survey on the effects of glyphosate spraying on the villagers' fields.[12] In February 2016, villagers called TV journalists, who exposed their case to the whole country (ITV 2016). On 26 October 2016, TPRI concluded that KPL was not responsible for the loss of rice in the neighbouring villagers' farms, and no compensation was given to the villagers.[13]

Maasai pastoralists and Sukuma agro-pastoralists from Mgudeni village are also resisting. They have been occupying land and grazing with their cattle, while knowing the risks of being caught by the *askaris* (plantation guards) and of being fined heavily. A young Maasai herder explained:

> On the 12th March 2016, a security guard from KPL caught two of my cows who had run into the KPL farms that were not under cultivation. When females are in heat, they can run everywhere! The cows were grazing weeds, yet were taken by the guards, and I had to pay a 460,000 Tanzanian shilling fine. (Personal interview with a young Maasai pastoralist in Mgudeni village, 24 August 2016)

---

[12] Translation from Swahili, Letter from E.E. Kimaro, General Director, TPRI, No. TPRI/DG/OGC/VOC/VOL.XIII/80, dated 23 February 2016, entitled 'Maombi ya wataalamu kuja kuchunguza athari ya Kiuagugu ya Glyphosate iliyopuliziwa na ndege ya kampuni ya Kilombero Plantation Limited katika Kijiji cha Mkangawalo wilaya ya Kilombero'.

[13] Letter from Ernest R. Mkongo headed 'Uchunguzi wa athari ya kiuagugu aina ya gliphosate kwenye mashamba ya mpunga ya wakulima wa kijiji cha mkangawalo wanaolima pembezoni mwa shamba la kpl'. Information provided by village council members during a field visit to Mkangawalo, 1 March 2017.

Conclusion

While SAGCOT promotes poverty reduction, the case of KPL shows several negative impacts, notably through the increase of land conflicts. The investment has, as a result, led to increased socio-economic differentiation in the area. Different categories of 'squatter' have been generated, with different rights to land and compensation. Those with access to loans and with sufficient capital have been able to join the outgrower scheme, while others have missed out. There is differentiation between locals and outsiders, notably investors from urban areas, who have been able to acquire new land. These dynamics have resulted in multiple conflicts between and among farmers and pastoralists as access to land is contested.

The investment has thus reshaped the territory, redefining 'internal frontiers' (Kopytoff 1987b) through the expansion of exclusive areas. Asserting control has in turn required the use of force, and physical and symbolic violence. The violence of the evictions, the land scarcity that had been generated and the harmful environment impacts resulted in a variety of local reactions (cf. Borras et al. 2015; Hall et al. 2015a). Resistance has taken different forms, from land occupation and protests to legal actions. The atmosphere in the area has been very tense, with conflict, violence and fear dominating. The bankruptcy of Agrica Ltd does not mean that the rights of farmers and pastoralists will be returned. Even a failed investment massively reconfigures politics, authority and rights over land, as new actors arrive and new forms of social differentiation emerge (cf. Rasmussen and Lund 2018; Peluso and Lund 2011).

Understanding what happens to investments over time – in this case over thirteen years since inception – reveals important dynamics that a simple focus on the initial land acquisition does not show (Hall et al. 2015c; Cotula 2013). As investments become established, and conflicts are revitalised or created and processes of social differentiation occur, the social, political and environmental landscape is fundamentally reshaped, even when the investment – as in this case – ultimately fails.

7

Hosting Refugees as an Investment in Development

Grand Designs versus Local Expectations in Turkana County, Kenya

CORY RODGERS[1]

The expectation that large-scale investments will spur economic development and reduce poverty in Africa's drylands is not unique to the agricultural, extractives and renewable energy industries. This idea has also been embraced in the humanitarian industry, where organisations like the United Nations Refugee Agency (UNHCR) are seeking models of aid delivery that respond to both the immediate needs of refugees and to the longer-term development agendas of the countries and communities that host them. By re-conceptualising refugee aid as an investment in development, humanitarian organisations are attempting to rekindle enthusiam among fatigued funders and make the presence of refugees more palatable to host governments.

One of the most ambitious efforts in this regard has been the Kalobeyei Integrated Socio-Economic Development Programme (KISEDP), located in the drylands of Turkana West sub-county near Kenya's north-western border with South Sudan (see Map 7.1). KISEDP envisions a new model of refugee assistance that leverages humanitarian funding to promote local development and economic growth. The plan encompasses a territory of over 15,000 km^2, but its core vision has focused on a newly constructed 15km^2 settlement, located just 10 km from the decades-old Kakuma refugee camp. Like the camp, the settlement is designed as a place of asylum and protection for refugees. But it is also a site of investments in physical infrastructure and human capital that are intended to improve social service delivery to the local population, stimulate market activity, and attract the private sector to this economically marginalised area. These investments are substantial: implementation of KISEDP is expected to cost around US$500 million in the first five-year period (2018–2022).

[1] Fieldwork was made possible by a small grant from the Swiss Federal Department of Foreign Affairs and results were written up under the Pedro Arrupe Research Fellowship in Oxford. Additional support was provided by the World Food Programme, which commissioned researchers at Oxford's Refugee Studies Centre to conduct a study on self-reliance in Kalobeyei from 2017 to 2020.

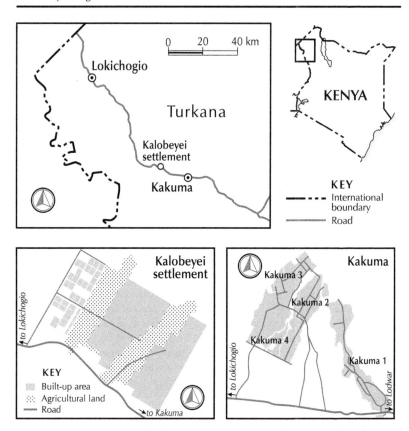

Map 7.1 Kenya, showing location of Kakuma and Kalobeyei Settlement, Turkana

Insofar as KISEDP covers just one of Turkana's six sub-counties, this is a steep increase from the US$750 million estimated for the entire county's development plan in the previous five-year period (2013–2017).

This chapter describes the vision for economic growth and regional transformation upon which the Kalobeyei Settlement was devised, as well as the perspectives of local residents whose needs and expectations do not align with the grand designs of planners and politicians. It draws on eight months of fieldwork conducted prior to the establishment of the settlement and throughout the first three years of its implementation. Interviewees ranged from agency employees to location chiefs, refugee leaders, business owners, shopkeepers and pastoralists.

It is too early to determine the success of KISEDP in achieving its objectives, but this chapter shows how the concerns of those affected by large-scale investments are overwritten by high-level narratives of growth and progress. In just three years, the sparsely inhabited plains on which the Kalobeyei Settlement was built have transformed into an urban space populated by over 40,000 refugees and boasting schools, health facilities and bustling market areas where both refugees and locals trade food, clothing and other wares. For some, this is evidence that international investments in Kalobeyei are working, but in many ways the growth of the new settlement is a result of local capital that refugees have been investing for decades in the nearby Kakuma camp. Moreover, local pastoralists express disillusionment at the lack of direct compensation for leasing out the land upon which the settlement was built, which was previously used as wet season pasture for dispersed households. The irony is that, while both refugees and pastoralists are being framed as attractive new frontiers for global capital, it is likely that many will be excluded from the benefits of this arrangement.

The problem with encampment in Kakuma

Two of the world's largest refugee camps – Kakuma and Dadaab – are situated in Kenya near the north-western border with South Sudan and the north-eastern border with Somalia, respectively. These camps were established in the early 1990s when wars in the Horn of Africa resulted in widespread displacement across the region, and they now host hundreds of thousands of people. The Kakuma camp in Turkana County consists primarily of people from South Sudan but also includes refugees from Somalia, Burundi, Democratic Republic of the Congo and other parts of the Horn and Great Lakes regions. According to UNHCR statistics, the refugee population grew steadily over the course of the 1990s, reaching over 35,000 by 1995 and 80,000 by 2000. The population decreased after 2005, when peace in Sudan made repatriation possible for many. However, following the outbreak of civil war in post-independence South Sudan the population again swelled, reaching nearly 200,000 by 2016.

Academics have long advocated against encampment policies, which force displaced populations into protracted dependency on aid providers (Verdirame and Harrell-Bond 2005), subject them to dehumanising practices of surveillance and management (Hyndman 2000) and prevent them from accessing more 'permanent' arrangements such as local integration (Hovil 2007; Kibreab 1989). Aid providers have also been criticised for paying little attention to host populations, to the extent that poorer members of host communities become the 'hidden losers' of refugee operations (Chambers 1986). A growing literature has highlighted the negative environmental consequences of hosting large, dense camp populations, especially where resource availability is already a problem (Martin 2005; Jacobsen 1997).

Nonetheless, many governments in sub-Saharan Africa continue to implement refugee encampment policies, often citing security concerns about foreigners hailing from conflict-affected areas. In Kenya, the national government prohibits most refugees from engaging in formal employment and strictly regulates their movement, forcing the UNHCR to operate under a 'care and maintenance' model that treats the camps as 'temporary' spaces of refuge. The UNHCR has itself been accused of perpetuating encampment, serving as a 'surrogate state' for camp populations rather than urging host governments to pursue more durable solutions to protracted displacement (Slaughter and Crisp 2009). International donor countries also support encampment as a strategy of border externalisation, encouraging asylum seekers to apply for resettlement from remote camps rather than invoking their right to asylum by travelling to the borders of destination countries in the global North (Hyndman and Giles 2011).

As a result of the long-standing 'care and relief' model for refugee services in Kenya, many UNHCR services remained restricted to the refugee camp. While hosts could often access health and education services there, other services such as food aid were provided exclusively to refugees. This is a point of persistent and occasionally violent protest among Turkana locals. Their county is among the poorest in Kenya, with some of the lowest education rates and worst health indicators. Border insecurity and worsening droughts have taken a toll on pastoralist livelihoods in the area, forcing many to seek alternative livelihoods in the meagre urban economies that have emerged in former colonial outposts and Catholic mission centres, including Kakuma. Locals have long complained that they face the same challenges as refugees; but because they have not crossed an international boundary, they do not receive UNHCR assistance (Aukot 2003).

An innovative alternative? The Kalobeyei Integrated Settlement

Recognising the problems inherent to encampment, UNHCR adopted its 'Alternatives to Camps' policy in 2014. While this policy advocates self-settlement in cities as an option for refugees, Kenyan law restricts refugee movement outside 'designated areas' (i.e. the camps). As such, UNHCR proposed a new model for refugee settlement that – while still enforcing the national government's containment policy – would turn away from the conventional 'care and maintenance' model. The model was inspired by Uganda's open refugee settlements, albeit constrained by the stricter legal framework in Kenya. Rather than segregating refugees in a camp, they would be encouraged to reside together with locals in a mixed settlement. Aid funding would be used to strengthen social services through integrated delivery to both populations. Moreover, instead of restricting refugees' economic efforts, they would be encouraged to engage in entrepreneurial activities in pursuit of self-reliance while also contributing to the growth of a regional economy.

In Kenya, the 2013 devolution of power and funding from the central government to newly established county governments provided a propitious moment for UNHCR to pursue its new settlement model. While the national government maintained its security-centric refugee policies, UNHCR found a powerful ally in the Turkana County Government, whose governor put the Kalobeyei Settlement alongside the county's nascent oil industry as a core aspect of his strategy to open up Turkana to private sector investments. In February 2015, UNHCR reached an agreement with host representatives – including a dialogue committee composed of local Turkana 'stakeholders' as well as representatives of the Turkana County Government – to set aside 15 km^2 of land for the Kalobeyei Integrated Settlement. The project was billed as a 'progressive' alternative to camps, based on integrated development for both refugees and their hosts.

To maintain enthusiasm, UNHCR was careful to brand the proposal not as another camp, but as an innovative new approach to refugee settlement, where the outdated model of 'care and maintenance' for a contained refugee population would give way to more inclusive, market-oriented approaches benefiting refugees and hosts alike. Although the settlement was constructed on a site that Turkana locals called Natukobenyo, the UN renamed it according to its location in Kalobeyei Ward.

As international enthusiasm grew and funding materialised from sources like the European Union Trust Fund for Africa and the World Bank, the UNHCR and Turkana County Government expanded the scope of their agenda. What began as plans for a 15 km^2 settlement quickly evolved into KISEDP, a fifteen-year vision for development that encompassed the entire 15,000-plus km^2 of Turkana West sub-county. In alignment with the county-wide development plan, the new settlement was strategically integrated into broader visions for infrastructural expansion in Turkana. This includes the highways, railways and pipelines of the LAPSSET transport corridor, which would pass through Turkana on the way to South Sudan. As described in the KISEDP Phase One document: 'Turkana County, with the strategic geographical position of Kalobeyei settlement, represents an epicentre which could act, through the infrastructure development plan, as a pole for distribution of services for the corridor' (UNHCR 2018: 68).

Aid as investment, refugees as resources

Investment is central to the vision for KISEDP – the term appears eighty-two times in the document outlining the KISEDP Phase One document mentioned above – but the precise form of investment varies. At one level, KISEDP is itself an investment of international resources in the infrastructure and human capital of Turkana County. Humanitarian resources have long fuelled local development in Kakuma through, for example, the construction of schools and clinics at the camp periphery (Sanghi et al. 2016). By making this a more explicit part of development planning, the large refugee population is reframed not as a burden on the local population, but as a source of funding from international donors. It is noteworthy that refugees are listed in the 'Natural Resources' section of the KISEDP Phase One document alongside the county's oil reserves and solar potential (UNHCR 2019: 10).

At another level, KISEDP is an attempt to make Turkana attractive to further investment by the private sector. In order to do so, UNHCR and its partners needed to frame the refugee population as an untapped opportunity. In 2016, the International Finance Corporation (IFC) commissioned a study on the scale of local demand. The resulting report (*Kakuma as a Marketplace*) sought to turn the conventional image of a refugee camp on its head:

> Rather than focusing on humanitarian or development needs of refugees and the host community, we considered Kakuma camp and town as a single commercial and financial market … present[ing] information for companies looking to enter the substantial, yet mostly untapped market, in Kakuma. (IFC 2018: 5)

The study concluded that Kakuma was ripe for investment, with sufficient market potential for major supermarkets, energy providers, banking and microfinance institutions, and telecommunications services, as well as a largely untapped labour force for potential employers. Through the Kakuma Kalobeyei Challenge Fund, the IFC will provide millions of dollars to stimulate private sector investment in the area.

However, the emergence of economies in refugee camps is not a recent revelation. Rural camps like Kakuma have long been recognised as a step towards urbanisation (De Montclos and Kagwanja 2000), insofar as they develop into busy social and economic milieus with a city-like quality that has been coined 'humanitarian urbanism' (Jansen 2018). As Kakuma expanded throughout the 1990s, people from across Turkana and other parts of Kenya were drawn to the camp in search of employment and business opportunities. Many refugees engaged in informal entrepreneurial activities, and some were hired by humanitarian agencies as 'incentive workers'. Poor Turkana people also came to Kakuma and surrounding villages to sell firewood, charcoal and their domestic labour to refugee households. Refugees and Turkana locals became economically and socially intertwined in an emerging informal economy (Oka 2011). Over the past twenty-five years, the Kakuma camp has expanded into a major economic hub for Turkana County, complete with busy marketplaces, wholesale depots, education and health services, churches and mosques, an airport and other marks of urban form.

Kakuma's economy emerged as the unplanned consequence of locals and refugees investing their capital in response to rising demand for goods and services. What is different about the Kalobeyei Settlement and the broader KISEDP framework of which it is a part is that UNHCR and the Turkana County Government are attempting to engineer economic growth through investments by humanitarian agencies and commercial funders. In the early phases of implementation, this includes two primary strategies for leveraging humanitarian resources to the ends of local development: by strengthening local infrastructure through the provision of integrated services, and by fostering self-reliance through investments in human capital and market-based approaches to refugee assistance. The next two sections consider each of these in turn, with particular attention to the expectations of and impact on the local population.

Uneven access to integrated services

Integrated service delivery is a key component of KISEDP and is specified in the 2015 Terms of Engagement, which provided official community consent for the construction of the settlement on local land. The agreement incorporated feedback through a community dialogue committee and was signed by representatives from the national government and UNHCR. Various expectations are laid out in the areas of education, water, health, income generation and employment, and environment. Some provisions are quantitatively specific, such as the stipulation that 70 per cent of all employment opportunities in the settlement should be allocated to the host community. Other provisions are less numerically defined, such as 'water trucking during drought', 'scholarships for students' and 'access to health facilities in refugee camps'.

More entrepreneurially oriented Kenyans were generally enthusiastic about the self-reliance agenda. The prospects of expanded access to social services, including schools, health-care facilities and water infrastructure was more widely welcomed. Nonetheless, the prospect of an expanding refugee settlement met with strong opposition, especially from Turkana pastoralists who exerted their claim to the area's rangelands.

Despite these divided opinions and interests, the local population was represented by a single dialogue committee during negotiations with UNHCR. Caught between Turkana demands for their own 'benefits' and the international community's vision for an integrated settlement, the dialogue committee conveyed a somewhat distorted public message. As implementation of the Kalobeyei Settlement began, many Turkana locals expected that they would receive their own benefits separate from and parallel to those of refugees, and not integrated services as such. This expectation emerged many times in individual interviews and focus groups:

> We Turkana have said that we want those things that were previously promised to us here. The houses that they said would be built – we want them to be built! The water that they said would be given – give it! The school as well that they said would be established, which would be our own and not for the refugees – they should establish that for us. (Interview with Turkana man, September 2017)

Besides the unclear communication, the planners also failed to assess the likelihood that Turkana people would not want to leave their current homes and move into the settlement. Early plans for the settlement envisioned a 'hybrid community' of both refugees and locals, who would live side by side sharing water, health and education facilities. However, many Turkana people – especially those with livestock – were unwilling to move into the planned settlement. Pastoralists who resided in Natukobenyo prior to construction gradually exited as refugees arrived. Some expressed fears of theft as the settlement provided a market for stolen livestock. Others decried the plastic waste that littered the grazing lands near the populated areas, which posed risks for their goats.

Even if locals had been interested in relocating to the settlement, an unexpected influx of new arrivals following the outbreak of civil conflict in South Sudan in 2013 quickly brought the new settlement to its maximum capacity of almost 40,000 people. Some arrivals were initially settled in Kakuma, but as the camp reached its saturation point in mid-2016, UNHCR was compelled to locate new arrivals in the unfinished Kalobeyei Settlement. Therefore, hopes for 'co-residence' were abandoned in favour of more modest calls for 'peaceful coexistence', which requires merely that people share resources and space while living apart.

The challenge now is how Turkana locals living outside the settlement will access services. For example, the Kalobeyei Masterplan envisioned that locals living in the settlement would be able to access water through the settlement infrastructure. Drilling them their own water sources outside the settlement is not an option because most boreholes in the area have not yielded water. Instead, water for the settlement is piped over a distance of 20 km from the Tarac River (also the source of water for the Kakuma camp) and distributed to holding tanks in the three sub-sections or 'villages' of the settlement. It is released to collection points where refugees come to fetch it in jerry cans, but there are no plans to pipe it to distant points beyond the settlement. Many Turkana locals have therefore been left feeling that the promise of improved access to water has not been met:

> What the refugees are given should also be given to us ... We gave our land to the refugees thinking that we would benefit from them. We thought that if they built a school, hospital or water source for the refugees, they would also do the same to us. But nothing has been done for us. (Interview with Turkana herder, September 2017)

Urban biases of market-oriented development

As with other investments in the drylands featured in this book, the refugee-focused investment drive obscured variations as to *who* within the local population can pursue these opportunities. The market-oriented approach has afforded business opportunities to local entrepreneurs, but many current and former pastoralists have had fewer opportunities to benefit. The two major self-reliance programmes in Kalobeyei Settlement are the World Food Programme's (WFP's) Bamba Chakula ('Get Your Food') and the UNHCR's Cash for Shelter. Bamba Chakula replaces conventional food aid distribution with a market system in which local traders provide food to refugee customers, who pay through electronic vouchers transferred by WFP each month. Similarly, Cash for Shelter provides funding for the construction of houses, which beneficiaries receive in three instalments. Recipients can purchase building materials and contract labourers from the local economy. Both programmes replace direct provision by agencies with market solutions that support local employment and the growth of a regional supply chain.

An early contingency of significant consequence for self-reliance programming was the influx of new arrivals from South Sudan, as described above. This prevented UNHCR from pursuing its original plan to populate the settlement with refugees possessing the capital and business experience required for self-reliance programming. As many of the arrivals from South Sudan have recently fled conflict and insecurity, they lack the required networks, capital and skills to become successful small-business operators, dashing the hopes of planners that the settlement would become an easy self-reliance success story. Instead, it is likely that many of the settlement residents will need relief support for the foreseeable future (Betts et al. 2018).

Nonetheless, implementation of the cash and voucher programmes went forward as planned, with refugees targeted as the direct beneficiaries and locals participating as the providers of goods and services. The scale of financial input has been substantial, with over 50 million Kenyan shillings (US$500,000) disbursed to Kalobeyei's refugees each month under the

Bamba Chakula programme. Under the Cash-for-Shelter programme, each household receives 140,000 Kenyan shillings (US$1,400) and, as of late 2018, over 1,000 households had benefited (UNHCR 2019). Entrepreneurs from both the refugee and the local populations have capitalised on the resulting markets for food and construction materials, and others have been hired as construction labour. And because retailers in Kakuma acquire most of their goods from trade hubs to the south of Turkana, the new business opportunities have swelled supply chains and increased the volume and variety of products in the county.

However, these benefits are not equally available to different segments of the local population. Among Turkana people, it is largely those with formal education and commercial experience who have profited from the self-reliance programmes. In the Bamba Chakula programme, only a limited number of food traders are contracted by WFP to receive voucher credit from refugee customers; as of 2019, there were about sixty traders in Kalobeyei Settlement, of whom about fifteen were Turkana. Although literacy was not an explicit criterion for selection, traders must procure the requisite government registration and food hygiene documentation, sign contracts and undertake book-keeping, all of which create a bias for urbanites with formal education and business experience. WFP has begun a transition to an unrestricted cash programme, which would potentially open up opportunities for a greater number of host and refugee entrepreneurs. But regardless, the programmes are not amenable to the livelihood competencies of current and drop-out pastoralists. As one Turkana woman from a nearby village explained:

> Those from town are the ones benefiting, because they use the pen. Not us, we don't know how to use the pen, and that is the thing that brings us down. Those in town benefit because of the pen, but as for us, we must struggle to sell our firewood. Or some might decide to go get married to a man from town. (Interview with Turkana woman, December 2018)

Similarly, in the Cash-for-Shelter programme, those gaining the greatest benefits are contractors and dealers of construction materials. Some former pastoralists have found temporary employment as builders, but even those who might be able to access labour can only do so if they live in the direct vicinity of the settlement. As one woman explained, regarding the rural–urban divide, 'Those in town are getting more help than those of us who live farther away. Some of them engage in small jobs, and they get something. But for us … we only depend on firewood' (Interview with Turkana woman, December 2018).

Conclusion

The enthusiasm for integrated settlements that provide services and social assistance to refugee and local populations alike is a response to tensions engendered by the older 'care and maintenance' model of assisting refugees in camps. Integrated settlements are cast as significant investments in pastoral drylands and catalysts for the growth of markets and development of infrastructure. This approach to refugee camps and integrated settlements bears similarities to discussions around enclave versus integrated investments in agriculture and energy. The thinking goes that to ensure local acceptance, refugee settlements must not be walled off from the surrounding society but rather used to leverage economic development and strengthen access to markets and services for local populations. Along those lines, Kalobeyei was planned as an integrated settlement in which refugees and locals would live as neighbours, running businesses and accessing the same social services.

Yet, like large-scale investments elsewhere in the region, including the Mgneta farm profiled in the last chapter or the story of the Bagamoyo sugar project told in Chapter 11, the Kalobeyei development has not advanced according to plan. Although the project is still in its first five-year phase and it is too early to determine if will ultimately be a success or failure, the opinion of many Turkana residents in Kalobeyei is that they have not benefited. Most Turkana have rejected the idea of integration, preferring their own allocations of services and assistance and living outside the boundaries of the settlement. Furthermore, the market-oriented programmes of KISEDP's self-reliance agenda have benefited entrepreneurial urban dwellers but largely neglected pastoralism, which remains the backbone of most Turkana livelihoods. This may be due to the oversight of planners who cannot 'see' significant local forms of social stratification and for whom the perception of a homogenous local population (i.e. destitute and in need of a new livelihood outside of pastoralism) is a convenient simplification (cf. Scott 1998). Coupled with the optimism for innovative market-based solutions, such simplifications tend to drown out local voices and to obscure the divergent consequences for 'winners' and 'losers' of investments. The risk is that investments in socio-economic integration for refugees and locals could exacerbate an already widening wealth gap between town dwellers and pastoralists in Turkana.

Despite problems with the early implementation of the Kalobeyei Settlement, UNHCR and the Turkana County Government are optimistic that KISEDP will ultimately be a 'win-win' development by encouraging refugee self-reliance while also supporting economic development that benefits the wider Turkana population. However, sustaining enthusiasm across multiple stakeholders has contributed to – and perhaps even required – some degree of historic myopia among planners. Even though Kalobeyei's backers strive to depict the investment as an innovative use of humanitarian funds that catalyses economic growth, camps have long provided large injections of international funding, markets for local goods and places to invest local capital. For decades, locals have supplemented their livelihoods by selling cooking fuel and construction materials in Kakuma or providing domestic labour to refugees. These relations arose organically and were largely below the radar of international relief agencies. The case of the Kakuma camp demonstrates how supposedly 'enclave' investments may be experienced locally as oases of opportunity, especially for mobile pastoralists. But plans that rely on large-scale external investments – like KISEDP – may overlook these opportunities, especially when they frame refugees, pastoralists, or other local populations not as endogenous investors, but as frontiers for external capital. By emphasising the novelty of designed 'investments' like the Kalobeyei Settlement, planners may be missing what was already working in Kakuma.

8

Negotiating Access to Land & Resources at the Geothermal Frontier in Baringo, Kenya

CLEMENS GREINER

Perspectives on large-scale investment in Africa's rural margins often start from the assumption that projects happen in socio-ecological and livelihood settings that were relatively stable and undisturbed until new developments. Yet in Kenya's northern Rift Valley recent large-scale infrastructural investments intersect with longer-term changes in land use, livelihoods and internal differentiation. Describing looming dramatic changes in this previously marginalised pastoralist hinterland, a 2015 headline in *The Economist* declared that 'a glimpse of Africa's future' was apparent in the region's transformation. Africa's largest wind energy development near Lake Turkana (see Drew, Chapter 5 this book), the planned Lamu Port–South Sudan–Ethiopia Transport (LAPSSET) regional corridor (see Chome, Chapter 2 and Elliott, Chapter 3), along with the massive expansion of geothermal power generation, are among the largest projects, all linked by the modernist longings of Kenya's Vision 2030. The pastoral rangelands of northern Kenya, a region hitherto bypassed by state or global capital investment in infrastructure or services, and characterised as impoverished, marginalised and peripheral, is being reimagined as a frontier brimming with resource wealth and new markets that can help fuel the country's economic development. However, while conjuring economic growth and transformation, new large-scale investments create anxieties around land grabbing, displacement and exclusions as well.

Based on fieldwork carried out in Baringo, in Kenya's northern Rift Valley (see Map 8.1), over different periods since 2009, this chapter explores how the rapid spread of dryland farming among the pastoral Pokot is happening alongside and entwining with the early development of geothermal power. It uses different concepts of the 'frontier' to examine the intersections of these processes and how they mutually reinforce each other in ways that lead to profound competition for and revaluation of land.

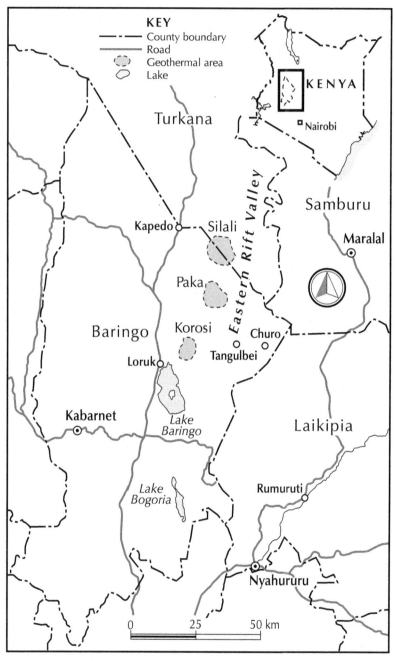

Map 8.1 Kenya, showing location of Baringo in the northern Rift Valley

Seeing the frontier

Recent attempts to conceptualise the spread of capitalist relations and state power in the rural margins have invoked the idea of an advancing resource frontier (Watts 2018; Li 2014a; Korf et al. 2015; Mosley and Watson 2016; Tsing 2003). An implicit assumption in many assessments is that communities in and around sites of new large-scale investment are bystanders in broader processes of transformation. Conceptualisations of the advancing resource frontier often start from Turner's (1894) analysis of settler expansion into the American West, a narrative criticised for, among other things, its supremacist and teleological perspectives (Geiger 2009; Klein 1996). Kopytoff's 'internal African frontier' (Kopytoff 1987a) provides a different take. He argued that processes of establishing frontiers at the margins of more established ethnic groups, which had no interest in policing the unused land, shaped political culture in Africa. He described the frontier as consisting of interstitial zones, core areas of more established polities, and emerging new boundaries. Similar versions of the frontier have been used to describe agricultural colonisation of previously uncultivated areas (Lane 2004; Netting and Stone 1996) and – more generally – changing land-use practices, migration and commodification of land in marginal rural areas (Amanor 2010; Guyer et al. 2007). Here, these processes are likened to the creation of an 'internal agricultural frontier'.

Intersecting temporal and spatial dynamics define the frontier. They are spaces in becoming, ultimately driven by processes of future-making (Appadurai 2013). The aspirations, anticipations and different temporalities of multiple social, political and economic actors drive transformations of frontiers, as Luning (2018) argues in the case of mining contexts. It is not simply large domestic and global capital; endogenous (or local) capital also plays a significant role in reconfiguring the frontier. Emerging, and sometimes simply imagined, economic opportunities as well as an institutional vacuum characterise these settings, which frontier capitalists exploit to their advantage. The transition away from customary tenure arrangements, and the precarity of new institutions, generates uncertainty that provides an opening for local grabbing and commodification of land (Greiner 2017). Thus, it is through not only the intervention of states and global capital but also internal processes and differentiation that frontiers are shaped and defined (Li 2014a). These processes relate to and reinforce each other, as they are interconnected through alliances that connect stakeholders at multiple levels, as developments in Baringo show.

The Baringo context

East Pokot is a rugged landscape of rolling hills and mountains rising from the lowland plains of the Baringo basin up to the Laikipia plateau bordering Baringo County to the east. In an area inhabited mainly by the Pokot people, specialised pastoralism has been the dominant form of land use over the past two centuries and still persists on the lowland plains up to today (Anderson and Bollig 2016). The latter half of the twentieth century, however, was characterised by a declining livestock/human ratio, growing malnutrition and poverty, violence and increasing environmental degradation (Bollig 2016). Even before recent geothermal developments in East Pokot, patterns of land use and tenure in the area had transformed significantly. Up until the 1990s, rights to land were communal according to the Pokot customary system. Communal tenure reflected the need for flexibility and opportunistic resource use by livestock-keepers. Since then, Pokot society entered a phase of rapid transformation characterised by increasing sedentarisation, privatisation of land and a growing awareness of territorial boundaries (Bollig et al. 2014). These changes are associated with livelihood shifts, particularly the spread of rain-fed cultivation.

These coincided with changes in the political administration, which had remained largely unchanged since Kenya's independence in 1963. East Pokot, which was part of Baringo District after independence, gradually gained greater political autonomy in the 1990s until it became an administrative district in its own right in 2006 (Österle 2007). Since 2013, after devolution reforms that saw the creation of forty-seven counties, each with their own executives and elected officials, East Pokot has been part of the newly established Baringo County. As elsewhere in northern Kenya (Lind 2018; Mosley and Watson 2016), devolution contributed to rising local expectations to benefit from infrastructure and other investments and to increasing political tensions over ethnic belonging and county boundaries (Greiner 2013). These changes provide the context for understanding negotiations of both the internal agricultural frontier and large-scale geothermal investment.

The internal agricultural frontier

Following the severe droughts of the 1980s, the Welthungerhilfe (German Agro Action), together with the Kenya Freedom from Hunger Council, promoted rain-fed maize cultivation as a famine relief measure in East Pokot. Except for some highland areas, however, farming did not gain traction. An evaluation of the project noted that 'after completion of the programme 1985/86 most of the communal plots were abandoned and reverted to fallow bushland' (Wirth 1988: 11). Farming began to take off on a larger scale from the late 1990s, more than a decade after Welthungerhilfe left the area. Initially, drought-related loss of livestock and poverty were the main factors driving people into taking up cultivation. This is no longer the case. Wherever cultivation is possible, a high percentage of households are engaged in agriculture. While cultivation until the late

1990s was mostly restricted to the highland areas around Churo, it spread down to the area around Tangulbei and even to the bottom of the Rift Valley around Loruk (Greiner and Mwaka 2016). An analysis of remote sensing data covering a period from 1985 to 2015 shows the dramatic increase in rain-fed maize cultivation in East Pokot over the past three decades. The area cultivated increased by a factor of 7.5 from 1,104 ha in 1985 to 8,176 ha in 2015. There was a dramatic, almost fivefold increase in the cultivated area within a five-year period alone between 1995 and 2000, coinciding with a serious drought in northern Kenya that pushed many pastoralists to look for alternatives.

In other contexts, such a dramatic expansion of the agricultural frontier into previously uncultivated areas followed the expansion of cash crops, such as cocoa in the case of Sulawesi (Li 2014a) or Ghana (Amanor 2010). In the literature on East African pastoralism, the spread of cultivation into rangelands has been associated with the gradual encroachment of non-pastoralist people into the drylands (Spencer 1998; Galaty and Bonte 1991). In East Pokot, however, there is no expanding market for cash crops, nor do cultivators from outside East Pokot seek land in the area. Rather, the rapid expansion of subsistence maize cultivation from within is the driver of transforming land use in Baringo since the late 1990s.

In this respect, the agricultural frontier in East Pokot is reminiscent of Kopytoff's (1987a) understanding of internal frontiers, where under certain conditions core groups split and reassemble as new social entities. Indeed, many of those Pokot who nowadays rely on more sedentary and agricultural-based livelihoods see themselves as socially distinct from their pastoral counterparts, although the differences are often not as clear-cut as some Pokot make out. Many Pokot cultivators, for example, still keep animals with their pastoralist relatives. Yet schools, churches and other new institutions have contributed to cultural and socio-spatial practices that are increasingly distinct from the customs, rituals and policies of their pastoral brethren (Bollig et al. 2014).

What is different from Kopytoff's understanding of the internal African frontier, however, is the lack of empty space in East Pokot. While Kopytoff (1987a) begins from the observation that '[e]stablished societies were surrounded by large tracts of land that were open politically, physically or both' (ibid.: 10), the expansion of cultivation in East Pokot is only possible at the expense of other land uses, particularly herding. This scarcity of land is made worse by the introduction of wildlife conservation areas, some of which exclude cattle grazing at particular times (Greiner 2012), and by vegetation changes, particularly bush encroachment (Becker et al. 2016; Vehrs 2016). Herders are increasingly pushed into more marginal areas. This pressure has spilled over in recent years, with herders invading private ranches in neighbouring Laikipia (Pas 2019; and see Gravesen, Chapter 12 this book).

Competing claims over arable land, particularly near to permanent settlements, has led to considerable conflict within Pokot society since the early 2000s. Although tenure is strictly communal, land has become a commodity, traded between Pokots. In the wake of these processes of endogenous commodification, conflicts at all levels of Pokot society – between individuals, families and clans – have unfolded in an institutional vacuum that is typical of many frontier situations. The rules and regulations that once served to regulate resource access for livelihoods centred on livestock-keeping are no longer recognised in a situation in which most people seek exclusive access to land on a permanent basis. Competing stakeholders often resort to violence (or the threat of it) to enforce their claims to land as the authority of customary male elders dwindles (Greiner 2017).

The area chiefs in the highlands, who are involved as mediators in many of these conflicts, have complained about the 'declining moral standard of the community' in the rush of grabbing and subdividing land, and by the fact that areas that formerly have been preserved are now encroached on by the growing population (Interview with Assistant Chief, Churo village, 10 November 2010). A local political administrative official complained that 'in the agricultural areas, we need the private land titles to prevent further quarrels and conflicts over land. The boundaries often are not well defined and are cause for much trouble among people. If there will be no demarcation, there will even be more trouble' (Interview with District Officer, Churo village, 19 October 2010). Hoping for an early announcement of land adjudication, he later advised the chiefs to freeze all the conflicting land disputes in which they were involved until further notice. They could not adhere to this instruction for very long, as by early 2019 still no surveyor had visited to start the process of adjudication.

These conflicting endogenous dynamics overlap with and reinforce the processes of land commodification brought about more recently by the advancing extractive frontier, which in Baringo centres on the development of geothermal infrastructure.

The geothermal frontier

In 2008, the Kenyan government incorporated the parastatal Geothermal Development Company (GDC) to facilitate the development of geothermal steam fields.[1] Infrastructural development for exploiting geothermal resources is a risky venture that bears high upfront costs, particularly in remote rural areas (Johnson and Ogeya 2018). The risks include resistance by local communities who are the rights-holders to the community land on which the infrastructure is developed. As the 'geothermal frontier' unfolds, institutionalising and legalising control of the area is a significant challenge for investors (Peluso and Lund 2011).

[1] www.gdc.co.ke/about_us.php, accessed 4 March 2019.

In East Pokot the first explorations into the geothermal potential of the Baringo–Silali Block were completed in the early 2000s. More detailed surface studies in 2013 indicated a potential of 3,000 MW centred on Silali, Paka and Korosi, three dormant volcanoes.[2] Infrastructural investments proceeded shortly thereafter in 2014 with the construction of access roads. The exploration demands enormous transport capacities, as the moving of one single geothermal drilling unit requires more than 150 truckloads. Therefore, more than 100 km of new gravel roads now connect areas that were formerly accessible only by foot. Large water reservoirs are being erected on top of the volcanoes, filled by a pumping station located on the shores of nearby Lake Baringo.[3] This newly created water infrastructure is of crucial importance for the technical operations.[4]

It also appears, however, to be a key argument in convincing local residents to accept the GDC's operations. To win over local opinion, the GDC has developed twenty community water points for human and animal consumption. An administration officer for the GDC's North Rift operations explained: 'The challenge on the ground is to buy in the community. This is a priority for the GDC, as infrastructure development is very expensive and projects will run on a long-term basis' (Interview with GDC official, Kampi ya Samaki, 11 January 2016). GDC community officers organise *barazas* (community meetings) involving area chiefs, leaders and elders, among other community members, to sensitise and inform residents about the development plans. While these meetings ostensibly are meant to give the impression of a 'participatory approach', the GDC officer acknowledged that there is considerable scepticism, especially among the illiterate and elderly: 'They ask: "Why do we need roads? What comes next?" They fear that ritual places will be affected. They say, "We do not need fire" [*ma*, which in Pokot language is synonymous with electricity]. But they agree that they need water, which comes along with the exploration' (ibid.).

The GDC has encouraged local residents to register in savings and credit cooperatives (SACCOs) to help the recruitment of day labourers at construction sites and to create a framework for paying compensation. The secretary of the newly formed Silali Development Trust, explained that people can still move into his ward, but that no more land is available around the larger settlements. He explained that local elites have already claimed all land along the newly built and planned roads (Interview with

---

[2]   www.gdc.co.ke/baringo.php, accessed 4 March 2019.

[3]   www.gdc.co.ke/blog/gdc-changing-fortunes-of-communities-living-in-the-north-rift-region, accessed 22 May 2019.

[4]   Geothermal energy is produced by tapping hydrothermal convection systems. These usually occur in areas with volcanic activity, such as the Rift Valley. In the process, cool water seeps into the Earth's crust, where it is heated by magma and forced to the surface as hot water or steam, which can be used to drive generators. (Information from www.ucsusa. org/clean_energy/our-energy-choices/renewable-energy/how-geothermal-energy-works. html, accessed 12 March 2019.)

Silali Development Trust official, Chemolingot, 12 January 2016). There are parallels with the situation in Isiolo, the putative hub for the LAPSSET corridor in northern Kenya, where people have rushed to secure plots as a way of staking a claim on the future city in the making (see Elliott, Chapter 3 this book).

According to National Land Commission official in Baringo County, there are also processes of land registration by some of these groups. Baringo is an adjudication area until September 2019 and thus open for assignments of land rights to groups as well as to individuals. But these processes, the official observes, are not very transparent: 'The people in Tiaty ... some have already identified themselves as a community and they like to go on with their land, but then they need to be sensitised so that they do not take advantage, especially in the management. Because what we fear is the elite capture' (Interview with Baringo County Coordinator, National Land Commission, Kabarnet, 12 March 2019). Concerns that local elites have a head start in transforming communal into privately claimed land have existed for many years, as an elder shared in 2010: 'Land might not be enough for everybody. The stronger families will be more successful than the weaker ones in privatising land' (Interview with elder, Churo, 21 October 2010).

The risk of conflict over land is especially acute where different ethnic groups meet. Both Pokot and Turkana, who inhabit areas west of Baringo County, claim Silali and the future geothermal operations in this area. Recent tensions that have arisen around Silali and particularly the nearby border village of Kapedo have renewed a much deeper Pokot–Turkana conflict that stretches back decades (McCabe 2004; Bollig 1993). Violent clashes, including livestock raiding and sieges of Kapedo by Pokot warriors have intensified over the past decade. This peaked in an unprecedented operation by the Kenyan army in late 2014, following the killing of twenty-two Administration Police officers by Pokot warriors in the Kapedo area (Vehrs 2018). Although often using livestock raids as cover, contestations over the border between Baringo and Turkana counties, and access to planned investment and infrastructural developments, play a crucial role (Greiner 2013, 2016). The widespread availability of automatic weapons has made the consequences of the conflict even worse (Mkutu 2007). These 'inverted capabilities for violence' (Geiger 2009: 111) can be found throughout dryland Kenya. They appear to create room for bargaining, as power is not *a priori* vested on one side. The state has no monopoly on violence. Investors are vulnerable and must negotiate their presence with care. Conflicts between communities and investors over oil extraction in Turkana County demonstrate that perceived injustices and unmet expectations of benefiting from oil development can lead to violence, with potentially serious consequences for investors' operations (see Okenwa, Chapter 4 this book; Mkutu 2017).

Conclusion

The current situation in East Pokot can be described as a convergence of different frontiers. An accelerating transition to rain-fed cultivation and sedentarisation has created an internal agricultural frontier as cultivation spreads across areas that were used for pastoralism. Although bearing a resemblance, this process is different from the 'encroachment hypothesis' (Spencer 1998; Galaty and Bonte 1991), which posits that pastoralism will be displaced into marginal areas by farmers migrating in from distant more fertile areas. The spread of dryland farming and land privatisation is squeezing pastoral Pokot. However, they are under pressure from neighbours and family members who are fencing plots to try their hand at farming. In contrast to the narrative that pastoralists are victims of recent frontier dynamics, the invasion of the Laikipia plateau shows that they are pushing into new territories, opening up a new pastoralist frontier. These dynamics resemble Kopytoff's (1987a) notion of the internal African frontier, where groups split from cores to open new frontiers in interstitial spaces that had been weakly controlled.

The advancing resource frontier, along with expectations of rising land values, accentuates the trend towards privatising land. From the investors' perspective, the geothermal frontier in Baringo primarily concerns political control over land and its incorporation into the Kenyan state, and is thus reminiscent of Turner's frontier logic. Global capital forces outside Pokot are driving the area's latest transformation to meet increasing national demands for energy. Both frontiers create an institutional vacuum and, in both frontier settings, violence or the threat of it plays a key role in negotiating land access.

Resource frontiers are often associated with asymmetric power relations between global capitalist forces and local populations. Pessimistic accounts of land grabbing, the denial of rights and displacement prevail in scholarly and advocacy work, whereas internal differentiation, acquiescence and participation is downplayed (Korf et al. 2015; Li 2010; Geiger 2009). East Pokot, however, demonstrates that commodification of and the scramble for land can predate the dynamics of the advancing extractive frontiers and entwine with them. This challenges normative understandings of rural frontier populations in the global South as being somehow passive victims of new political economies that are in the making.

9

The Berbera Corridor Development & Somaliland's Political Economy

AHMED M. MUSA

In September 2016, the Somaliland government agreed a thirty-year concession with DP World, the Dubai-based ports operator, to develop and operate the port of Berbera. The US$440 million expansion will transform Berbera – already a significant hub for the Horn of Africa's regional livestock trade – beyond recognition. The two-phase development incorporates plans for a new 400m quay, a 250,000 m² yard and upgrades to the city's airport. The Berbera corridor will expand port access for neighbouring Ethiopia, which has a 19 per cent stake in the development. With Somaliland holding a 30 per cent stake, this leaves DP World as the majority stakeholder. The United Arab Emirates (UAE) has committed over US$100 million in additional investment to upgrade the 250 km road connecting the port with Hargeisa, Somaliland's capital, and Togwajale, a town astride the border with Ethiopia (see Map 9.1).

The Berbera corridor development is part of a wider drive by Gulf rivals the UAE and Qatar to cement their geostrategic standing in the Horn of Africa. Through large-scale investments in infrastructure, they seek to secure preferential access to potential developments and trade under China's Belt and Road Initiative (International Crisis Group 2019). Yet, these large-scale investments are being pursued in 'ways that increase rather than decrease regional polarisation', with political considerations to squeeze rivals trumping economic interests (Verhoeven 2018: 334). Tensions engendered by new large-scale infrastructural investments reach more deeply into Somali society itself, with concerns that Gulf investments and funding will deepen pre-existing societal divisions and, thus, foment instability (Meester et al. 2018).

The UAE's large-scale investments, unprecedented in Somaliland's history, have precipitated a scramble among the region's clan-based economic networks. Past patterns of exclusion, and intense competition to command a favourable position in regional trade networks, influence new struggles to capture the expected windfall of Berbera's development. This chapter examines the political economy of the Berbera corridor and the competition and conflict it has unleashed.

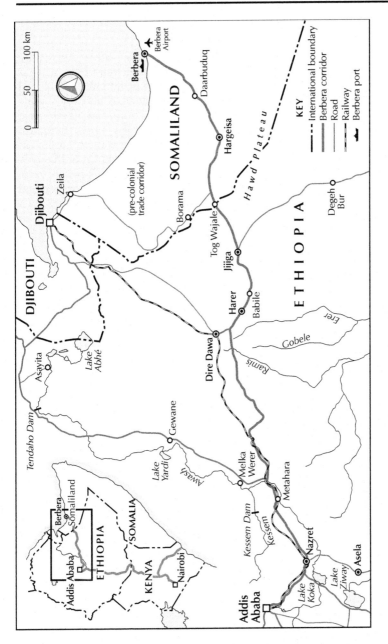

Map 9.1 Somaliland, showing location of the Berbera corridor

History of corridor contestation

By the early 1900s, Berbera and Zeila ports on the Gulf of Aden were already established as key ports for caravan-based trade from what is now Somaliland, as well as neighbouring areas of Ethiopia (Mohamed 2004). During this period, Zeila remained a principal port for exports of coffee, gum, hides and skins, ivory, livestock, guns and slaves, most of which came from Ethiopia via Harar (Pankhurst 1965). European colonialists (Italy, France and the United Kingdom) as well as the ancient sultanates and chiefdoms in the region competed for control in the trade routes (see Barnes 2000; Ram 1981). The fortunes of the strategic Zeila corridor changed in subsequent years with the expansion of French and British influence in the region and development of infrastructure such as the Ethio-Djibouti railway. It assumed a more political character as both the British and French contested to influence the direction of the infrastructure due to its economic importance (Ram 1981).

The opening of the Ethio-Djibouti Railway in 1917 changed the importance of the Zeila corridor as this infrastructure drew trade away from nearby Zeila port under the British to Djibouti under the French (Dua 2013; Ram 1981), while the establishment of a British military garrison in Aden across the Red Sea in Yemen, at the beginning of the second quarter of the twentieth century, cemented Berbera's significance (Dua 2013). Berbera served as the capital for the British Somaliland Protectorate, while Hargeisa and Burao were administrative centres for the western and eastern hinterlands respectively (Samatar et al. 1988). Helped by their administrative status, the towns experienced steady growth as market centres that connected pastoralists to a wider regional livestock trading system (ibid.).

Over time, the Berbera corridor has constituted a 'negotiation arena' (Hagmann and Péclard 2010: 550) in Somaliland's politics since the break-up of Somalia in 1991. According to Hagmann and Péclard 'negotiation arenas represent a broader political space in which relations of power and authority are vested ... negotiation arenas are embedded in the social relations between contending groups and are characterised by spatio-temporal dynamics and a certain informality' (2010: 551). In Somaliland's early state formation, President Egal took advantage of embedded clan relations to remove roadblocks from this main economic corridor (Balthasar 2013: 224). The port has been, and still is, instrumental in Somaliland's state formation and development as a centre for a regional livestock trade that connects it and neighbouring pastoral regions of Ethiopia with markets in the Arabian Peninsula (Yacob Aklilu and Catley 2009). Livestock exports from the port, the president's hometown, generated US$10–15 million in revenue for the Egal administration in the early 1990s (Balthasar 2013: 223).

Much of the port infrastructure and connecting road links were established by the 1970s. The corridor assumed greater geopolitical significance by the late 1990s as a trans-shipment route to supply food aid to eastern Ethiopia (Gaani 2002) following its war with Eritrea and the ensuing loss of Massawa port. The economic importance of the corridor has only expanded since. The road that connects Berbera–Hargeisa–Wajale is the country's main economic corridor (Balthasar 2013: 224). Whoever controls the corridor commands considerable political and economic power.

In Somaliland, the segmentary clan structure provides the social foundation for constituting political and economic power (Lewis 1961). Competition between clan-based networks is therefore the basis to understand struggles over Berbera's development and patterns of exclusion and inclusion arising from it. Much of the competition and contestation over Berbera is between central Isaaq sub-clans. Isaaq is the largest clan in Somaliland and is divided into a number of sub-clans that have vied for a commanding economic position (Huliaras 2002). The Habar Awal sub-clan is predominantly agro-pastoral and town-based and is concentrated in settlements along the Berbera corridor. The Garhajis sub-clan is predominantly pastoral and resides mainly in areas removed from the Berbera corridor route. The import and export of goods is the main source of revenue in the corridor. Historically, the Habar Awal dominated the import economy, while the Garhajis controlled the livestock export economy (Interview, businessman and former minister, Hargeisa, March 2018).

Conflict between the Habar Awal and the Garhajis in the early 1990s turned on control of the corridor (Balthasar 2013; Bradbury 2008). Dubbed the 'Berbera conflict', tensions erupted in 1992 after interim President Abdirahman Ahmed Ali Tuur, from the Garhajis sub-clan, tried to wrest control of the port, an important source of revenue collection for the fledging Somaliland government (Phillips 2013). Mohamed Haji Ibrahim Egal, the so-called 'master manipulator of clans' (Balthasar 2013: 231), succeeded Tuur as president in mid-1993. Egal was from the Habar Awal sub-clan, who resisted Tuur's rule. Egal mobilised his supporters and Habar Awal business elites against the Garhajis, triggering a more serious civil war between 1994 and 1996 and a flow of refugees into Ethiopia (Balthasar 2013; Phillips 2013; Huliaras 2002). During the civil war, the Habar Awal strengthened their dominance in the import sector while also, together with the Habar Jelo clan, taking control of livestock exports from the Garhajis.

The political and economic reconfigurations resulting from the civil war reverberate up to now. Despite the widely held view that Somaliland's post-war reconciliation was successful (Jhazbhay 2008; Bradbury et al. 2003), there is a growing sense of political and economic inequality resulting from the state formation process. In the early years of Somaliland's state formation, through clientelism Egal received loans from businessmen who in turn received tax exemptions and tools for long-term corridor and market control (Balthasar 2013; Bradbury 2008).

Egal was also able to encourage fighters from his Habar Awal sub-clan to demobilise by offering job opportunities derived from the revival of economic infrastructure, such as the port of Berbera and customs collection along the corridor. Promising long-term control over the port to senior business and political figures was also a way to cement the demobilisation and wider security-strengthening efforts (Musa and Horst 2019).

Egal thus used the Berbera corridor as an 'object of negotiation' in Somaliland's state formation, linking investment with security (Hagmann and Péclard 2010: 552). The corridor – and the associated processes of investment, revenue-raising and political manoeuvring – can therefore be understood as a source of friction (Tsing 2011), centred on contestation and alliance-making among competing sub-clans, powerful businessmen, politicians and contractors, all suggesting a particular politics of investment linked to the corridors.

Inclusions and exclusions from the corridor development

The DP World Berbera port development is Somaliland's largest investment since it declared independence from Somalia in May 1991. Owing to Somaliland's political status as a self-declared state, and recognised internationally only as an autonomous region, it did not previously attract substantial foreign direct investment. The new investment changes the game substantially. Not surprisingly, it has brought many past tensions and conflicts to the surface and created new forms of inclusion and exclusion, as competition to capture the benefits of the investment is heightened.

Stepputat and Hagmann (2019: 806) explain that the development of the Berbera corridor has produced a 'politics of circulation' at the local and regional levels, as dynamics of exclusion and inclusion arise from 'attempts to upgrade and rescale' the corridor. This section assesses these dynamics, contrasting state and investor narratives, which claim that the corridor will lead to economic transformation, with varying local perspectives and concerns, which present a more mixed picture.

State and investor proponents of the Berbera corridor development have emphasised the positive economic benefits and transformative potential of the corridor, pointing to similar developments elsewhere in the Horn of Africa, such as the Lamu Port–South Sudan–Ethiopia Transport (LAPSSET) corridor in Kenya (see Chome, Chapter 2 this book; Enns 2018; Laher 2011). Proponents have stressed that the corridor will create jobs in shipping and containerisation. At a ceremony in February 2019 to lay the foundation stone for the Berbera corridor development, Somaliland President Muse Bihi, from the Habar Awal sub-clan, stated that the Berbera corridor development would contribute to economic growth and create jobs for the youth:

We are here to witness the laying down the foundation stone for the Berbera–Wajale road, known as the Berbera corridor. This is 250 km road that will connect Somaliland to Ethiopia, a country with a growing economy and a population of over 100 million. Ethiopia needs access to the sea; we need compete with neighbouring countries to serve for Ethiopia and its growing economy ... The Berbera corridor development is part of other economic infrastructure development projects and will play a role in the regional economic integration ... this road development will strengthen and promote the strategic Berbera port. Berbera corridor development will reduce youth unemployment, as a result of economic growth and, with increase in trade volume, youth unemployment will reduce.[1]

Beyond the corridor's economic promise, Somaliland government officials and their political allies have appealed to nationalism and aspirations for sovereignty to mobilise support for the corridor, which they see as a way of furthering the region's political recognition on the international stage. Although there is wide public support for the corridor development, many question the official narrative that its economic benefits will be widely shared. Local critics from different backgrounds are suspicious of the development's impacts, as well as of government and investor intentions. Government shared only a summary of the agreement with the parliament and as of today the detailed agreement remains unknown.

The secrecy of the deal reached between DP World and the Somaliland government has fuelled suspicions, as well as competition between clan groups. Berbera is mainly inhabited by the Issa Muse, a sub-clan of the Habar Awal, while other local clans are Habar Yonis, a sub-clan of Garhajis and Habar Jelo. Clan dynamics around Berbera have become more intense since 1991 when the Issa Muse strengthened their control.

The port is a major source of employment for Berbera residents, with 80 per cent relying in part on income generated from work associated with port operations (Interview, Berbera port authorities, Berbera, July 2016). Before investment was first mooted, most of the port labourers were from the Issa Muse sub-clan, while management jobs for locals were exclusively captured by the Issa Muse (Interviews with local residents, Berbera, 16–19 July 2016). The Issa Muse clan has resisted the proposed transfer of the port to DP World (Hangoolnews 2016), fearing a diminishing influence over the port's management. Meanwhile, members of other clans in Berbera, who have felt excluded from work opportunities in the port, have backed the investment, seeing it as a way to promote equal opportunities in finding work. Young people pin their hopes on DP World recruitment practices, which they expect will be merit-based and so diminish the importance of clan identity and patronage in allocating coveted jobs (Musa and Horst 2019: 46)

---

[1] President Muse's speech at the Berbera corridor development ceremony, from www.youtube.com/watch?v=1lIJAByGrPs, accessed 6 April 2019.

Competition and tensions around the Berbera corridor development are rooted in the territorialised nature of Somali clan identity. As something inherently spatialised, investments in the port and other corridor infrastructure are contested along lines of clan membership (Interview with development practitioner, Hargeisa, 15 February 2016). Clan identity, as the basis for configuring certain stakeholders in economic development projects and opportunities such as contracts and tenders, has been a constant in political struggle in post-war Somaliland. As a common saying in Somaliland goes: 'He who sits close to the cooking pot gets a good bone' ('*Dheri ninkii u dhow baa lafaha kala baxa*'). Some clans that inhabit areas removed from the corridor infrastructure fear that they will be excluded from the investment benefits.

Seen from this perspective, the corridor development will result in new patterns of accumulation that create longer-lasting social, economic and political inequalities. Fears of exclusion, and attempts to be included in the benefits generated by Berbera's development, are reminiscent of corridor developments elsewhere in sub-Saharan Africa, including in Lamu and Isiolo as detailed in this book (see also Enns 2018; Smalley 2017; Laher 2011). Actors in peripheral areas may relocate to gain access to benefits that arise from corridor development, while those near the corridor attempt to consolidate their hold. Corridors are not simply large investments; rather, they result in profound social and political reconfigurations at regional, national and local levels. At the national level, they represent an exercise of power, as national-level politicians seek alliances with sub-national figures to exercise control over both territory and populations.

These dynamics of contestation are evident in the Berbera port development. Issa Muse elders have sought not only to guard their privileged access to work and other opportunities, but also their political influence and territorial control. This contrasts with the leadership of other clans in Berbera, who have given enthusiastic backing to the port as a way of levelling the playing field and yielding new political influence and identity-based claims.

A wider 'politics of circulation'

Beyond the sharp territorial politics in and around the port, the 'politics of circulation' play out at a wider scale in the region. A senior Somaliland politician voiced a common refrain that the Berbera corridor development is unlikely to benefit pastoralists in the Hawd area (Interview with former minister, Hargeisa, 13 August 2018). Hawd is an extensive semi-arid area in the south-west of Somaliland and south-east of Ethiopia, stretching to the Ethiopia–Kenya border, and a key area supplying the regional livestock trade. Hawd has remained the centre of Somali's rural economy over the years, as the Hawd–Hargeisa/Burao–Berbera–Arabia corridor is historic and gives the rural economy access to the markets of Arabia (Ahmed 1999).

Instead of the Berbera corridor development, some politicians and development practitioners from the Garhajis clan advocate for a southern corridor that would connect the pastoral areas in Hawd to both the Berbera and the LAPSSET corridors. Proponents believe that this will result in 'spatial inclusion', with the potential to transform the economic structure of the pastoral areas (Interview with former minister, Hargeisa, 13 August 2018).

In 2012, the Edagale, a Garhajis sub-clan dominant in the livestock trade corridor, built local committees to mobilise resources for the development of Wadada Cad, a historic and 'indigenous' road network that connected the Berbera export–import economy to Hawd and south-central Somalia before the development of the current contemporary road networks. In this ambitious plan, the local committee intend to develop 80 km of tarmac road that would connect southern Hargeisa to the Ethiopia border via pastoral rural areas dominated by the clan. Speaking at a ceremony held in southern Hargeisa to lay the foundation stone for the road construction, the former minister of planning, who was from the local clan, said that 'road construction benefits the local community, communities in the vicinity of the road and the whole region and this road is key for the livestock trade, which is the backbone of Somaliland economy'.[2]

The Edagale sub-clan is not the only group with an ambitious plan to develop road networks in their localities; Sa'ad Muse and Gudabursi clans also had similar plans to develop road networks that would connect both north-western Hargeisa and Borama cities to Djibouti. Several explanations can be provided for these ambitious clan efforts. First, in the absence of state projects to develop key economic infrastructure, clans have taken on the responsibility of developing their own economic corridors to improve their economic status by attracting a flow of goods and people to their corridors. Second, local clans are announcing the strategic and economic relevance of their corridor, so that in the future the national government or international investors can step in. Third, these clan corridor development initiatives have a political dimension, as major clans are negotiating for political leverage through increased economic development in their respective localities.

In Somaliland, livestock production is concentrated in the Hawd plateau and most livestock exported through Berbera originates from the peripheral Hawd rangelands. Currently, livestock destined for Somaliland terminal markets, for export through Berbera, are trucked hundreds of kilometres along undeveloped clan corridors (Umar and Baulch 2007). Critics of the Berbera corridor development point to the economic

---

[2] Former Minister of Planning speaking at a fundraising event for the development of Wadada Cad road in 2012; see documentary on Wadada Cad road at www.youtube.com/watch?v=SzBryEkjRoM, accessed 6 April 2019.

potential of pastoralism, which already generates considerable national wealth for Somaliland through the export economy, and suggest that development of a southern corridor would have a more transformative impact than the Berbera corridor.

The direct impacts of the Berbera corridor development on Somaliland's predominantly pastoral and agro-pastoral economies are unknown. Somaliland consists of ten ecological zones, eight of which are arid and semi-arid where pastoralism is the main source of livelihood and the economic backbone. Mixed farming and herding systems are prevalent in the north-western plateau, consisting of Gabiley and Morodijeh, dominated by the Habar Awal clan. These areas are nearer to the proposed routing of the corridor and thus are positioned to benefit more than more peripheral pastoral areas. Some proponents of the Berbera corridor development, including some from the Garhajis, stated that, besides the economic benefits that come with close proximity to the physical infrastructure itself, which will concentrate along the corridor, the development will spur the growth of institutions and services that will be of benefit to society in Somaliland more widely (Kunaka and Carruthers 2014).

Wider benefits that could arise from Berbera corridor development include formalisation of the international livestock trade. Currently, livestock are traded informally across the Somaliland–Ethiopia border, which bisects the pastoral rangelands in Hawd and surrounding areas, owing to the absence of functioning customs, banking and border arrangements between the two countries. Like the regional cross-border trade, the international livestock trade between Somaliland and the Arabian Peninsula countries has been informal (Costagli et al. 2017: 17). The international informal livestock trade may benefit from the agreements between the states that have stakes in the Berbera corridor development.

In April 2019, Somaliland and the UAE agreed to establish a 'joint livestock export bureau' that will regulate animal health to enable Somaliland to access the UAE livestock markets (*East Africa Business Week* 2019a). However, the formalisation of the livestock trade will also change patterns of accumulation by accruing revenue to formal institutions and major livestock exporters, while other players in the wider livestock economy will remain on the periphery for the benefits that will come with livestock trade formalisation.

There are different perspectives on patterns of differentiation that result from the corridor development. Some interviewees were of the opinion that a concentration of benefits, entailing the exclusion of many, was inevitable since the siting of the corridor infrastructure is mostly in areas dominated by the Habar Awal. A development practitioner commented:

> From Berbera town to Togwajale, the Berbera corridor passes through eighteen towns and villages that are dominated by the Habar Awal.

This huge foreign investment will go into the territories of this one sub-clan. The increase in economic activities will transform these villages into larger economic centres and this will change the power and economic balance between the clans. (Interview with development practitioner/academic, Hargeisa, February 2019)

It is not only proponents of new corridors from the 'central' clans that are concerned about power and economic imbalances. Politicians and traditional elders from the *'beelaha darafyada'* (peripheral non-Isaaq clans) also questioned why historic corridors connecting to the coastal towns of Zeila and Lughaya, inhabited by the Gudabursi and Esse, on the Gulf of Aden in Somaliland's far west, had no planned investments. In their view, the Berbera corridor development was irreparably politicised and being pursued by Somaliland government elites from the Isaaq clan in order to consolidate their economic and political power.

Geopolitical contexts

Clan rivalries in anticipation of the port's benefits sit alongside wider geopolitical tensions in the Horn of Africa and Arabian Peninsula. The spatial definition of the corridor has been determined not by Somaliland alone, but also through regional and international relations, as mentioned previously. In low-income countries, the spatial definition of corridors reflects the interests of the proponents of the corridor – typically global capital and large domestic political and economic interests (Kunaka and Carruthers 2014: 14).

Despite its strategic location, Somaliland's political status and relatively weak institutions were major obstacles to the export sector and investment. Since 1991, there has been no formalised economic co-operation between Somaliland and its key trading partners, including Ethiopia and countries in the Arabian Peninsula. The absence of official cooperation hampered Somaliland's participation in international trade and restricted its access to key regional and international markets. This is likely to change with the large-scale investment in Berbera's port and related corridor infrastructure, marking Somaliland's emergence as a key economic partner. According to Somaliland's Minister of Transport and Road Development, upon completion of the Berbera corridor development, planned for 2022, the volume of trade between Somaliland and Ethiopia will increase by 30 per cent (*East Africa Business Week* 2019b).

Ethiopia is the fastest growing economy in the Horn of Africa, averaging growth of 10.3 per cent per year between 2006 and 2017, according to the World Bank (2019). Since Ethiopia's war with Eritrea between 1998 and 2000, Ethiopia has relied on Djibouti port for 95 per cent of its international trade (Norton 2018). Ethiopia's Growth and Transformation Plan II identified Berbera as a strategic corridor for trade and a way of reducing its dependence on Djibouti. However, rapid change is now afoot following the historic peace deal signed between Ethiopia and Eritrea in late 2018. To fuel further economic expansion, Ethiopia is negotiating access to Eritrea's Assab and Massawa ports. This development, alongside the opening of the new Addis–Djibouti railway, and other infrastructural upgrades to this primary supply corridor, does not diminish the importance of the Berbera corridor, however. Rather, Ethiopian planners continue to look at the Berbera corridor as significant for eastern Ethiopia and its booming livestock economy.

All three countries with stakes in the Berbera port development share an interest in the Berbera corridor becoming a trans-shipment route. Somaliland authorities are interested in competing with neighbouring Djibouti ports to serve Ethiopia's growing economy. Ethiopia has over-lapping interests, including reducing its overdependence on Djibouti port, while aiming to emerge as a regional power, both militarily and economically (Cannon and Rossiter 2017). Through DP World and its own investments, the UAE also has political and economic interests in the Berbera port and corridor, part of a wider regional strategy (ibid.; Larsen and Stepputat 2019). The geopolitical interests of the countries involved in the Berbera corridor development are a cause of suspicion for those sceptical about the corridor development.

Conclusion

The Berbera corridor development demonstrates the political and economic realities that surround large investment projects in the region. State and investor narratives of corridor development run up against more complex political economy realities and risk upsetting power dynamics in corridor development. The politics of circulation play out as the background to the political economy of investment projects, producing new patterns of accumulation alongside processes of inclusion and exclusion (Stepputat and Hagmann 2019).

In Somaliland, proponents of different corridor developments under-stand that infrastructural developments offer the potential to increase the volume of the flow of goods and people and create new spatial economics and politics, with implications for economic and political imbalances in the longer term. This explains the inherent social and political friction that surrounds corridor development projects. As well as local concerns about the imbalances that are likely to result from corridor developments, regional and neighbouring states could also harbour similar concerns and fears. The inherent concerns about exclusion and inclusion underlie informal narratives that run up against the formal narratives that proponents of corridor development try to advance.

In order to achieve the economic and political stability that corridor development promises, it is important to address historic grievances, concerns and conflicts that emanate from the development. Investors also need to be aware of the complex local realities that disturb and challenge official narratives, and the tensions that can develop, which may cause conflict and insecurity in the longer term.

10

State-building, Market Integration & Local Responses in South Omo, Ethiopia

FANA GEBRESENBET[1]

Conflict, violence and other forms of struggle are often associated with the extension of centralised state power at the pastoral margins. The South Omo region of southern Ethiopia is one such place, where large-scale investment in hydropower and commercial agriculture has been part of a broader push by the state to transform pastoral environments and livelihoods. Large-scale state investments have entailed the increased presence of state security, if not the use of outright force against local populations. Pastoralists and agro-pastoralists have been displaced and pushed into alternative livelihoods that are more 'legible' to state power. Yet violence and resistance is not the end of the story of state-building in Ethiopia's southern pastoral margins. Closer inspection reveals a more mixed picture of transformation happening at different speeds, with varying degrees of support by local populations, and diverse outcomes for livelihoods, food security and state–society relations.

This chapter reviews the diverging pathways of expanding and deepening state power in two parts of South Omo: Benna-Tsemay and Salamago districts (see Map 10.1). Although they are geographically close, processes of state-building and responses by local populations are distinct. The state has arrived with a bang in Salamago through the establishment of a large estate by the Ethiopian Sugar Corporation, occasioning resistance by local Bodi herders. By contrast, the state's presence has extended gradually in Benna-Tsemay through the deepening of political administration, road-building and improving transport links to larger towns and markets in the region. These diverging pathways are associated with very different livelihood prospects and 'security' as experienced by the region's pastoral and agro-pastoral inhabitants.

The chapter draws from long-term fieldwork stretching back to 2012. The most recent data, collected in 2018, included participatory group exercises, interviews with district- and zone-level government officials and other community leaders and livestock traders, and systematic observations.

[1] The fieldwork for this chapter was made possible by funding from the Agricultural Policy Research in Africa programme based at the Institute of Development Studies. I acknowledge the assistance of Jeremy Lind, Ian Scoones and Andy Catley at different stages of the research.

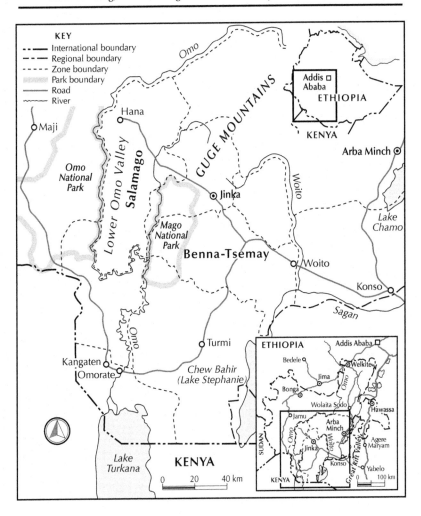

Map 10.1 Ethiopia, showing location of the South Omo valley

Background to South Omo

Situated in Ethiopia's far south-western margins, South Omo takes its name from the Omo River that bisects the region from north to south as it flows towards Lake Turkana across the border in Kenya. Much of the region lies to the east of the river; Nyangatom district makes up the area west of the river up to the border with South Sudan. The Woito River cuts across the region's eastern flank as it flows southwards into Chew Bahir, a large swampland and basin straddling the Ethiopia–Kenya border. The Bodi, Mursi, Dime (a small agrarian group) and Kwegu (a fishing group) inhabit Salamago district, whose western border is defined by the Omo River. Benna-Tsemay district on the eastern side of South Omo is named for the area's Benna and Tsemay agro-pastoralist inhabitants. The Omo and Woito rivers are the backbone of livelihoods in the region. Customarily, flood retreat agriculture along these rivers was crucial for agro-pastoralist diets. The rivers also gave life to riparian resources that were critical drought reserves for the region's large livestock population.

Successive regimes have regarded the diverse ethnic groups inhabiting South Omo as 'backward' and in need of modernisation and pacification. These outlooks persist. In recent years, tour companies have marketed the region's cultural richness and heritage as a type of primitive identity belonging to remote peoples. The views of government officials were that agro-pastoralism, the backbone of the region's economy and livelihoods, was irrational and an unproductive use of resources. Up to the 1980s, the state was mostly absent from the region, its presence restricted to a few civil servants. Postings to the region during imperial times (up to 1974) were taken as a form of punishment. Officials rarely ventured outside of towns, fearful of the area's pastoral and agro-pastoral inhabitants. State development efforts barely registered and were mostly limited to managing pastoral conflicts, a state of affairs that did not change until after the 1974 revolution (Markakis 2011). This legacy of underdevelopment is apparent even now. While some parts of the region have become more closely incorporated into national development and the wider economy of southern Ethiopia, large parts of South Omo remain far from administration and markets. The following sections describe the different experiences of and responses to state integration and large investment in Benna-Tsemay and Salamago.

Gradual incorporation of the Tsemay

Tsemay's earliest direct contacts with the state were in the late 1960s when Ethiopia was ruled by Haile Selassie. Civil servants stationed in the area, most coming from Ethiopia's highlands, sought to 'civilise' the Tsemay by instructing them in ox plough farming as well as in modern dress (Interview with trader from central part of Ethiopia, Woito town,

28 July 2018). It was around this time that road construction began, with residents coerced into volunteering their labour for the effort. A Tsemay informant recalls: 'Haile Selassie flogged us if we did not take part in the construction' (Interview with a past Tsemay *Kebele* administrator,[2] Duma village, 30 July 2018). The road was constructed not to directly 'secure' or extract wealth from the Tsemay but instead to reach areas further south in Hamar and in Teltele, an area inhabited by the Borana across the Woito River (ibid.). In the years after a military junta, the Derg, seized power from Haile Selassie in 1974, the state renewed its road-building efforts in the region. A gravel road was constructed to connect Arba Minch (a large town in the nearby highlands) with Konso, Woito town and Jinka in South Omo. Transport services to the region grew slowly at first when the road was finished in the mid-1980s, easing access to Tsemay and neighbouring areas. Investment soon followed. A North Korean-owned farm was established further south in Omorate (in what is now Dassanech district), ensuring a steady flow of officials and traders.

By the time an ethnically based opposition movement allied under the Ethiopian Peoples' Revolutionary Democratic Front (EPRDF) overthrew the Derg in 1991, an Ethiopian investor established a 5,490 ha commercial farm. An estimated 2,000 labourers, mainly from Wolaita and Konso in the southern highlands, were brought in to work the farm (Yacob and Basechler 2002; Melesse 1995); the promised services and other support for displaced Tsemay people failed to materialise, breeding resentment (Interviews with traders from central part of Ethiopia, Woito town, 28 July 2018; interview with a past Tsemay *Kebele* administrator, Duma village, 30 July 2018). The loss of grazing land and the destruction of beehives added to Tsemay discontent (Interview with highlander trader 2, 28 July 2018). Tensions spilled over in 1994, culminating in a heavy-handed government response that resulted in many deaths, including those of Tsemay and migrant labourers (Interview with a past Tsemay *Kebele* administrator, Duma village, 30 July 2018; focus group discussion with elders, Duma village, 29 July 2018).

In the decades since, relations between the Tsemay and migrant populations, notably the Wolaita, have improved markedly through various exchange relations, including intermarriage. In the words of a Tsemay elder, the Wolaita and Tsemay are now 'mixing ... like blood and milk' (Focus group discussion participant, elder, Duma village, 29 July 2018). The outlooks of elders towards state-building efforts have mellowed over time as the benefits of the road-building, improved access to markets and opportunities to trade have grown. One compared a road to a 'shed in your homestead that saves you from direct sun' (Interview with a past Tsemay *Kebele* administrator, Duma village, 30 July 2018). Others explained that the investments and roads brought government nearer

---

[2] *Kebele* is the lowest administrative level in Ethiopia, often corresponding to a small set of villages (about four or five).

through the improved delivery of services, particularly education, which
had a dampening effect on tensions with neighbouring Konso and Borana
(Focus group discussion with elders, Duma village, 29 July 2018). Tsemay
elders view the state's presence as also providing protection against
attacks by Konso and Borana, who are more populous and better armed
than the Tsemay. As views of the state have softened and even warmed,
attitudes to investment have also evolved. The acquisition of 3,500 ha
of land by the government in 2009 for two commercial farms, Nassa and
Sagla, happened peacefully. Displaced Tsemay were relocated to Gisma
village between 2011 and 2014. Promised services never materialised
(Various interviews in Woito town and Gisma village, July 2018; see also
Asebe Regassa et al. 2018). Regional drought and the overutilisation of
water by commercial farms in the area led to the drying up of the Woito
River in 2016, preventing the river from flowing to Gisma village, and
pushing the government to distribute food aid and fodder. Still, while the
conditions generated unease, there was no open violent protest against
the state or commercial farms, with area residents instead putting their
complaints to the zonal government (Interview with head of Zone Water
Bureau, Jinka, July 2016).

State-building and rupture in Salamago

The Bodi people inhabit a fertile but remote rangeland that is bordered
to the south and west by the Omo River. Until recently, Hana, the small
town that serves as the administrative centre for Salamago district, was
the last point for anyone travelling from the highlands that lie to the
north and east of the area. The state's presence was minimal, and mainly
limited to preventing Bodi raids on the Dime, an agrarian society that
inhabits the mid-altitude areas of the eastern side of Salamago. The
Bodi acquired firearms from the *Neftegna*[3] who settled in neighbouring
highlands, including Dime territories. The Bodi first encountered
the 'forces of modernity' in the late 1960s when William Muldrow,
a missionary, established an airstrip in the area to serve a mission
he established in the nearby highlands.[4] Since the late 1890s and up
until the latter years of imperial rule, Bodi interaction with the state
was short-circuited by the devolution of tax collection to the *komorut*,
'the holder of a hereditary office whose role is to insure the well-
being and prosperity of the land' (Buffavand 2017: 21). Although this
gave the *komorut* more power, their efforts to collect tax were mostly
unsuccessful. Besides evading the payment of taxes, the Bodi openly
resisted the *komorut*, even killing some occupants of the office as a way
of attacking the state (ibid.: 209). The state's presence began to deepen

[3] Literal translation is 'one who carries gun', but the term is used in reference to settlers from
northern parts of the country representing the state.
[4] See Buffavand 2017 for a detailed ethnographic account of the Bodi.

slowly during the period of the Derg, when the government distributed clothes and famine relief (Interview with key informant, Hana town, 6 August 2018). Police were stationed in Hana from the early 1970s to curb Bodi–Mursi conflict (Buffavand 2017). Besides security, the other state interest in the area was conservation around the Omo and Mago National Parks (Turton 2011). From the perspective of conservationists and the state that hoped to benefit from increased tourism, the very isolation of the area was desirable. This meant there was little push for infrastructure development or administrative integration.

The early 2000s saw quickening change and intensifying state-building efforts. Similar to the Tsemay experience decades before, the state's growing presence was initially felt through road-building efforts when the road connecting Hana to Jinka, a larger town, was upgraded to facilitate the resettlement of food-insecure households. In 2004, following an initial consultation with the Bodi, 826 Konso households were resettled in mid-altitude areas of the district, near to the contested boundary between the Dime and the Bodi (Ayke 2005). Other Konso soon arrived, encouraged by the success of the original settlers. The regional government then expanded the resettlement programme, supporting a further 1,857 households to settle in the area in 2012. However, owing to Bodi resistance, the government resettled the new arrivals deeper in Dime territory.

The resettlement efforts widened in spite of conflict that had opened up in preceding years between the Bodi and the Konso. At the root of the conflict was the Bodi's understanding that the Konso were being relocated on a temporary basis, estimated to be a five-year period, until they became food secure. However, it quickly became evident that the relocation was permanent, as more Konso arrived on the back of the initial resettled households. Some Bodi felt the alienation of more land and the growing influx of migrants from the highlands as an existential threat. They objected to the intensive land utilisation of the Konso settlers, the cutting of trees causing particular consternation. By 2011, the Konso armed themselves with newly found wealth from the sale of sesame. The power balance shifted to the Konso, whom the regional government favoured.

In 2011, in a speech in Jinka to celebrate National Pastoralists Day, the then Prime Minister Meles Zenawi announced government plans to introduce industrial sugar-cane production in South Omo, including in Salamago. Meles Zenawi argued the ambitious plans would see South Omo become 'an example of rapid development' (Meles Zenawi 2011). The development of industrial sugar-cane production in the region was made possible by completion of the upstream Gibe III hydroelectric dam, which regulates the river's annual flow to permit downstream irrigation in the Omo Valley. The plans were an extension of the developmental state approach and high modernist vision pursued under the EPRDF (Mosley and Watson 2016). The proposed sugar-cane estates and factories in South

Omo were part of a broader push by the state to lease as much as 3 million hectares of land, mostly in the pastoral lowlands, to an array of investors (MoFED 2010), leading to a geographically differentiated development policy of setting aside pastoral areas for large-scale plantation agriculture (Makki 2014). In total, the estates in South Omo were to cover 175,000 ha, including 50,000 ha in Salamago, 25,000 ha in Bench Maji Zone and 100,000 ha across the Omo River in Nyangatom district. Moreover, a massive labour influx was expected to work the plantations and sugar mills, with one estimate that up to 400,000 jobs would be created (Kamski 2016; Tewolde Woldemariam and Fana Gebresenbet 2014).

The alienation of land and the influx of labourers from central parts of the country created a sense of becoming a minority on one's own territory and entrenched the Bodi feeling of being existentially threatened. Although advanced in the name of enabling service provision, the state-orchestrated sedentarisation of agro-pastoralist Bodi further signalled the state's ambition of limiting Bodi mobility and changing their economy and culture. This, coupled with repeated accidents involving vehicles hitting Bodi individuals and livestock, triggered conflict in the environs of the sugar plantation and Hana town. By 2016, Hana town was under curfew.

The implementation of this modernist vision was a textbook example of 'breaking every rule in the book', and what followed is an example of 'how not to do development' (Turton forthcoming). The Ethiopian government could not convince the Bodi to agree to the land expropriations for the sugar-cane plantation, nor to the accompanying sedentarisation scheme, officially dubbed 'voluntary villagisation'. Thus, these 'development' interventions co-occurred with security measures, including campaigns organised by the sub-national political administration to bring men suspected of ambushes to prison, to instil fear and obedience and to break resistance.

In this context, the development has advanced more slowly than planned. By February 2016, 10,000 ha of land were planted and an additional 13,000 ha cleared in Salamago (Kamski 2016). Only two of the five factories originally envisioned were operational at a limited capacity by 2020. Besides Bodi resistance, the project has faced other hurdles, including inimical relations with the existing sugar bureaucracy and the swindling of the funds by powerful officials in the then military-run Metals and Engineering Corporation. Revised plans have seen the area for plantations reduced to less than 100,000 ha, and four factories are anticipated instead of five (Kamski 2016).

Responses to state-building and market integration

Although both located within South Omo region, the experience of state-building has been very different for the Tsemay and Bodi. The key

Table 10.1 Comparison of the 'state experience' of the Bodi and the Tsemay

	Tsemay	Salamago
Time and nature of earliest state contact	1960s, consistent direct contact, no extraction interest	1960s, intermittent contact, through missionaries and *Komorut*
State contact, 1970s–2000s	Continuation, commercial farming, sedentarisation	Intermittent, Konso settlement
State projects, 2010 onwards	Continuation, commercial farming, sedentarisation	Sudden intensive interaction, large-scale sugar-cane plantation and factory, plan to sedentarise the entire Bodi
Perception of 'state experience'	Continuity, evolutionary	Rupture

differences, summarised in Table 10.1, concern both the speed at which state interventions unfolded, as well as the existence (or not) of a state-valued resource. The first distinction is the pace of state-building. State interventions have evolved over time in Benna-Tsemay, starting with road-building in the 1970s and 1980s, accompanied by the increased presence of political administration, and grew over time to incorporate irrigation schemes and attempts to promote sedentarisation. State-building was both evolutionary and sedimentary; earlier interventions became embedded in the landscape and socio-economic life over two decades before the state's focus widened to include taking land for commercial agriculture schemes in the area. This incremental deepening of the state's power minimised resistance as the Tsemay adapted to creeping state presence, which at least some Tsemay came to regard as a bulwark against more powerful Konso and Borana neighbours.

By contrast, many Bodi have felt state-building as a rupture in both their lives and livelihoods. After decades of neglect and minimal contact with the state's political administration and security forces, beginning in the early 2000s the state intervened on multiple fronts. Resettlement of Konso in 2004 happened in a contested boundary area between the Bodi and neighbouring Dime, thereby generating tensions at the start of a period in which many successive developments were about to unfold. As more Konso moved into the area and expanded the area under their cultivation – in mid-altitude areas that were key resources for pastoral Bodi, state plans to develop industrial sugar estates and factories announced in 2011 were taken by the Bodi as a direct threat to their way of life. The plans were announced at a time when the conflict between the Bodi and Konso peaked: the Bodi fighting against what they perceived as Konso expansions, and Konso fighting to firm up the area where they were resettled by the state.

The second major difference between Tsemay and Bodi experiences is the existence of a state-valued resource. In Tsemay, state-building involved investments in infrastructure along with slowly deepening political administration to open up the area. The state did not seek to extract resources or acquire land, at least not at first. The Tsemay, although treated as backward, were not seen as a threat, and therefore while the state leaned on coercion and disciplinary practice at times to enlist labour for road-building, and in sedentarisation efforts, it did not resort to the use of violence. In Bodi, the existence of state-valued land for resettlement and industrial farming has been the basis of struggle. The acquisition of large land areas, along with investments in irrigation infrastructure and roads, happening in tandem with resettlement of Konso from the southern highlands, has led to resistance as well as the increased presence of state security and use of force to protect the state's investment.

These diverging state-building trajectories are associated with very different local responses. The Tsemay, being nearer to the densely populated southern highlands, knit more closely into wider livestock marketing and trade. Since the 1970s, livestock traders from the southern highlands would buy animals from the Tsemay and other groups in South Omo and contract the Tsemay to rear the animals before they were trekked to large markets further afield. In recent years, Tsemay traders have emerged to wrestle some of the business away from outside traders. Each week, a Tsemay trader in Woito town supplies a truckload of goats to exporters based in Modjo.[5] The trader works with other Tsemay buyers who purchase animals from livestock-keepers across Benna-Tsemay and beyond in Arbore and Hamar. At first, the buyers borrowed money from the Tsemay trader, but now they have turned enough profit to purchase livestock with their own money, thereby increasing their own returns. Local buyers invest their profits in other schemes to make money, notably mills and property in Woito town.[6] Young men also seize on an increasing local demand for goats fuelled by the growth of towns and need for cash to meet expenses for food, fuel and rent.

Tsemay social and economic life is increasingly monetised. Although most households still rely on their own production, women now almost exclusively go to grain mills owned and operated by rich households.[7] By

---

[5] About 180 goats, worth (after deducting vehicle rental and fuel expenses) 150,000 birr (c. US$5,175 at the exchange rate of March 2019 applied to all conversions in this chapter).

[6] These traders purchase most of the parcels at auctions for urban land (informant, Woito Municipality).

[7] Paying 45 birr for 50kg of maize, for example (focus group discussion with women). Each mill costs about 100,000 birr (US$3,500).

2018, there were twelve mills in Duma village alone, with the first one opening less than a decade ago. Moreover, there is increasing utilisation of donkey-powered carts to transport grain to and from mills and to fetch water.[8] The use of motorbikes has also proliferated in Woito town both for private use and to operate as taxis. As the use of motorbikes has spread, fuel kiosks have opened to meet the increased demand for fuel, first in Woito and now beyond, including Gisma (the resettlement village) and other sites where the state is encouraging sedentarisation. All of these changes, which point to the absorption of the area into wider markets, influence Tsemay socio-cultural norms. According to elders, since 2010 cash has been accepted as a form of bride-wealth payment.

The damaging consequences of large-scale investment and related state-building efforts in Salamago continue to reverberate through Bodi society. Livelihoods were compromised by the ending of the seasonal flooding of the Omo River (since 2015, after the completion of the Gibe Dam), which has meant diminishing opportunities for flood retreat cultivation, as well as the loss of resource access in mid-altitude areas where Konso were resettled. The combined pressure of insecurity, food shortages and resource alienation is pushing the Bodi to sell animals faster, and at prices lower than offered in Tsemay. Hunger is the primary reason for livestock sales, according to ranking exercises carried out with groups in July 2018, while raising funds to visit family members detained in Jinka ranks second. Since construction works began on the sugar estate in 2012, more than 300 young Bodi men have been imprisoned, a significant number considering the entire Bodi population is estimated to be around 10,000 (Interview with key informant, Hana town, 6 August 2018). While the crackdown aims to stamp out resistance to the development, it is also damaging the Bodi social fabric, specifically the culturally sanctioned birth cycle. Cultural expectations are that a married woman will give birth every two and half to three years, since children constitute a significant part of a household's wealth. The families of Bodi prisoners have had to sell cattle to earn cash to pay police bribes to arrange conjugal visits. Other costs to be covered include travel to Jinka with a male relative. Conjugal visits were suspended in 2016 after prisoners from other ethnic groups protested to be granted the same rights. Interviewees indicated that an average of one to two cattle were sold each year to finance travel and bribes to facilitate visits.

The government foresaw the influx of workers for the sugar plantations as a positive for livestock sales by creating market linkages in a remote area. Indeed, in spite of the project unfolding at a slower pace, business has boomed in Hana, with many new hotels, cafes and rental accommodation opening to cater for labourers and other plantation workers. In 2018, a branch of the Commercial Bank of Ethiopia opened in the town, the area's first. In addition to the new road connecting Hana with Jinka, a

---

[8] Such carts cost about 5,000 birr (US$175).

further road was completed to connect the town with Nyangatom, and roads within the town were being tarmacked. The Bodi are supplying cheap meat to the workforce in the area, as well as town residents and restaurant owners, but mostly because of distress and need for cash and not primarily because of new marketing opportunities. The mixture of factors outlined above show that the Bodi economy is suffering, as they have to continue selling animals to sustain their lives and social fabric. The only recognition they get is when they do not sell. Some local officials complain that the Bodi do not sell enough animals and that the Ethiopian Sugar Corporation and other contractors have to buy cattle from afar to meet the need for meat. Yet the limited number of buyers (mainly restaurant owners) have a comparative advantage in price negotiations. As such, the Bodi are being impoverished, while they continue providing the unrecognised subsidy to sugar industrialisation, by supplying meat at relatively cheaper prices to consumers brought to work in the sugar plantations.

A lasting consequence of these varying state-building experiences is shifts in how Tsemay and Bodi see their own relations with the state. Elder Tsemay men, recalling their earlier marginalisation, more readily accept that the Tsemay are subservient in the wider national political and economic picture. They accept the need for adopting modern ways in lifestyle, language and culture as a way of 'catching-up' and ridding themselves of their 'backward' customs. Whereas a longer and more benign state-building process contributed to the 'sedimentary' type of local elite development among the Tsemay, the Bodi still strongly contest for their economic, cultural and political autonomy. Bodi leaders reject 'underdevelopment' as their identity; however political administration in the region as well as large state capital sees the Bodi as resistant to change and modernity and a risk to plans to accumulate capital.

Conclusion

This chapter has uncovered the very different experiences and responses to state integration and large-scale investment at the margins – even within the same sub-national region. The development of local capital in Benna-Tsemay over decades of state-building has now positioned the Tsemay as benefactors of more sweeping transformations that are occurring. By comparison, among the Bodi, the lack of local capital aligned with the state, and the sudden expansion of state capital into the area by force, has inevitably led to resistance, conflict and the use of violence by the state to protect its capital. In Salamago, sugar industrialisation is also indirectly coercing the Bodi to increasingly sell livestock. This is leading to a collective impoverishment of the Bodi, while they are providing an inadvertent, invisible subsidy to sugar industrialisation through the continued sale of good quality meat at relatively cheap prices. Recent smaller-scale investment in Tsemay is experienced as an intensification of a longer evolutionary state-building process. Deepening state presence, far from being something that threatens society and livelihoods, is instead something more benign and even potentially favourable to local elites.

11

The Impacts of Delay | Exploring a Failed Large-scale Agro-investment in Tanzania

LINDA ENGSTRÖM

I look out through the open car window over the wide, flat grasslands of northern Tanzania, home to Barabaig pastoralists and smallholder farmers. We have stopped to make way for cattle crossing the dirt road, herded by a young Barabaig boy. As we continue north, we see the area with scattered sheds and houses where I have been doing my research. A *dala-dala* (public-service minibus) overtakes us. It is overloaded with people and goods from Bagamoyo town and Dar es Salaam, two hours' drive to the south.

We are driving through the investment project site, the area where 20,374 ha of land were selected for investment by a Swedish investor in 2006, through a Memorandum of Understanding (MoU) with the Tanzanian government. In 2013, the company was provided with its Right of Occupancy, a 99-year lease, to develop 7,700 ha of sugar cane and a processing plant. Promises were made to produce hundreds of thousands of tonnes of sugar, millions of litres of ethanol and electricity for the national grid, as well as providing the state with US$30 million in yearly tax revenues, creating 12,000–15,000 jobs and contributing at least US$10 million per year to the local communities. Resettlement was to take place in line with international best practice.

Yet, more than a decade after the MoU was signed, no sugar cane was planted. None of the residents had been resettled. Instead, people waited for many years, with increasing uncertainty about when and where to move, how to plan their agricultural production, and what the rate of compensation would be. The result of the delayed development was deteriorating livelihoods.

Since the food, fuel and financial crises of 2007–08, huge attention has been paid to the rush for land for large-scale agricultural investment in Africa. Yet many of these investments never got beyond the plans, and others are stalled or have failed to materialise (Hall et al. 2015b). Tanzania is no exception to this pattern of failure (Abdallah et al. 2014). In this chapter, I contribute to our understanding of why such failures happen, drawing on the case of a planned sugar-cane project in Bagamoyo district.

In particular, I explore how simplifications in project design interact with the complex implementation context to produce repeated delays and, ultimately, the project's failure to materialise. Such simplifications, as discursive practices, are used to render complex contexts of people and their environment legible for intervention (Scott 1998), rendering political contexts technical in order to achieve legitimacy (Li 2007) and, in turn, conveying a potent message on how to achieve modernity and progress.

The Bagamoyo sugar investment

The Bagamoyo project was situated within the Razaba Ranch (Ranchi ya Zanzibar Bagamoyo) in Bagamoyo district, north of Dar es Salaam in Pwani, Tanzania's Coast Region (Map 11.1). The project was initiated by the Swedish company SEKAB Ltd in 2006 and was later sold to Bagamoyo Eco Energy Ltd, although it has been run by the same management team throughout. Initially, the project was geared towards producing ethanol for the European Union market, but it later shifted focus towards producing sugar for the Tanzanian market. The sugar outgrower programme was anticipated to supply approximately 30 per cent of the company's total sugar production. It entailed organising smallholders living in villages adjacent to the ranch into companies, where each company would take loans to irrigate a plot of 100 ha of sugar cane (EE 2010: 9).

The land targeted for investment has been farmed and utilised for seasonal grazing by pastoralists for at least 1,500 years (Mwasumbi et al. 2007). The name Razaba Ranch stems from the period between 1974 and 1994 when the Revolutionary Government of Zanzibar bought the land from mainland Tanzania to be run as a cattle ranch. In 1994, the project was abandoned owing to tsetse fly infestation and attacks on the cattle by leopards (ibid.). Around 300 workers and their families were permitted to live on the land until the farm was repurposed for other activities (Chung 2017; Mwasumbi et al. 2007).

The approximately 1,400 people residing on the land today represent a wide range of ethnic groups and a mix of pastoralists, farmers and former ranch workers (Engström 2018; Chung 2017). Since the ranch closed, there has been an influx of pastoralists from Arusha and Manyara, encompassing traditional areas of the Barabaig pastoralists from where they were pushed out by a large wheat scheme in the late 1980s (Lane 1994). There has also been an increase in people from adjacent villages using the land for hunting, shifting cultivation and charcoal burning (ORGUT 2008). As is so often the case in post-colonial settings, there are competing claims over the land. While some farmers refer to customary rights or other clauses in the current land law to claim rights over land (Chung 2017), these claims have not been officially recognised. Rather, the land was handed to the company by the government as 'unused'

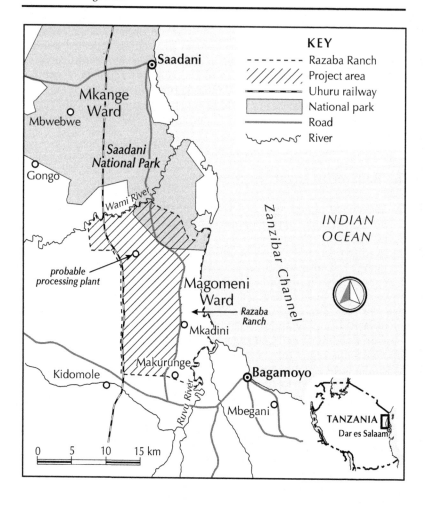

Map 11.1 Tanzania, showing location of Bagamoyo sugar-cane investment, Coast Region

general land under the management of the state.

The company's initial timeline was that about 3,000 ha of plantation would be developed in 2008, and the remaining plantation would be developed in 2009 and ready for ethanol production in 2010 (ORGUT 2008: 18). This assumed a finalised resettlement process by 2008, only two years after the MoU was signed. A six-year period was anticipated for developing the outgrower programme. However, the timeline of the project changed repeatedly and substantially.

Why did these delays occur? Despite the fact that the company's chief executive officer and the managing director had a background in ethanol production from northern Sweden, they had never invested in Africa. As the company discovered, starting up a complex greenfield sugar investment, building operations from the ground up, is a challenging task.

Yet the investment was supported by a range of powerful actors, including President Kikwete (2005–15) and the Minister of Lands at the time. Bagamoyo is the home district of Mr Kikwete, and he wanted to deliver development to his district before stepping down as president. The project also had strong support from the African Development Bank, which offered to put together a consortium of development banks to provide the funding necessary for the plant and plantation. Moreover, in February 2014 Sida (the Swedish International Development Cooperation Agency) decided to support the project with a guarantee of US$16.2 million from its development budget (Sida 2015: 5) in order to create job opportunities and contribute to increased incomes among poor people (Sida 2014: 3).

The analysis below builds on a discourse analysis of sixty-nine interviews: out of these, thirty-nine interviews were conducted with project proponents (mainly state officials at district and central government levels, Sida employees and company representatives) and the remaining thirty interviews were conducted with rural residents targeted by investment, living in and around the project site. Key policy documents and corporate documents were analysed, combined with observations during repeated visits to the project site between 2012 and 2017 (Engström 2018).

Privatisation in agriculture and development policy

While large-scale agricultural investments are not new in Tanzania, the context for such investments has changed. As a result of neoliberal policies, there is today a great focus on private investment and public–private partnerships.

Neoliberal policy has had a major influence on agriculture in Tanzania. For instance, under President Kikwete, the three key agriculture strategies were: Kilimo Kwanza (Agriculture First), the Southern Agricultural Growth Corridor of Tanzania (SAGCOT) and Big Results Now (BRN). Creating a conducive business environment to facilitate foreign investment was heavily promoted. Big Results Now had an ambition to develop twenty-five commercial farming deals on 350,000 ha by 2015 (BRN 2013: 15–17).

A focus on sugar aimed to fill a domestic demand gap and thus reduce import costs because, in 2010, Tanzania produced only around 60 per cent of the domestic non-industrial demand for sugar (Sulle and Smalley 2015: 118). The Bagamoyo project was seen as an important way to fulfil this aim, selected as a high potential farming deal within BRN and included as a partner of SAGCOT. An increasingly neoliberal agriculture policy in Tanzania dovetails with the privatisation trend in development assistance. This is the context in which the Bagamoyo project gained financial support from Sida in 2014. Encouraging private investment is promoted as a means to increase resources to accelerate the work towards inclusive development and poverty alleviation (Sida undated).

In this context, public–private partnerships have gained strong support, broadly defined as a 'cooperative institutional arrangement between public and private sector actors' (Hodge and Greve 2007: 545). Such partnerships can be seen as a kind of neoliberal 'roll-out', the active construction of modes of governance involving a neoliberalised state (Peck and Tickell 2002: 384). As an example of a public–private partnership for development, the Bagamoyo project was referred to as 'state of the art' by Sida (Interview with Sida officer, Stockholm, 12 December 2014) and an 'iconic project' by the Tanzanian government (BRN 2013: 23), with a vision to become a 'role model' for agro-energy production (EE 2010: 6).

The Bagamoyo sugar project thus enjoyed unprecedented political support in Tanzania. Yet, over a decade later, the gap between proposed and achieved outcomes was striking. What happened?

Framing development

Discourse analysis across multiple interviews revealed that the Bagamoyo project, and the associated overarching framing narrative about large-scale agricultural investment as a development strategy, built on a number of simplifications. Not least, these included simplified assumptions about people and their environment.

For instance, one critical simplification underpinning the narrative is the belief in a linear development path, drawing on Enlightenment ideas, Darwinian theories of 'progressive' evolution and development modernisation concepts (Nyamnjoh 2000). This belief envisions a set of stages, a predefined development ladder, on which every society will progress upwards, with the final stage being the 'modern' 'Western' society associated with industrialisation and urbanisation (Escobar 1993). For instance, one Sida official stated: 'It's hard to imagine Tanzania in 10 years remaining in a situation where every family lives on 0.5 acres [0.2ha]. Just like Sweden changed with land consolidation. It goes hand-in-hand with natural development. But of course it cannot be forced' (Interview with Sida official, Stockholm, 12 December 2014).

The strong emphasis in Tanzanian rural development policies on large-scale agriculture as an efficient and modern production system (SAGCOT 2011) stems from this simplified image. A company executive stated: 'If you want to create a heated debate, discuss the implications of what comes out of talking about that we should not develop or modernise and have large-scale agriculture' (Interview with company executive, Dar es Salaam, 16 March 2016).

Another important, and interlinked, simplification is the framing of the backward smallholder farmer, a kind of backward 'other' (Said 1978), using ancient agricultural methods and lagging behind. A company employee explained how they see farmers in the planned outgrower villages as currently living in a 'black hole' from where they 'cannot see straight', with a need to 'rise up': 'You can look up and you might see an object moving, and *we* know it's an airplane, but if you were just in that hole you wouldn't know it's an airplane, you would just see *pshht!* You know what I mean? 'Cause you can't fill in the gaps' (Interview with company employee, Dar es Salaam, 10 April 2014). Similar descriptions of the backward farmer were frequent in interviews with all project proponents, although particularly evident among company representatives (Engström and Hajdu 2018).

Simplifications in project planning

Beyond these broad simplifications in framing narratives about modern development and the backwardness of local recipients, there were also simplifications in the process of project planning. Simplified project plans promised efficient, large-scale sugar-cane production, thousands of jobs and poverty reduction in Bagamoyo, but they were undermined by unexpected events and were intersected by other processes, causing a cascade of second- and third-order impacts. In turn, these produced repeated delays and ultimately the failure of the investment to materialise.

The first simplification was the disregard of environmental complexity. Even though knowledge about soil properties was an important prerequisite, neither the company nor the state properly investigated soil properties in the early planning phase. Rather, it was investigated in detail for the first time many years after the MoU was signed, with surprising findings:

> Then when you start to do all of this soil investigation – it showed that, OK, the land is not all that good, they said you can't grow crops on all the types of land anywhere, so when they did the soil study you found that you had salinity and other problems, so – we have a mosaic of land that is good to use, a lot of land is not really good for farming

at all. (Interview with company managing director, Dar es Salaam, 10 April 2014)

In fact, assessments found that the soils in the area were poor, with high deficiencies in nitrogen, phosphorous and potassium (Sida Helpdesk 2012). This fact contributed to a drastic reduction of the area planned for sugar cane, from the 18,000 ha initially planned (ORGUT 2008: 17) to 7,700 ha (EE 2010: 8). This had one important downstream effect; since the funders required a minimum area of fertile land, the company was forced to search for additional land outside its estate, and approached adjacent villages.

However, in these adjacent villages, the company's request for land brought to the surface contesting land claims that escalated into a time-consuming dispute resolution process. Moreover, there were different opinions regarding who would compensate the villages for any potential land loss – the company or the state – and how much. While these conflicts were ongoing, the company did not have access to enough land to secure funding from the African Development Bank. Thus, the initial disregard for soil fertility caused a range of second- and third-order impacts, together drastically reducing the initially planned plantation size and delaying the company's operations.

Conflicting claims to land point towards the second key simplification in project design: the disregard for socio-political contestations and multilayered land governance. The simplified notion of vast tracts of unused or available land has been persistent since the colonial era (Baglioni and Gibbon 2013) and has frequently been found in the Tanzanian context (e.g. Bergius et al. 2018; Walwa 2017; Maganga et al. 2016; Coulson 2015). Nevertheless, one Swedish company executive had strong convictions about the availability of land: 'There is no lack of land! If you have travelled so much in this country now, you have been here so many times ... If you travel around by car everywhere and fly over the country, you can see that there is no lack of land!' (Interview with company executive director, Dar es Salaam, 16 March 2016).

In fact, there were many land conflicts in the area, and simplified assumptions about land governance and use do not hold up. One particularly influential conflict originated in north-eastern Razaba Ranch, where some residents claimed they were never part of the ranch and should therefore not be resettled. In the time gap between when residents on the ranch were officially informed about the project (in 2011) and the formal allocation of land to the company (in 2013), three elders from one of the sub-villages sued the company and the Tanzanian state for trespassing, thereby disrupting their historical claims to the land. In 2015, the Tanzanian High Court ruled in favour of the state and the company, stating that the land was general land without any formal rights ascribed to the sub-village residents (BEE 2017: 16). A court ruling on this conflict was one of the conditions set by Sida and the African Development Bank to provide funding, and so the case delayed the investment by a little over three years.

A third simplification entails the disregard of potential external events. The financial crisis of 2008, for example, led to the withdrawal of investment banks that had indicated their support for the project, and the company was forced to start looking for financial support elsewhere. It was at this stage that the African Development Bank offered to support the investment. However, there were two conditions. First, an external consultant should evaluate the resettlement process to ensure its compliance with international best practice in the form of the International Financial Cooperation Performance Standard on involuntary resettlement. This standard sets stricter demands than the national Tanzanian legislation, especially concerning compensation. In turn, this caused debate within the state apparatus, for example between district and central government, about the implications for the cost of resettlement elsewhere in Tanzania.

These debates delayed the resettlement process further. Linked to the same condition to ensure compliance with best practice, a consultancy firm entered the scene in September 2011. It was contracted to evaluate the existing resettlement action plan in what was intended to be a ten-day assignment. However, the consultant thought the government resettlement action plan needed to be complemented with a detailed socio-economic investigation of affected people. Moreover, the state and the company debated where to resettle these people. Because of this, the consultancy assignment was extended. Yet only half of the new resettlement action plan was complete when the contract was ended in 2015.

This is a clear example of how one external event – the financial crisis – caused multiple downstream effects, which all contributed to repeated delays in project implementation. It also shows how a range of factors interfered with the simplified technical solution of compliance with international sustainability criteria. With more delays, the company's resources ran out and it had to cancel the consultant's contract, which meant that resettlement planning was stalled. Ultimately, without a completed resettlement plan, the company would not be able to start constructing the plant or planting sugar cane on its estate. Thus, the initial timeline to finalise resettlement in 2008 was postponed, and by 2015 the process had stalled completely.

Delays are not innocent

Throughout the implementation of the project, various forms of simplification interacted with complex, more or less unpredictable, contextual factors to produce repeated delays. Such delays are, however, not innocent; rather, delays produce a range of sometimes detrimental impacts. Delays created space for messiness, contributing to more delay; for instance, where the time lag between informing people about resettlement and the company's formal access to land provided space for residents to sell land and initiate a court case.

Importantly, however, the company attempted to manage delay. In fact, it was with direct reference to delay that the company decided to apply for the loan from Standard Bank, for which Sida decided to provide a guarantee. The direct link to delay was expressed by one company executive: 'Because we are late – this government has been late taking a number of decisions – and we don't want to delay the project ... we took this bridge financing to be able to do early works, and by doing that we still should be able to start production in 2016' (Interview with company executive, Dar es Salaam, 10 April 2014).

The early works entailed, for instance, training provided by the consultancy firm administering the resettlement process, such as health screening or tailored courses in driving and construction, to facilitate a 'seamless transition of livelihoods' as required by the standards (Interview, Bagamoyo town, 4 July 2014).

The delays constituted an important reason for Sida's decision to halt the payments of the guarantee, since there were severe delays in fulfilling the loan conditions. Therefore, Sida withdrew funding and pulled out of the agreement in May 2015. Lack of funding meant that the resettlement consultant was fired, with a subsequent halt in training activities and a stalled resettlement process. Moreover, this all meant that Sida has a credit of US$6 million to collect from the company.

Another implication of delay was that monitoring of socio-economic effects of the project was postponed. In 2014, a Sida officer stated that monitoring agreements had been 'put on hold' since 'we don't know what will happen' (Interview with Sida official, Stockholm, 12 December 2014). In the end, the socio-economic monitoring never started. A Sida officer in 2017 stated: 'As regards the monitoring assignment, we never initiated it, since the project never materialised' (Email correspondence with Sida official, 12 February 2017).

Meanwhile, the stalled resettlement had a major impact on local communities. In interviews, Razaba residents' main complaints were about the delayed resettlement process. For instance, one male farmer living in the area for eleven years stated that the major problem was not that he was going to be moved, but that he still did not know where or when (Interview, Razaba Ranch, 28 January 2014). Some farmers left their land and took low-paid jobs with the company. At the compensation valuation of their assets in 2011, they were encouraged not to plant perennial crops and were informed that they would not be compensated for any investment in farmland or buildings. This had various impacts. For example, farmers had fewer perennial crops to fall back on when annual crops failed. People also postponed development of their farms and houses. Another concern was that inflation had increased the value of their assets over the years but no information had been provided as to whether there would be compensation for this. Thus, living with the uncertainty about when and where resettlement would take place caused severe mental stress. A sub-village chair commented: 'As the days go the impact becomes higher. You can't even think about developing the area, you just think about the shift that is coming' (Interview, Razaba Ranch, 19 March 2016).

Eventually, these delays contributed to the failure of the investment to materialise. In November 2015, nearly a decade after the MoU had been signed, President Kikwete, an eager supporter of the project from the onset, was replaced by President Magufuli. The latter brought with him an important shift of ideology in Tanzanian rule, with a more restrictive attitude towards foreign private interests. This would have a decisive impact on the project. In November 2016, the company received a letter revoking its land title, indicating that that the government no longer had an interest in the project.[1] Since then, part of the land (allegedly 10,000 ha) has been offered to a domestic company, Bakhresa Ltd, to initiate sugar production.

Conclusion

This chapter has outlined how different types of simplification, reflected in the Bagamoyo project design, interacted with complex contexts to produce repeated delays in project implementation. Simplified planning assumptions are evident in other cases detailed in this book, including the development of the Berbera port and related corridor infrastructure, the Ethiopia Sugar Corporation investment in South Omo, and oil exploration in Turkana. In all these cases, critical social complexities were missed or ignored in designing large projects, with consequences for implementation years after projects had commenced. In Bagamoyo, delays had a wide range of downstream effects: on project implementation, on relations between actors and on the livelihoods and well-being of rural residents. Together, these delays contributed to the failure of the project to materialise.

The chapter has emphasised the importance of delay, and its drivers and effects, when understanding the dynamics of failed land deals. Delay should not be treated as something unexpected, inevitable and innocent. Delays have real, tangible material effects on all involved actors and most profoundly on the assumed beneficiaries living on the project site. Non-action, not least concerning Sida's monitoring of these impacts, is a consequence of delay. When delayed, stalled or failed, projects are not reviewed and we risk losing out on learning about their diverse and often severe impacts.

---

[1]   Statement in an extract of the letter from Government of Tanzania to Eco Energy Ltd, provided in email correspondence with Managing Director, 22 February 2017.

12

Twilight Institutions   Land-buying Companies
& their Long-term
Implications in
Laikipia, Kenya

MARIE LADEKJÆR GRAVESEN

Kenya's protracted struggle over post-colonial land redistribution remains
a complicated story. Following the country's independence in 1963, the
government led by Jomo Kenyatta encouraged investment in companies
to buy land belonging to white settlers and subdividing these to meet
smallholders' demand for land (Boone 2012). However, the impacts of
the government's land redistribution and resettlement schemes were
ambiguous (Leo 1989). Nowhere is this more evident than in the northern
county of Laikipia (see Map 12.1). Currently, Laikipia's landscape is
divided into an array of enclosures, where smallholders settle according
to shared ethnicity and land-use practices on the margins of neighbouring
large-scale private conservancies, ranches and national parks. Wedged
between these settler categories are pastoralists who negotiate access to
pasture on large landholdings by force, through consented arrangements
with private land claimants or simply by occupying seemingly vacant
plots of absentee landowners (Letai 2015). Interrogating the origins of this
fragmentation reveals the county's history of differentiation and shifting
domination.

Land-buying companies (LBCs) remain at the centre of land-use
fragmentation, ambiguous ownership and disputes in Laikipia. Kenya's
independence ushered in a new political class with the financial means
and entrepreneurial skills to establish LBCs in the 1960s and 1970s.
In Laikipia they were able to purchase large tracts of former colonial
ranches via loans from the Agricultural Finance Corporation, offering the
government a crucial role as creditor in private land transfers – a role that
it was unable or unwilling to take advantage of. The high demand for land
eased the process of recruiting shareholders, with landless rural dwellers
and smallholders making up a significant portion of those who sought land
through LBCs. It was in this manner that land became an instrumental
actor in Kenya's political life, with LBCs harnessing desperation for
land shares towards patronage and electoral votes (Branch 2011). This
chapter shows how these companies operate as shadow institutions with

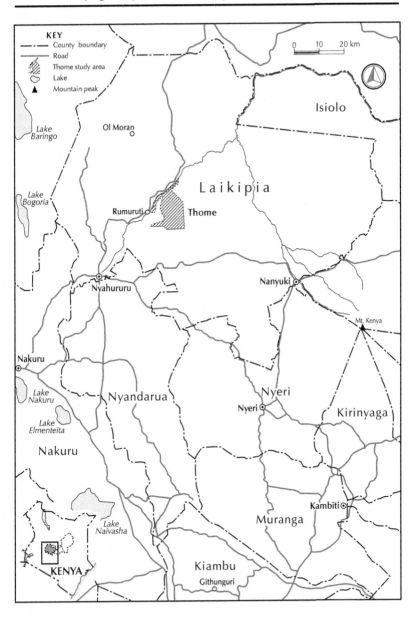

Map 12.1 Kenya, showing location of Laikipia

a political clout that enables an evasion of accountability. The twilight practices of LBCs have fostered an uneven playing field where losers and winners are defined not by their willingness to follow the legal frameworks, but by their capability to seize the opportunities created by recondite authority and legal frameworks.

Exploring these dynamics is key to understanding the historical formation and current issues in Laikipia and in Kenya more broadly. The chapter draws on detailed fieldwork carried out between 2014 and 2016, including biographical interviews with a wide range of parties involved in the land disputes, as well as a review of archives and media records. Central to the chapter is the case study of one LBC and the repercussions of its operations. These include the rise of absentee landlords, precarious settlements without title deeds, the creation of vernacular land markets, and how these factors create space for a new pastoral frontier.

Institutional pluralism and land-buying companies in Laikipia

Laikipia is positioned in the frontier where state presence can seem fragmented. Some 200 km north of Nairobi, the semi-arid Laikipia plateau borders the pastoral areas in Samburu, Isiolo and Baringo counties. Land-use fragmentation in Laikipia is itself a manifestation of the region's legacy as a contested frontier. White Africans on large landholdings live next to subdivided ranches belonging to small-scale farmers and herders (Letai 2015). Additionally, since the 1990s the county has seen an increasing influx of pastoralists and agro-pastoralists from neighbouring counties. For many years, Maa-speaking herders have moved opportunistically onto large ranches to access grazing and in more recent times to stake rights to land (Letai and Lind 2013). In 2017, large-scale 'invasions' by pastoralists from neighbouring counties onto large ranches raised the stakes over land contestations even higher (Gravesen 2018).

Laikipia holds no more available land suitable for redistribution through prospective companies. Taking an official stand on land issues can have long-term consequences for political leaders based on the multifaceted land ownership structures (Mburu et al. 2013). Politicians might be in need of votes from one ethnic group, making them unwilling to sanction land claims from another group. Such cases are numerous and frequent in Laikipia, exacerbating divisions in towns and hostility between communities. This in-between positionality in relation to the state is definitive of frontiers where services and control are fragmented (McDermott Hughes 2008). In such vacuums of state absence, other forms of authority often fill the gap, leading to legal and institutional pluralism (Berry 2002). In parts of Laikipia, state authority is replaced by vernacular land markets in which people negotiate their access to the resources in lieu of secure statutory land rights. In other places, however, institutional infrastructure is well functioning and police support is efficient.

These current circumstances have been formed and fostered by a momentum for political opportunism in the independence years, allowing the extensive progression of ambiguity in tenure security, land investment and support for the new political elite. Aspiring politicians in the 1970s took advantage of the pent-up demand for land among smallholders who had not benefited from the government's resettlement schemes. The public discourse on land scarcity made them extremely willing to acquire a share in the private LBCs. Many were willing to make a financial commitment even before a suitable piece of land was allocated. However, relations soured when many shareholders discovered they had effectively purchased a pile of rocks instead of fertile land. Unlike the resettlement schemes, where the ecological conditions were evaluated for their suitability for small-scale farming, LBCs acquired whatever ranch land became available (Kanyinga 2009; Leo 1989). The large ecological variations meant that prospects of an investment would depend greatly on where a shareholder's share was placed. A former director of Mutokanio Farmers Company explained that the process of distributing land shares was designed to be random through balloting. Yet the outcome was often given beforehand:

> Balloting was done and people picked plot numbers … Since we were the directors, we had picked our plot number in advance … When you are able, you must make out something good for yourself. By then they used to pay us peanuts as directors. So, I had to pick the best; I won't lie. I told the guy who was indicating the plot numbers not to drop my plot numbers in the box. Even before balloting, I had a complete house there. I got six acres. (Interview with former director of Mutokanio Farmers Company, Ol Moran, 2015)

Consequently, in Laikipia's drier areas, the reality for many shareholders was that the land held low economic potential, which effectively locked them in poverty traps (Interview with respondent, Nyahururu, 2015).

In addition to the consequences of the quest for political support, the slow processing of title deeds made it possible for company directors to continue the sale of shares beyond capacity (Kanyinga 2009). Since a surveyor can only be commissioned to undertake subdivisions for titling when all shares are sold, the directors would typically maintain that not all shares had yet been sold in order to evade pressure to process the title deeds – a process that could last decades. The directors had little incentive to finalise the process as they gained financially from renting out the unsettled land during this time (Interviews with multiple respondents in Rumuruti, Thome, Githunguri and Nanyuki, 2014–15). In 1981, the chairmen among twenty LBCs included three ministers, two leading political administrators, one leading party official and one member of parliament. In Central Province, members of registered LBCs had contributed 475 million Kenya shillings (US$64 million) by the early 1980s, and LBCs operating in Laikipia District had collected between 170 million and 240 million Kenya shillings ($23 million and $32 million) between 1962 and 1980 (Kohler 1987).

The LBCs are based on elite structures imposing authority upon smallholders. Owing to their political links, they exist in between the legal frameworks of what can clearly be termed public or private institutions. Falk Moore (1973) describes the dichotomy between expectations of legal state practice and the actual social contexts that it is supposed to control, and how, if the gap between the two is too large, a vacuum can be produced in which social engineering can take place. Lund determines such practices as twilight institutions taking on state-like functions. They prescribe norms, procedures and hierarchies formed around a new locally based power centre, flexible enough to fill the gap when formal procedures are at a loss (Lund 2012). As a type of parastatal twilight institution, the LBCs are not state institutions but are nevertheless lawfully wielded authority over land (Lund 2006).

Today, these types of LBCs still exist, even though they were ever only meant as a means for the smallholder members to acquire land. Shareholders often continue to live on land that is not yet legally theirs, despite having paid for it decades earlier, because the lands are not yet surveyed, subdivided and titled. Without a title deed, they are unable to acquire bank loans to invest in their lands and unable to obtain police protection in case of pastoralist trespassing – an increasingly frequent event in Laikipia as the ambiguous legal status of the land attracts especially pastoralists from neighbouring Samburu County (Interviews with respondents in Thome, Lorien and Ol Moran, 2015). State institutions are reluctant to get involved to support the shareholders' protests against the LBCs because this would mean interfering with a private company. Therefore, where politicians' opportunistic establishment of the LBCs in the years following independence was strategically motivated, the smallholders' opportunistic present-day settlement is often their only option.

Thome: a case study of Laikipia's land-buying companies

Thome is a sublocation 25 km west of Rumuruti on the western extent of the Laikipia plateau. Its challenging semi-arid conditions force the mixed ethnicity population of small-scale farmers to diversify into contract labour. Those farming are heavily dependent on irrigation from the neighbouring Ewaso Narok Swamp and increasingly challenged by encroachment on their fields by the growing population of pastoral livestock in the area. Part of what makes the situation peculiar is that the LBC offices are situated in Githunguri, a town located 250 km south of Thome in Central Province and thus far removed from the settled shareholders and the crisis point.

Arthur Magugu founded Thome Farmers Company in 1976. The land was purchased from Carr Hartley who ran a business selling wildlife. Hartley's ranch was excluded from the resettlement scheme extended to white settlers because it was not based on mixed farming. The introduction of the hunting ban in 1973 complicated the wildlife trade (*Daily Nation* 2013a) and might have inspired Hartley to sell to a wealthy Kenyan with political connections in order enable him to salvage some capital to export abroad. As part of the known circles of the 'Kiambu mafia',[1] Magugu's political aspirations drove him to secure land and establish a company that could give him an edge over his political rivals (*Daily Nation* 2013b). Though his constituency of interest at the time of the 1979 elections was Githunguri, land scarcity in the area led him to consider options elsewhere. However, if shareholders settled after acquiring shares, they would become voters in another constituency and no longer be of value to him. By targeting people in Githunguri who already owned land there Magugu speculated in creating absentee landlords. Additionally, he located the company office in Githunguri rather than in Laikipia and prolonged the process of transferring the land into private titles in order to stop people from settling. That way, he could sell to a considerable number of shareholders in his constituency and preserve them as 'voting cattle' for as long as he needed (Interview with respondent in Rumuruti, 2015).

In contrast to Magugu's Thome Farmers Company, the Mutokanio Farmers Company and the Laikipia West Farmers Company opened five offices in Laikipia mandated to sell shares (Interview with respondent in Ol Moran, 2015). The founders of these two companies, Kihika Kimani and G. G. Kariuki, were keen to settle their shareholders, in contrast to Magagu's delay tactics.[2] Both politicians, Kimani and Kariuki were looking to run for seats in the Laikipia constituency and needed the new shareholders to become voters in Laikipia. To this end, they established several offices in Kikuyu-populated areas around Laikipia assuring interested shareholders that useful farmland was ready for immediate settlement. Despite their promises of quick subdivisions, both companies continued to recruit members even after all shares had been sold. Unlike in the case of Thome Farmers Company, where the majority of shareholders were absentee landlords based in Central Province, the majority of shareholders in Mutokanio Farmers Company and Laikipia West Farmers Company bought shares because they did not have land

---

[1] In the independence years, and through the 1980s, groups of powerful Kikuyu politicians referred to as the 'Kiambu mafia' were known to exercise their influence on government policies.

[2] 'Kenya Land Transfer Programme: John Alison Dykes, Marmar Ranching and Trading Ltd, and Andrew Dykes, Melwa Ltd, Laikipia'. Foreign and Commonwealth Office records for 1975–6, reference FCO 141/19572, held by the National Archives, Kew, UK.

elsewhere and needed to settle immediately (Interviews with respondents in Ol Moran, 2015).

A fair portion of shareholders in Thome Farmers Company also wanted to settle immediately – contrary to what Magugu intended. A share was estimated to include one acre (0.405 ha) and set to cost 500 Kenyan shillings (c. US$50 in 1976). However, it soon proved impossible for everyone to get one acre per share because of the excessive number of shares being sold. This realisation blocked the land from being surveyed and individually titled, leaving the shareholders with tenure insecurity despite having paid for the land they had settled on. Nonetheless, some of the settled shareholders still maintained a high regard for Magugu as their patron. As the vice-chairman for Thome Farmers Company explained: 'Honourable Magugu did everything for us and we just came in to buy shares. He was the one sourcing land for people' (Interview, August 2015). Magugu achieved his political ambition and won the constituency over former Vice-President Karanja in both the 1979 and 1983 elections. Serving as the Minister for Health in 1979 and Minister of Finance in 1983, he was considered a political giant right up until his death in 2012 (*Daily Nation* 2013b).

Initially, many of the relationships in the companies took the shape of patron–client relations. Magugu was the patron providing land for the shareholders, who in turn secured him political support. Today, the vast discrepancy between Thome's total acreage of 37,676 and the total number of shareholders of 53,138 make it unrealistic for the shareholders to maintain their share size. Yet, even after decades of tenure insecurity, politicians would retain their image as patrons, while shareholders blamed the company directors for the prolonged proceedings (Kanyinga 2009). The physical distance between directors and shareholders and the directors' lack of engagement in the challenges of the shareholders has negatively affected the trust relations (Luhmann 1982). Shareholders have learned to treat whatever is communicated from the directors with suspicion, and trust in patron–client relations has degraded, leading the LBCs to become incapable of functioning (Interviews with respondents in Thome, 2015).

As for the settled shareholders in Thome, they continue to dream of getting their title deeds, anticipating that this will provide them with tenure security and increased agricultural yield from their land. Nevertheless, where the title deeds may provide security for some it would reduce it for others owing to the imbalance between the number of shareholders and the size of the land. Therefore, the directors have continuously attempted to convince the shareholders to accept a reduction in the share size.

The legal ambiguity of shareholders' land rights also makes land transfers problematic. However, just because the process for converting share certificates into individual title deeds may have stopped, it does not mean that the land among shareholders has not changed hands since the

1970s. The legal way to transfer land is to register it at the company offices because the LBC still legally owns the land (Interviews with respondents in Rumuruti and Nanyuki, 2015). However, for a smallholder in Thome it is a considerable expense to travel to the office in Central Province merely to complete formal registration with a rubber stamp and possibly pay a bribe (Interviews with respondents in Thome, 2015). Instead, transactions take place via local vernacular land markets and include local witnesses and documents with thumbprints or signatures. For this reason, the legal titleholder or shareholder and the actual land user are often not the same person. In contrast, vernacular land markets consist of people known and trusted by the sellers, lenders and buyers. As such, the authority in land matters has changed, transforming shareholders into semi-autonomous appropriators of informal institutions formed according to bottom-up principles rather than top-down convenience (Shipton 2009; Chimhowu and Woodhouse 2006).

In this environment, the livelihoods of the settled shareholders remain precarious. The high number of absentee lands, in Thome as well as on other LBC land, has created vast areas of seemingly vacant land and attracted Samburu pastoralists to settle on what has effectively turned into a new pastoralist frontier (see Greiner, Chapter 8 this book, for a comparison with neighbouring Baringo). The high number of pastoralist settlements since the early 1990s has made the grass insufficient in these seemingly vacant areas, and the pastoralists' grazing has increasingly included the settled shareholders' farms and the neighbouring ranches. This leads to ethnic tensions that sometimes spill over into violent confrontations (Letai and Lind 2013). The police are reluctant to get involved because of the shareholders' lack of title deeds and ambiguous private property rights. In contrast, the Samburu have taken advantage of the ambiguous conditions in the authority and legal status of the land, adding further pressure on the shareholders.

Repercussions of private land distribution: social and ethnic differentiation

After decades of living under the same conditions, the settled shareholders have come to relate strongly to one another. Yet their mutual trust seems born out of necessity. They acknowledge that they are stronger together, while simultaneously opposing intermarriages (Interviews with respondents in Thome, 2015). The limits to their trusting relations are also illustrated in how they position themselves during meetings and in the settlement patterns. In Thome, Kikuyu settle in some places, Kalenjin in others, while Samburu non-shareholders cluster their settlements in yet other sections. This division has contributed to turning the LBC lands into sites of ethnic competition. This can also be seen in the Lorien Ranching Company towards the south of the county, where shareholders are composed of Kalenjin and Kikuyu. Both groups were resourceful in terms of their links to political circles, reinforcing the connection between ethnicity and politics (Kanyinga 2009). Politicians used existing land conflicts to consolidate their bases of support, instrumentalising the strife for political gain (Leo 1989). Therefore, the shareholders' intentions to add weight to their claim through political associations effectively turned them into puppets for political power schemes.

For those with no land elsewhere, their land relations are comparable to serfdom. They have to develop their land despite ambiguous land rights. Much scholarly work has dealt with the precarious relation between property and resource access. As several scholars argue, one may have property rights but no access to the property's resources, while others may have access to resources yet no property rights to the accessed land (Li 2014a; Lund 2012; Ribot and Peluso 2003). For Laikipia specifically, shareholders have been unable to invest in the land despite having bought it. As Shipton argues, the acquisition of a title deed and tenure security can affect 'decisions to fertilize, to enclose, to subdivide, to buy or sell, to migrate' (2009: 234). So, shareholders who have settled without an individual title deed are limited in creating security and investments at a fundamental level.

Another aspect of the social differentiation of the shareholders is the concept of the absentee landlord. As products of unequal power relations they fall into three overall groups (Mburu et al. 2013). The wealthy absentee landlords bought shares in LBCs for investment purposes and had no intention to settle. This group is often settled in Central Province and does not depend on their land being productive, nor are they concerned by pastoralists settling on the land. The second group of landlords from Central Province were keen to settle after making their investment in 1970. However, the dry conditions of the land made it difficult to make a living through farming. Some settled for a short period before relocating to areas with better ecological conditions. The last group of absentees also bought land with the intention to settle. Many were among the poorer Kikuyu, who settled in Laikipia having been outbid in land acquisition by wealthier shareholders elsewhere. However, tensions with pastoralists and political bias eventually forced them to leave. Like other absentees, they left their land in Laikipia as seemingly vacant grazing resources to be used by pastoralist settlers (interviews with respondents in Rumuruti and Githunguri, 2015; Throup and Hornsby 1998). Common to all three groups of absentees is that, even when they decided to move, few were willing to sell their land. Consequently, large tracts of land in between ranches and smallholder areas were left idle as open-access resources for whoever was interested in making use of it.

The existence of unfenced LBC land has aggravated tensions among different land and resource users (Interviews with respondents in Ol Moran, Thome and Sugoroi, 2015). In the 1980s, unoccupied and unfenced areas in Laikipia were used for livestock grazing and collection of firewood to the benefit of settled shareholders (Kohler 1987). More recently, pastoralists in search of grazing resources have laid claims to and settled on the absentee lands – Pokot in the eastern parts and Samburu in the northern and central parts of Laikipia. Owing to challenges that include ecological pressure and large-scale investment in neighbouring Baringo and Samburu counties (see Greiner, Chapter 8 and Drew, Chapter 5 this book), the option to claim these vacant lands through physical occupation is not simply motivated by potential gains. Instead, similar to the smallholders' reasons for settling in spite of tenure insecurity, these pastoralists have settled opportunistically out of necessity and argue for their right of presence based on historical marginalisation and exclusion from what they consider their former territories. As ambiguous access is preferable to deprivation, the absentee lands of Laikipia open up a new pastoral frontier, in which ambiguity of land rights and twilight practices create possibilities for expansion. In 2017, the expansionist potential of these lands once again became apparent in a wave of politically incited land occupations by other groups of pastoralists, especially Samburu. In contrast to the settled groups, these pastoralists were not motivated by long-term strategies to secure resources but were rather incited to rebel against their exclusion from resources with the short-term goal of claiming re-election for certain politicians (*Star* 2017a).

A development in recent years that compounds tensions is the practice of some absentee landholders buying up land from other absentees in order to create larger landholdings for commercial farming (Letai 2015). Still without intentions to settle, they instead fence the land, hire a manager and invest in machinery to increase productivity. Such strategies make the land investments pay off instantly. Yet many of the settled pastoralists consider it immoral to deny someone access to water, grass and passage through fencing. This moral register is directly opposed to the farmers' rights-based principles of private property.

Conclusion

This chapter has highlighted the ways in which ambiguous authority in land matters produced winners and losers based on the willingness or lack thereof to exploit loopholes rather than follow the absent state's legislation. These present-day dynamics offer a critical perspective on the impact of land acquisition over the course of several decades. Redistribution schemes reproduced the social inequality and ethnic difference they set out to address. This chapter also underlines the different ways of perceiving and making use of land resources at the frontier. For aspiring politicians such as Arthur Magugu, frontier lands were seen as bankable assets. Acquiring peripheral land in Laikipia, much of which was unsuitable for smallholder farming, was a way to woo unsuspecting shareholders among the many smallholders in Central Province who were in search of land. As LBC founders amassed influence and a shot at political office by selling shares to unsuspecting smallholders, they offered little accountability in return in the form of secure tenure. This one-directional chain of value shows how frontier resources are open to appropriation through their very nature of being located at the margins of the state's reach.

For wealthier shareholders, shares in LBCs were assets to be used as collateral for other financial transactions rather than to establish new homesteads. Large tracts of land were left seemingly vacant and unfenced, permitting the passage of livestock and the settlement of some herders in a new pastoral frontier. The pastoralists saw the unused lands as an opportunity to make up for their exclusion from the redistribution of lands in the years following independence. Their decisions to move into and settle on Laikipia's absentee lands have further complicated the livelihoods of the settled shareholders who lack secure tenure. At the time of their share acquisition, the poorer shareholders saw the land at the frontier as an opportunity to settle and secure their livelihood. However, without the state or the founding politicians to ensure their rights, the social dynamics around the lands have thickened, and vernacular responses have become the only way for them to maintain a form of control over their precarious land relations. To them, it is not an option to wait for the title deeds before settling and making further transactions, since waiting may leave them without income for years. All the while, the directors have appeared as a form of broker, whose position in the LBCs provided them with an opportunity to acquire the most fertile land plots and afterwards benefit from the continual land uncertainty through rental income from the unused lands.

Set in the context of a frontier, the opportunism to access land in Laikipia has changed from being prompted by political interests as had occurred in the 1970s. Instead, present-day actors in Laikipia navigate access to land opportunistically and out of necessity. Yet opportunistic actions do come with certain implications. For the shareholders, although offering an income from farming, settling without a title deed limits protection of what they consider their property. In turn, this creates an opportunity for pastoralists to challenge the shareholders' rights to the contested lands. To the directors, maximising profits by extending the company's life comes with the uncertainty that protests may attract media attention and political interference – even though authorities rarely interfere in the affairs of private companies. Ultimately, the effects of both sets of practices are undeniable. The future for both shareholders and pastoralists on these lands will depend on whether formal authorities intervene or continue to practise inaction.

13

Farmer-led Irrigation Investments
How Local Innovators are Transforming Failed Irrigation Schemes

GREGORY AKALL

Turkana County, one of the driest regions of Kenya, has a long history of irrigation interventions, extending from the colonial era to the present. In this chapter, I pose the following questions: How has irrigation development in Turkana changed, and what does it look like today? What are the impacts of recent private-led irrigation development on livelihoods and local economies? How do local Turkana people perceive contemporary irrigation projects and their outcomes? These questions are explored in the context of irrigation schemes along the Turkwel River in Loima sub-county.

The Government of Kenya has prioritised irrigation development as part of its Vision 2030 national development strategy, and considerable sums have been earmarked for irrigation investments. This renewed attention to irrigation and agricultural water management more broadly dovetails with wider trends across governments in sub-Saharan Africa to rehabilitate and develop new schemes (Harrison 2018; Woodhouse et al. 2017; Mutambara et al. 2016). International donors are equally enthusiastic about irrigation development as a route to addressing climate change and generating resilience in dryland areas. The 2013 discovery by the Kenyan Government and the UN Educational, Scientific and Cultural Organisation (UNESCO) of two huge aquifers in Turkana – the Lodwar and Lotikipi basins (Avery 2013) – has added to the notion that irrigation represents an excellent solution to the multiple problems in the region. This is in spite of a history of failed irrigation developments in Turkana (Hogg 1987a). However, while state and donor visions of development promote an idea of large-scale, top-down irrigation schemes as a way to provide alternative livelihoods in the region, it is bottom-up efforts by individuals and groups in Turkana that are showing a different way that irrigation could be developed.

This chapter offers details of farmer-led irrigation development at three sites in Loima as shown in Map 13.1. It compares current efforts to develop irrigated plots with the Turkwel Irrigation Scheme Association

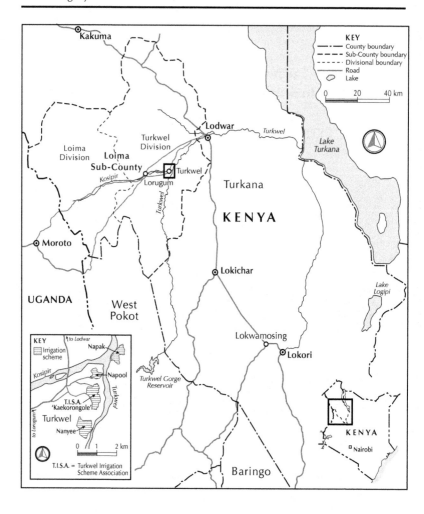

Map 13.1 Kenya, showing location of Loima sub-county in Turkana County and location of study area in Kaekorongole (Turkwel)

(TISA), one of the earliest interventions to promote large-scale irrigation in Turkana. TISA was established in 1966 but fell into disuse in the 1990s. It is now being revitalised under a new wave of informal farmer-led irrigation development.

According to Woodhouse et al. (2017: 216), farmer-led irrigation development 'is a process where farmers assume a driving role in improving their water use for agriculture by bringing about changes in knowledge management, technology use, investment patterns and market linkages, and the governance of land and water'. Outside formal schemes, and with limited external support, such irrigation provides opportunities for accumulation for those able to purchase pumps, rehabilitate canals and sell high-value produce to nearby market centres. This style of irrigation creates a new form of 'endogenous capital' (Korf et al. 2015: 883), linking agriculture to pastoralism and urban development in new ways.

Irrigation in Turkana from a broad perspective

Irrigation has long been promoted in Africa's drylands as a means to improve food security and livelihoods. Turkana was no exception. Pastoralism was seen as an 'abuse and move' livelihood that was not ecologically or economically sustainable (Turner 2011: 474). This strong environmental narrative shaped and influenced policymakers' understanding of Turkana. Irrigated farming was believed to provide an alternative livelihood to livestock-keeping. This was encouraged alongside a broader push to sedentarisation in order to make it easier for the state and other actors to provide services (Catley et al. 2013b). However, Turkana pastoralists saw irrigation schemes as a means of re-establishing the capital necessary for herding and not as a viable alternative to pastoralism. Destitute formerly nomadic Turkana tried their hand at farming, but once they had accumulated sufficient livestock for subsistence, they re-entered pastoral production. In this way, people moved in and out of irrigation schemes (Anderson and Broch-Due 1999; Adams 1992; Hogg 1987a).

Since the 1960s, many irrigation schemes have been constructed. These range from a few large-scale donor-funded projects to numerous small-scale local initiatives (Stave et al. 2005; Adams 1992; Adams 1989). Following years of disappointing results, and the dependency of many scheme farmers on food relief, outside funding for irrigation development all but dried up by the early 1990s. Irrigation infrastructure fell into a state of disrepair in subsequent years, as farmers lacked the resources to repair broken pumps. Donors began to support irrigation again from the early 2000s as a way of supporting adaptation to drought and improving food security. In 2019, there were fifty-six formal irrigation schemes in Turkana County, which are registered as water users associations (WUAs) with the Water Resource Management Authority, the Kenyan formal institution responsible for managing water resources, which expects irrigators to obtain permits and pay for their water usage through formal WUAs (Interview with County Executive Committee Member for Agriculture, Pastoral Economy and Fisheries, Lodwar, 20 May 2019). Scheme farmers are levied about 90,000 Kenya shillings (US$1,026 in 2019) for initial water investment, particularly canal systems.[1] However, in most cases, development agencies supporting water projects within the Turkwel River basin pay this start-up amount. Subsequently, irrigators are expected to pay the annual fee of $1,026, although this is often not paid.

More than twenty schemes were established in a five-year period alone up to 2019. Most are located along the Turkwel River, where the estimated number of farmers is over 10,000 (Ocra 2013: 50), with a smaller number of schemes established along the Kerio River. Outside formal schemes, there are also a string of smaller farmer-led schemes along the lower Turkwel River. These are not recognised by the National Irrigation Board (NIB) because they are unregistered as WUAs.[2] These schemes are managed without outside subsidy and remain invisible to policymakers. Most are thriving without outside support and represent a new form of private entrepreneurial investment and a focus for accumulation by pastoralists and others.

Formal irrigation: the Turkwel Irrigation Scheme Association

The Turkwel Irrigation Scheme Association (TISA), previously known as the Kaekorongole *Harambee* ('pulling together' in Swahili) irrigation scheme, is based along the Turkwel River in Loima sub-county in Turkana. The Government of Kenya and the Food and Agriculture Organization (FAO) supported the establishment of the scheme in 1966 targeting 175 destitute households as a famine prevention measure.

Hogg (1987a) observed that farmers in Kaekorongole invested more time and energy in their traditional rain-fed sorghum plots than in the formally irrigated scheme. The *Ng'imonia* Turkana (one of the nineteen Turkana sub-groups who historically inhabited the Kaekorongole area and who focused on both agriculture and livestock) and Turkana settlers (a mix of six Turkana sub-groups, including *Ng'ikamatak*, *Ng'isiger*, *Ng'ilukumong*, *Ng'ibilae*, *Ng'iesetou* and *Ng'ipucho*) worked as labourers and did not own plots in the Kaekorongole irrigation scheme. They started their own farms in Nanyee and Napool because the FAO restricted the growing of traditional Turkana sorghum in the scheme. The Turkana settlers joined the irrigation scheme between 1966 and 1972; many were people who had lost livestock through drought, conflict or disease. They

---

[1] Historical exchange rate, https://fxtop.com/.
[2] On 16 August 2019, NIB was renamed the National Irrigation Authority (NIA) in response to the enactment of The Irrigation Act, 2019 No.14 of 2019 on 29 July 2019.

became referred to as '*Amasikin*', a term that combined the idea of 'people of the scheme' together with the Swahili word for 'poor', *maskini*, and became a new Turkana sub-group. The FAO managed the scheme until 1978, when it was handed over to the Ministry of Agriculture.

In 1982, the Norwegian Agency for Development Cooperation (NORAD) under the Turkana Rehabilitation Development Programme (TRDP) provided a fresh infusion of funding for the scheme. The scheme was reengineered from a furrow-based to a basin-based system in order to reduce the reliance on heavy machinery, cut overhead costs and encourage participation by individual plot owners (Interview with former TRDP programme manager, 3 September 2013). In 1984, NORAD, through the Turkana Rehabilitation Project, an offshoot of the famine relief efforts of 1981–82, also introduced to the area *Prosopis juliflora*, originally from tropical America (Maundu et al. 2009), known locally as *etirae*, in order to counter degradation. According to a former TRDP forestry adviser, the tree was believed to be a means to restore vegetation, to take pressure away from indigenous trees and to provide fodder for livestock (Interview with former TRDP forestry adviser, Cambridge, 4 September 2013). But today, unfortunately, people report that *Prosopis* has become a problem for crop and livestock production. The thorny, invasive species has colonised large tracts of cropland inside and outside the schemes as well as dry season grazing areas, particularly along the Turkwel River (Focus group discussions with irrigators and pastoralists, Turkwel, March–August 2014). In Turkana, *Prosopis* has displaced indigenous species, particularly fodder species (e.g. grass, acacia trees and herbaceous plants) and edible wild fruits important for local livelihoods (Maundu et al. 2009: 44).

In 1990, NORAD withdrew its funding as a consequence of a diplomatic dispute between Norway and Kenya that led to a severing of bilateral ties. In the following years, up to 2003, there was little to no external support for Kaekorongole, yet farmers continued to make use of the scheme infrastructure (Interview with Aboi Louruka, former chairman of Kaekorongole scheme, Turkwel, 14 June 2014). They sought their own ways to manage a scarcity of water by constructing an ancillary canal from the main channel. Between 1992 and 1995, farmers cleared parts of the scheme and set up plots in eight blocks. Ninety farmers benefited from these plots, with each owning a quarter of a hectare (Interview with retired agricultural extension officer and a farmer, Turkwel, 7 March 2014).

In 2003, the Kaekorongole irrigation scheme was renamed Turkwel Irrigation Scheme Association (TISA) and registered as a WUA under the District Gender and Social Services unit in response to the reforms brought about by the 2002 Water Act, which liberalised the water sector, particularly the management of river basins. The creation of TISA was to enable the scheme's members to access external support as a communal group. This meant that the new TISA had to be managed through a formal and bureaucratic conventional administrative structure, as per rules and regulations pertaining to WUAs (Interview with Francis Esibitar, Turkwel, 7 March 2014).

In 2003, the NIB announced plans to revive the scheme and expand the area under cultivation from 45 ha to 120 ha. This began a period of renewed external assistance; yet various problems dogged these efforts. To prepare for the scheme's expansion, the land was cleared using food-for-work labour, but there was no investment in basin maintenance. The NIB's capacity on the ground was small with only one irrigation engineer to oversee these developments. According to farmers, progress was slow, and by 2014 only 1.2 km of canal was completed. The contract for the work was given to a local contractor, who did not consult with the locals on where the canal should pass. Farmers were stopped from questioning the lack of progress and the limited Turkana involvement in jobs and consultations (Interview with Chairman of TISA, Turkwel, 11 March 2014).

Other support came from the Catholic Diocese of Lodwar, which installed 400 metres of fencing to the scheme in 2005. The parish priest provided vegetable and fruit seeds to farmers before leaving the area in 2008 (Focus group discussion with TISA farmers, Turkwel, June 2014). Caritas Lodwar provided additional support in 2012, including repairing two pumps and providing water pipes and horticultural and agricultural training programmes; they also constructed five greenhouses (Interview with Caritas official, Lodwar, 7 September 2014). However, the greenhouses sat empty for over a year while farmers continued to struggle with a lack of water, a problem that was compounded by the breakdown of the solar water pump (Interview with scheme official, Turkwel, 11 June 2014). Furthermore, by 2013, 75 ha of land that had been cleared years before was again unfit for cultivation owing to the rapid spread of *Prosopis*. The National Irrigation Board supported fresh bush clearance to try to contain the problem, while connecting 2.5 km of canal and fencing farmland to prevent livestock incursions. Despite allocating money to clear the *Prosopis*, very little has happened on the ground. Turkana has the second-highest allocation of devolved funds in Kenya, after Nairobi, and in the 2014/15 financial year it received 9.1 billion Kenya shillings (c. US$100 million in 2014) (Lind 2018: 142). However, the Turkana County Government has not committed to the renewed investments in irrigation.

Outside efforts to establish irrigation as an alternative to livestock-keeping were high cost and failed to establish a sustainable livelihood for farmers. As in the past, irrigated farming has never covered the food needs of scheme households, especially for the large polygamous households that are common in Turkana. Even now, most farmers survive by combining income and livelihoods from a number of tasks for cash, such as brewing, charcoal production, touting for passengers for *matutu* (public service vehicles) and selling firewood, alongside cultivating plots and keeping animals. Today, TISA has a membership of 450 farmers. Some twenty households receive cash transfers through the Hunger

Safety Net Programme, while others receive occasional relief food (Interview with irrigation schemes' coordinator, Turkwel, 22 February 2014). Rather than formal, externally driven irrigation development, whose fixed, standardised and controlled (Scoones et al. 2019a) design features are hard to implement in highly uncertain drylands like Turkana, more encouraging outcomes are apparent in farmer-led irrigation efforts, as explored below.

New irrigation entrepreneurs: possibilities for accumulation

It is not all doom and gloom for Turkwel farmers, however. Outside the failing formal schemes, a number of initiatives have emerged led by people with start-up capital, including retired civil servants and other Turkana who had lived outside the county in other parts of Kenya and returned in recent years, many after the country's post-election violence in 2008. They have used a combination of their own investments and some external support to invest in entrepreneurial activities, often including fodder production to link to the wider pastoral economy. They have used old irrigation infrastructure but rehabilitated it in ways that can be sustained, often by linking it in innovative ways with elements of the flood cultivation system. They have invested in pumps and other equipment and have begun to make profits from their businesses, which are a mix of individual and collective enterprises.

Several cases from Napool, Nanyee and Napak introduced below illustrate these dynamics. All three schemes have their roots in the efforts of groups in the 1950s and 1960s who aspired to increase returns from customary flood retreat cultivation along the banks of the Turkwel River. Napak was the first farmer-led scheme to be established in the 1950s by a local agro-pastoralist group that combined growing sorghum with grazing livestock seasonally in the riverine forest. Membership of the 40 ha scheme jumped threefold from 120 in 2001 to 360 in 2014. Napool's scheme began in 1966 when founding members of the scheme dug a canal system from the Turkwel River to supply water to their plots, fenced the scheme to keep off livestock and over time cleared more land to expand the cultivated area. It currently covers 20 ha and has a membership of around 250. Nanyee irrigation scheme was also started in the 1960s by a group who relied on seasonal sorghum cultivation. In 1982, the NORAD-funded Turkana Rehabilitation Project used farmers to build the canal and introduced a basin irrigation system. Some 762 members now cultivate 40 ha. Most farmers till between four and twenty-three basins (0.08–0.46 ha), alongside herding small stock.[3] In 2000, farmers constructed their own secondary canal that serves up to 200 farmers. The FAO provided

---

[3]   A basin measures 20m by 10m.

additional support in 2003, installing intakes and check boxes on the canals (Interview with an elderly founder of Nanyee scheme, 4 July 2014).

The move to establish WUAs in all three schemes in 2005 has encouraged better governance and efforts by scheme members to rehabilitate and expand irrigation infrastructure. The Nanyee association created a sanction, a fine of 500 Kenya shillings ($5.70)[4] for members who divert water without the water committee's consent (Interview with former chairman of the Nanyee irrigation scheme, 4 July 2014). Further, members who do not contribute to communal efforts to desilt the canal are fined 500 Kenya shillings or even risk having their farms denied water (Interview with scheme member, Nanyee, 4 July 2014). The scheme's water management committee uses a block or tertiary system to supply water to the plots. The scheme's management committee meets twice a month to enforce the scheme's by-laws. The chair of the Napak association mobilised farmers to redig the main canal, started by the Anglican Church of Kenya, which supplies water to all the plots in the scheme (Interview with Napak irrigation scheme chair, 5 July 2014). The scheme members contribute 100 Kenya shillings per harvest (approximately six times a year), raising an estimated 216,000 Kenya shillings for the association. Members' dues are used to rehabilitate the canal and clear the plots (Interview with Napak irrigation scheme secretary, 5 July 2014). The association also issues sanctions. For example, livestock owners must pay an average fine of 1,000 Kenya shillings or between one and three goats if their livestock invade farms.

As in the formal schemes, the per capita area of land under cultivation is very small, and insufficient on its own to support the food needs of households. Most Nanyee farmers also engage in basket making, collecting and selling roofing materials from doum palms (*Hyphaene compressa*; *engol* in Ng'aTurkana), burning charcoal, collecting and selling gravel that is used in the construction sector in Lodwar (the administrative and commercial centre of Turkana, about 30 km away) and other growing towns, as well as working as casual labourers. Some also receive cash transfers through the Hunger Safety Net Programme (Focus group discussion, Nanyee, 4 July 2014). Farmers with large families rely on family labour to plant, weed, guard plots against intrusions by livestock and harvest. Others employ labourers seasonally, who are paid in farm produce. Horizontal forms of labour exchange are also important among farmers to help with particular farm work.

For most scheme members, the potential of irrigated farming comes from the ways it is combined with other livelihood and economic activities. One example is Simon Ekadeli, aged fifty, a member of the Napool scheme since 1990, who is married with two wives. He owns twelve basins and harvests six bags of maize cereal in a good season. Ekadeli combines farming with running a food kiosk in Turkwel trading

---

[4]   Historical exchange rate, https://fxtop.com/.

centre, as well as livestock-keeping. Like many Turkana farmers in the past, he invests profits from farming and his business in growing his herd (Interview with Simon Ekadeli, Napool, 5 July 2014). Another example is Lomong Emase, aged fifty-four, a farmer, who joined the Napak scheme in 1992. Lomong grows green maize and produces ten bags in a good harvest and six bags in a bad season. She sells the surplus to earn income to buy books and pay school fees for her children. Apart from maize, she also grows green grams, cowpeas and onions for local markets. She combines farming with keeping thirty sheep and goats, which are grazed in an enclosure on her farm during the day and driven home in the evening.

Several farmers have turned to growing vegetables as a way of supplying growing local markets, particularly in nearby Lodwar. One of these is Lopira Loleny, aged seventy-four, who was one of the labourers who helped construct the Kaekorongole scheme. Unable to get a plot in the formal scheme, he helped found the Napool scheme. He owns forty basins, from which he produces between fifteen and forty bags of cereal. In 1987, he was able to acquire plots in Kaekorongole to raise vegetables using water drawn from a borehole. Vegetable production has compensated in part for losses from his diminishing herd, which he attributes to recurring drought and to the spread of *Prosopis*, which has reduced grazing areas, and its pods, which after being eaten by livestock result in teeth loss and block the rumen causing death. Another farmer, a retired police officer, purchased a diesel water pump for $570, which he now uses to grow kale, tomatoes and onions for the Lodwar market. He also harvests between twelve and fifteen bags of maize and cereal annually from other plots that are fed with canal water. He generates enough profit to cover school fees, buy farm inputs, especially seeds, and purchase fuel and cover repairs of the diesel pump. Inputs, particularly seeds, are difficult to come by for horticulturalists. In 2014, there were no seed stockists in all of Turkana County; the nearest were in Kitale, some 350 km away. Some farmers have found ways to improve supply by using mobile-phone money transfers to courier seeds to Lodwar, where farmers arrange to pick them up. One farmer in the area has started a business supplying other farmers in the area with surplus seeds for which he has arranged delivery (Interview with scheme member, Napool, 5 July 2014).

Other farmers are finding success by developing connections with the livestock economy. In 2013, Lopira (the farmer mentioned previously) sold one of his plots to a women's group for US$1,284.[5] The group sought the land for growing fodder after completing a Vétérinaires Sans Frontières Belgium training course. In 2014, the group harvested 625 bales of fodder in their first harvest, which they sold to the Turkana County Government at 200 Kenya shillings ($2.28) a bale, turning a profit of 125,000 Kenya shillings ($1,426). Since then, the group produces fodder four times a year, earning returns of 500,000 Kenya shillings ($5,703) annually (Interview

---

[5] Historical exchange rate, https://fxtop.com/.

with local women's group, Napool, 10 July 2014). Another farmer leases his enclosure to pastoralists who pay 1,000 Kenya shillings ($11.41) or a goat to access the individually owned enclosure (Interview with scheme member, Napool, 7 March 2014). Most farmers in the area, including in Napool, permit pastoralists' livestock to forage on sorghum or maize stalks after harvesting, which is free for members. However, non-members are charged a fee of 1,000 Kenya shillings to graze their livestock.

Like Simon Ekadeli, the Napool farmer introduced above who invests in livestock, many farmers carry on the tradition of Turkana farmers who seek to convert farm surplus into growing their herds. To take another example, Emase Lokuda, aged fifty-nine, is a Napak farmer who used irrigation as a way back into livestock-keeping. Emase left Turkana in the 1960s, spending many years in Kitale, Kisumu and other large 'down country' towns working as a security guard. He returned to Turkana in 1978 and within two years had enough savings to start farming at Napak. A few years after settling at Napak, he was imprisoned for a brief period in Lodwar after his camels invaded plots at the nearby Kaekorongole scheme. He returned to Napak and eventually took over as chair of the WUA. After mobilising scheme members to redig the irrigation canal, farmers enjoyed a bumper harvest. Emase and his brother, also a scheme member, generated enough surplus to purchase forty shoats (sheep or goats) each.

Irrigators in the three case study sites are able to accumulate because of the flexibility of their irrigation practices and the links to the livestock economy. This contrasts with their counterparts in TISA, who have been less successful because of control by the state and donor aid agencies of production practices in the irrigation scheme.

Conclusion

This chapter shows that Turkwel farmers have persisted with irrigation, in spite of a history of low yields, large family sizes and the uncertain provision of outside relief and technical assistance. Although over-shadowed by formal schemes, farmer-led irrigation has always been a fallback for local Turkana, whose livelihoods combine both livestock and agriculture. However, since the 1960s, following the introduction of modern small-scale irrigation schemes, the indigenous irrigation system has been ignored by developers, which saw it as 'traditional' and 'informal'. Larger irrigation developments implemented by the state and international organisations in Turkana have been characterised by delayed infrastructure development, high investments and poor outcomes – factors behind failed investments elsewhere in the region, as seen in Bagamoyo sugar project detailed in Chapter 11. Meanwhile, Turkana farmer-led irrigation initiatives have thrived, sustaining local livelihoods and contributing to lasting transformations in Turkana.

Taking the examples of the Turkwel Irrigation Scheme Association alongside the Nanyee, Napool and Napak farmer-led irrigation schemes, this chapter has shown how local farmers were able to thrive with only limited outside support. Turkwel farmers crafted their own strategies when the scheme 'collapsed', including acquiring plots in more than one scheme, digging new canals and using motorised pumps to irrigate plots. Some of them shifted to fodder farming as an enterprise, selling hay to pastoralists and supplying the Turkana County Government and livestock-keepers in Lodwar town.

As this chapter shows, irrigation has therefore been the basis for local accumulation, with irrigators purchasing motorised water pumps, investing in horticultural production, and investing in livestock. Some private irrigators represent the emergence of 'endogenous' or 'local capital' through accumulation. This has implications for local politics and patterns of investment in the area, as evident in other cases profiled in this book including Benna-Tsemay (see Chapter 10), Baringo (see Chapter 8) and Isiolo (see Chapter 3). The staying power of farmer-led irrigation in the past six decades and the links to the wider pastoral economy show new potential for transforming livelihood and economic settings of Turkana.

14

Shifting Regimes of Violence within Ethiopia's Awash Valley Investment Frontier

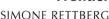

SIMONE RETTBERG

Over the past fifteen years the Ethiopian state has greatly increased its investments in the sparsely populated arid and semi-arid pastoral lowlands where land is deemed as 'unused' (Lavers 2012). Guided by export-oriented agro-industrial development strategies and a modernist development ideology, the state has embarked on large-scale mechanised schemes to expand commercialised irrigation agriculture. Land investments focus on the large river basins such as the Wabi-Shebelle, Nile, Omo and Awash, all of which are considered to have high irrigation potential. With the construction of large dams and the conversion of prime grazing areas along large rivers into farmland, conflicts with dispossessed and resettled local pastoralists and agro-pastoralists are on the rise (Fratkin 2014). While the Ethiopian government has trumpeted double-digit national economic growth rates, critical perspectives are that pastoral livelihoods have experienced a 'negative' structural transformation characterised by widespread impoverishment, increasing social inequality and rising levels of destitution (Rettberg et al. 2017). Most pastoralists are currently excluded from the benefits of large-scale land investments pursued in the name of 'growth and transformation'.

Land investments and large-scale enclosures in marginal dryland areas are not a new phenomenon in the Ethiopian lowlands. They map onto the historic Ethiopian centre–periphery dynamics between Muslim mobile pastoralists inhabiting the lowland areas and the ruling Christian Orthodox regimes familiar with farming in highland areas. Previous regimes under Emperor Haile Selassie (1930–74) and the socialist military junta of the Derg (1974–91) also pursued investments in large-scale cotton and sugar estates in the lowlands, leaving a legacy of displacement and dispossession in the pastoral frontier (Makki 2012). The state conceives arable land in the lowlands as 'underutilised', 'untapped' and relatively abundant compared to the densely populated highland areas where land is scarce, as we saw in Fana Gebresenbet's chapter on South Omo in this book. At the same time, large-scale agricultural investments in Ethiopia have always served as a tool for state-building and the consolidation of power in its periphery, countering the widespread assumption that land grabs undermine state sovereignty (Lavers 2016). An authoritarian high-modernist state mainly concerned with control and appropriation often uses the establishment of large-scale schemes as a way to increase the legibility of frontiers (Scott 1998). Pastoralists uniquely challenge state sovereignity as their mobility undermines the state's capacity to tax, conscript and otherwise regulate the population. This explains the continuity of governmental policies for an expansion of the plantation economy in the pastoral frontier in spite of its lack of profitability compared to pastoralism (Behnke and Kerven 2013).

In the face of increasing resource appropriation by the state, this chapter examines the impact of past and contemporary state-driven land investments on regimes of violence and forms of local conflict and contestation in the pastoral frontier of the Awash Valley. As Hagmann and Alemmaya Mulugeta (2008) argue, the drivers of conflict and violence in Ethiopia's lowlands have changed through the process of increasing political and economic incorporation of pastoral areas into the state. In 2014 the Awash Valley accounted for 50 per cent of the national irrigated area (Fratkin 2014). Having unfolded over a period of nearly sixty years, the impacts and influences of large-scale investments in the Awash Valley are readily apparent. Once known as an area of exceptional pastoral wealth due to preferential grazing areas along the river, pauperisation and food insecurity have substantially risen during the last decades, with new forms of local conflict emerging. Therefore, the case of the Awash Valley can also be read as a cautionary story of how lives and livelihoods in other drylands in the Horn of Africa that are experiencing new, more recent large-scale investments may develop, including in South Omo (Chapter 10), Lamu (Chapter 2), Turkana (Chapter 4), and Kilombero (Chapter 6).

Conceptually, frontiers are understood as symbolic and material spaces at the margins of the state where 'authorities, sovereignties, and hegemonies of the recent past have been or are currently being challenged by new enclosures, territorialisation, and property regimes' (Peluso and Lund 2011: 668). They are zones of contact between two previously distinct social orders, where governmental and autochthonous forms of political organisation compete and multiple regimes of violence, power and territoriality overlap (Korf et al. 2015; Hagmann and Korf 2012).

The transformation of regimes of resource control goes hand-in-hand with the conflictive establishment of new property rights and regulations of access. Territorialisation, the embedding of social relations in bounded space, is the defining strategy to gain resource control, to consolidate state power in frontiers (Vandergeest and Peluso 1995) and to increase the legibility of the society (Scott 1998). It refers to the 'creation of systems of resource control – rights, authorities, jurisdictions, and their spatial representations' (Rasmussen and Lund 2018: 388). Therefore, territorial reordering for the allocation of rights, authority and control presents one of the main features of national governance in pastoral areas where national sovereignty is contested. Recent studies increasingly include indigenous discourses and practices so that territorialisation appears as a co-constitutive process of governmental and non-governmental actors within the frontier (Korf et al. 2015). The centre represents frontiers as zones of backwardness, disorder and insecurity. However, from the perspective of local inhabitants, the frontier is not a backward, marginal territory needing to be controlled but a threatened homeland at risk of being invaded by external powers.

The hegemonial discursive construction of the frontier as 'no man's land' is constitutive for the legitimate use of state violence and authoritarian interventions in the name of 'civilisation' and modern development, for example, through sedentarisation (Asebe Regassa et al. 2018). While violence is often the outcome of conflicts over resource control and sovereignty within the frontier, it can also serve as a tool to establish the frontier. A 'state of emergency' characterised by violence, disorder and insecurity is often a constitutive means of governance for the anchoring of state presence in areas where the state lacks the monopoly of power (Hagmann and Korf 2012; see also Chapter 10 on South Omo).

Historicising conflicts over land control in the Awash Valley

The Awash is the longest river in Ethiopia (1,200 km), originating in the highlands where mean annual rainfall reaches 1,200–1,400 mm. It descends the escarpments of the Awash Valley as it makes its way to Afar, a hot lowland region bordering Djibouti and Eritrea. The land-use potential for irrigation and grazing along the river has made it a bone of contention between the state and Afar pastoralists inhabiting the riverine areas. The fertile seasonally inundated floodplains along the Awash River became the earliest focus for agricultural investments under the imperial regime of Haile Selassie in the second half of the twentieth century. These floodplains constitute a small area but are highly significant resources for Afar pastoralists as dry season grazing and drought refuge. Customarily, access to and use of resources in the floodplains was governed by a communal clan-based system of granting land rights. The only area where Afar practised agriculture along the river was the powerful Sultanate of Aussa located in the lower Awash Valley (around Asayita), where agro-pastoralists engaged in small-scale irrigation in the inland river delta.

Another group who claims resources along the Awash are Issa-Somali pastoralists. With the flare up of Somali irredentism in the second half of the twentieth century, Issa violently displaced the Afar far towards the west, so that Afar clans of the middle Awash Basin lost access to a major part of their rainy season grazing areas (Rettberg 2010). Issa even managed to establish several settlements along the main road to Djibouti (Undufoo,

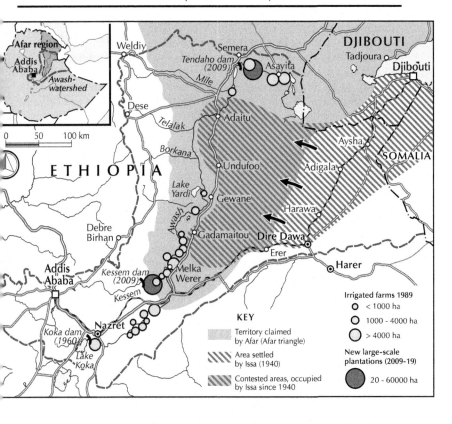

Map 14.1 Ethiopia, showing the Awash Valley as a conflict hotspot

Adaitou and Gadamaitou). The area where Afar and Issa currently come into contact and violent contestation overlaps with the development corridor along the Awash River where small towns, administrative centres, major transport routes and large-scale farms are concentrated (see Map 14.1). Recurrent clashes along the main road threaten Ethiopia's foreign trade, which relies disproportionately on access to the Djibouti port that is reached by road through Afar.

Imperial and military rule: geopolitical threats and securitisation

State land investments in the Awash Valley were initiated by the Abyssinian imperial government as part of its nation-building efforts and as a way of asserting its economic and political power in the pastoral frontier (Markakis 2011). The establishment of commercial farms on the banks of the Awash in the 1950s and the completion of the Koka Dam in 1960 marked the start of an agro-capitalist exploitation of the floodplains (Kloos 1982; Bondestam 1974). The main body responsible for the planning and implementation of development programmes in the Awash Valley was the Awash Valley Authority (AVA), a parastatal agency founded in 1962. The government transferred the land rights along the Awash to AVA in order to modernise the agricultural economy through the cultivation of cash crops and to generate foreign currency. In the following years, the Awash Valley became Ethiopia's most intensely used river basin. This was also owing to its relative proximity to ports along the Red Sea and the strategic location of the valley between the Ethiopian highlands and the Red Sea, which made it an important transit region for overseas trade. Under Haile Selassie large concessions were granted to foreign investors, primarily British and Dutch. By 1971 the irrigated farm area had expanded to 48,900 ha, of which 60 per cent was used for cotton and 22 per cent for sugar cane (Maknun Gamaledin 1987). In 1989 the Awash Valley accounted for approximately 70 per cent of the country's total irrigated area (68,800 ha).

The Awash Basin also served as a security buffer for the Ethiopian state. The securitisation of the Awash Valley was of major importance in defending Ethiopian territory against the irredentist ambitions of Somalia, which claimed the Awash River as the western border of a 'Greater Somalia'. Even though the overall size of irrigated farmland increased (especially under Haile Selassie), the state's prime interest was not resource accumulation, but rather to protect national security in a politically fragile, war-ridden region. Against this background, the Ethiopian state employed divide and rule tactics to isolate the Issa-Somalis. Ethiopia selectively supported the Afar in their conflict with the Issa, while the Somalia government lent military assistance to the Issa. Consequently, the conflict between Afar and Issa-Somali pastoralists deepened and morphed into a proxy conflict between Ethiopia and Somalia. On several occasions over the years, buffer zones were established to separate the Afar and Issa, but this was above all motivated by the Ethiopian state's interest in halting westward Issa expansions.

Ongoing violence between Afar and Issa and repeated attacks on trucks and trains provided cover for autocratic governmental interventions, including the occasional proclamation of martial law and the deployment of violence as a means of political rule. For local communities, the state's presence was manifest above all in the military (Markakis 2011). Large-scale state violence was directed against Issa who were perceived as state enemies because of their Somali background. Notable episodes include the killing of hundreds of Issa civilians by troops of Haile Selassie in Aysha town in 1962 and the 'Getu war' (named after Colonel Getu, Police Chief of Chercher, Adal and Garaguracha Awraja) in 1972, when the army, led by Colonel Getu, in alliance with Afar and Oromo launched an attack on Issa who had settled close to the Awash River. In comparison, Afar suffered relatively more from structural forms of state violence, namely the dispossession from their key dry season pastures in the Awash floodplains to make way for large plantations. It can be concluded that the Ethiopian state under Haile Selassie and the Derg instrumentalised and used pastoral violence and disorder within the Awash frontier for its own ends: to defend its external borders against Somalia and to gain a hold over land resources for the sake of national economic development and modernisation.

The developmental state: geo-economic opportunities and infrastructural violence

The territorialisation of social relations and processes of land commodification in the Awash Valley intensified in the early 1990s following ruptures in state power. After the removal of the Siad Barre regime, Somalia descended rapidly into civil war, which meant a dampening of the irredentist threat inside Ethiopia. Around the same time, the Derg regime collapsed and the Ethiopian People's Revolutionary Democratic Front (EPRDF), an alliance of ethnically based opposition movements, assumed power in 1991. The government under the leadership of Prime Minister Meles Zenawi (1995–2012) adhered to a strategy of 'Agricultural Development-Led Industrialisation' (ADLI) with land remaining the property of the state. The policy encouraged land investments by foreign or domestic investors, which were centrally managed by the state (Lavers 2012). Adopting a developmental state model in the first decade of the twentieth century, the EPRDF embarked on a mission to consolidate its political power in the peripheral lowlands and to integrate Ethiopia in a global neoliberal market economy (Rettberg et al. 2017). The overarching interest of the Ethiopian developmental state focuses on export-oriented catch-up development in 'unused' areas of the lowlands. While security remains a major strategic objective, the expanded commercial exploitation of water and land resources, as well as extending the reach of state institutions, has become a further priority.

Against this background, practices for territorial reordering have received increasing attention in the Awash Basin frontier. The first phase of territorialisation aimed to create the base for an enhanced regulation of resources and pastoralists. It was marked by the institutional formalisation of a new administrative structure in 1994 based on ethno-territorial units (so-called ethnic federalism) and the decentralisation of political power so that state presence expanded significantly. This undermined customary institutions and created a class of Afar politicians highly loyal to the state. The second phase of territorialisation (since 2000) has focused on investments in commercial agriculture, water provision and transport infrastructure. Bearing the hallmarks of earlier large-scale resettlement programmes pursued by the Derg regime, since 2010 the EPRDF has pursued a villagisation programme in which pastoralists are encouraged to settle voluntarily in new settlements. Here, the provision of water and schools, as well as access to other basic services including health and social assistance, serve as a main incentive to encourage pastoralists to settle. This is linked to a formalisation of land rights and property regimes through land titling, the distribution of one-hectare riverine plots to newly settled pastoralists, and the commodification of water provided by new water supply schemes.

Decentralisation, an increasing literacy of the pastoral population and improved accessibility due to the expansion of transport infrastructure have increased the capacity of the state to penetrate civil society and to implement political decisions. A proliferating number of infrastructural state investments in the region indicate the state's intent to deepen its presence also in areas outside of the development corridor along the Awash River. This thickening of state presence is also apparent in other pastoral areas of Ethiopia, notably in the South Omo valley (see Fana Gebresenbet, Chapter 10 this book). Recent investments include the expansion of the rural roads, the completed rehabilitation of the Addis–Djibouti railway, and schemes to develop the region's groundwater supplies as well as tributaries of the Awash for irrigated agriculture.

In 2010 the EPRDF regime began construction of two large dams (Tendaho and Kessem) in the middle and lower Awash Valley with the capacity to irrigate up to 80,000 hectares of land. The Tendaho Dam and Irrigation Project aims to develop 50,000 ha for sugar-cane production along with 10,000 ha for fodder for displaced (agro-)pastoralists. Riverine forests were flooded or cut and existing cotton farms and key patches of communal dry season grazing areas were transformed into a fully state-owned and federally managed sugar-cane plantation. This dispossession from key rangelands has disturbed seasonal migration patterns, as pastoralists have been forced to move to other, less productive grazing areas for extended periods, leading to localised overgrazing in some places and declining herd sizes. This, in turn, has contributed to widespread impoverishment, chronic food insecurity and a high dependence on food and cash transfers (Rettberg et al. 2017; Müller-Mahn et al. 2010).

A large majority of the pastoralists have not reaped any economic benefits of agro-capitalist irrigation developments so far. Without formal land titles over their communal grazing areas they received no compensation when the land was expropriated and they were displaced (Dessalegn Rahmato 2008). They also have not benefited from employment opportunities on the plantations, as it is mostly incoming labour migrants from highland areas who are recruited. Afar only get low-paid jobs as guards, as they lack the agricultural skills and qualifications required by recruiting agencies; exclusion from higher paid work in this case mirrors the experience of residents living near to large projects in other contexts covered in this book, including oil installations in Turkana (see Chapter 4), the wind farm in Marsabit (see Chapter 5), and the Mngeta commercial rice scheme in Kilombero (Chapter 6). As in these others, lack of access to good paying and longer-lasting jobs for local residents has nurtured the perception that the state excludes them from economic development. Seen from the margins in Afar, the promise of large-scale plantations has turned into infrastructural violence (Li 2018; Zoomers 2018), as benefits are only captured by a narrow, predatory elite.

Resistance within the frontier

State interventions to firm up its economic and political control in the frontier are conceived by pastoral groups as massive threats. Most pastoralists experience the state as an external, colonising invader whose interventions have undermined local institutions and livelihoods. While pastoralists are often portrayed as victims of land grabs, local agency in resisting and adapting to the state's expanding presence has been evident in the Awash Valley over time. During the imperial and military regimes, local resistance within the Awash Valley was mainly directed against political control and state sovereignty. High on the political agenda of Afar and Issa was the quest for self-rule in autonomous regions. Various ethnically based insurgent movements offered armed resistance to state power.

At the same time, endogenous forms of territorialisation emerged to counter the ongoing and anticipated land losses through large-scale enclosures by external actors. Land investments had a notable impact on the wealthy Aussa sultanate where the granting of a concession to the British Mitchell Cotts Tendaho Plantations Share Company in 1961 led to dispossession and dislocation of the Afar (Cossins 1973). Against this background, the Sultan of Aussa, Ali Mirah Hanfere, who controlled most of the land in the lower Awash Valley, became one of the largest investors in order to prevent a further expansion of multinational investments onto 'his' land (Maknun Gamaledin 1993). This agrarian development led to a stratification of society in Aussa consisting of marginalised labourers, relatively affluent agro-pastoralists who cultivated small areas (<10 ha), and a wealthy upper class. The latter consisted of customary authorities and relatives of the sultan who controlled most of the irrigated land and were comparable to feudal lords (Bondestam 1974).

Processes of counter-territorialisation intensified after the EPRDF came to power in 1991. The new political context of ethnic federalism increased exclusive ethno-territorial claims to land. It induced processes of voluntary sedentarisation, which has also been encouraged by state development policies for pastoral areas. In a context of insecure land rights in the Awash frontier and an outstanding border demarcation between Afar and Somali regional states, Afar and Issa rushed to establish settlements along the main road to Djibouti as a way of staking territorial claims based on physical presence (Markakis 2003; Rettberg 2010; see Chapters 3 and 8 this book for parallel developments in Isiolo and Baringo, respectively). For the Issa these settlements also perform an economic function by providing an outlet for contraband items coming from Djibouti and Somaliland. In this context, the conflict between Afar and Issa pastoralists turned more and more into a political conflict involving also the Afar and Somali Regional States. It was the contested administrative status of the road settlements inhabited by Issa that led to severe fighting in 2018–19 between pastoralists as well as regional security forces.

Pastoralists also increasingly engage in small-scale subsistence farming (mostly maize and vegetables) on their clan land along the Awash River. Individual and communal enclosures for livestock and farming have become a new phenomenon in recent years, a further indication of local grabbing to stake exclusive land claims, minimise the risk of land losses to competing groups and diversify their livelihood. The main actor in this was the new local Afar elite that emerged after 1991. They included individuals who benefited from political positions in the regional administration and from their involvement in land deals with investors mainly from highland regions (Rettberg 2010). Many profited from their own agricultural investments as well. From being a collective resource, a 'gift of Allah' to be shared, land has turned into a valuable commodity and political resource, just as it has elsewhere in dryland eastern Africa (see Elliott, Chapter 3 and Greiner, Chapter 8 this book). The accompanying monetisation and spread of predatory dynamics have eroded the social capital and the overall well-being of the Afar. In a speech to mark his coronation as the new Aussa sultan in 2011, Hanfare Ali Mirah spoke of the worsening inequalities and social divisions:

> Formerly virility, bravery and a fighting spirit were the most laudable qualities among the Afar … Today we have entered into an age where merit and reputation are based only on the wealth one has amassed and the power one has obtained by intrigue. Today the descendants

of the Afar live in poverty, their livestock decimated, and everyone knows that their agricultural lands on both sides of the river, despite an increase in the area cultivated, have shrunk in size through land grabbing ... People have no mutual trust because of their fear, poverty, lack of faith and ignorance combined. This is due to a lack of spirit of resistance and solidarity leading to the total debility of individuals. A condition in which anything can happen without anyone making the least attempt to protest.[1]

With their integration in and growing economic dependency on state structures, the Afar leadership is increasingly co-opted and tamed. This has resulted in a crisis of both representation and political legitimacy. The interests of Afar elites who have amassed significant wealth from agricultural investments as well as political budgets are in opposition to the majority of Afar livestock-keepers who are dispossessed from key rangelands and are the losers within Ethiopia's developmental state model. The lines of conflict have shifted, with the state now embedded and allied with Afar leadership and pastoral frontier capitalists. The new wealthy Afar elite, which has benefited from its association with political administration and land deals, has emerged as a type of enemy from within as perceived by the majority of disempowered and dispossessed pastoralists. The insecurity and loss of solidarity this has generated has weakened customary institutions, undermining the potential for a unified resistance and easing the way for further investment in the future.

Conclusion

A long-term perspective highlights that land investments and the appropriation of communal land have been going on since the Ethiopian state first sought to expand into the pastoral lowlands in the mid-twentieth century. Shifting geopolitical and geo-economic conditions have seen the Awash Valley evolve from a security buffer zone against Somalia's irredentist ambitions into a frontier for grabbing resource wealth to the advantage of state development aims. While frontier interventions by the imperial and the Derg regimes were mainly guided by concerns of national security and territorial integrity, the state's objective since the early 1990s has shifted to expand and deepen its resource control and political domination as part of a broader vision of economic growth and structural transformation. The periodic coercive use of state violence and the instrumentalisation of pastoral conflicts have remained central strategies to consolidate its power and enforce processes of commodification and territorialisation in the frontier.

---

[1] Official speech of the new Sultan of Aussa, Hanfare Ali Mirah, on his coronation in Assayita, 10 November 2011. From 1995–96 Hanfare had also served as president of the Afar Regional State.

A new dynamic is the emergence of capitalist social formations in the context of land dispossession through enclosures. Under these conditions, new types of pastoral conflicts in the Awash investment frontier have evolved as territorial claims multiply. Ongoing processes of social differentiation that are marked by new inclusions and exclusions challenge the assumption that pastoral society is egalitarian. These dynamics underline the need for a critical agrarian political economy perspective in the context of understanding the impacts and influences of investments in pastoral settings. Land investments, rather than being seen only in terms of external state grabs of frontier resource wealth, must also be understood as an investment strategy by new pastoral and post-pastoral capitalist elites in the frontier.

Currently, local forms of resistance do not challenge power structures, as the state has effectively created a class of domesticated capitalists among the Afar who are closely allied with the exercise of state-building – a dynamic similar to what is unfolding in South Omo (see Fana Gebresenbet, Chapter 10 this book). Rather, increasingly individualistic adaptations to a changing institutional context of conjoined state–local elite power are a reflection of a fragmented pastoral society, and one of the few options for most people to build secure lives and livelihoods. With no end in sight to the state's investment push at the frontier, further inequality, social division, violence and conflict in the Awash Valley are likely.

REFERENCES

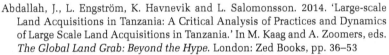

Abdallah, J., L. Engström, K. Havnevik and L. Salomonsson. 2014. 'Large-scale Land Acquisitions in Tanzania: A Critical Analysis of Practices and Dynamics of Large Scale Land Acquisitions in Tanzania.' In M. Kaag and A. Zoomers, eds. *The Global Land Grab: Beyond the Hype.* London: Zed Books, pp. 36–53

Adams, T., J-D. Gerber, M. Amacker and T. Haller. 2018. 'Who Gains from Contract Farming? Dependencies, Power Relations, and Institutional Change.' *Journal of Peasant Studies* 46(7): 1435–57

Adams, W. M. 1989. 'Dam Construction and the Degradation of Floodplain Forest on the Turkwel River, Kenya.' *Land Degradation & Development* 1(3): 189–98

Adams, W. M. 1992. *Wasting the Rain: Rivers, People and Planning in Africa.* London: Earthscan Publications

Adams, W. M. and D. M. Anderson. 1988. 'Irrigation Before Development: Indigenous and Induced Change in Agricultural Water Management in East Africa.' *African Affairs* 87: 519–35

Adepoju, A. 1995. 'Migration in Africa: An Overview.' In J. Baker and T. A. Aina, eds, *The Migration Experience in Africa.* Uppsala: Nordiska Afrikainstitutet, pp. 97–108

Adusah-Karikari, A. 2015. 'Black Gold in Ghana: Changing Livelihoods for Women in Communities Affected by Oil Production.' *Extractive Industries and Society* 2(1): 24–32

Agrica. 2011. *Sustainable African Agribusiness: Agrica Business Plan.* Dar es Salaam: Agrica

Ahmed, I. I. 1999. 'The Heritage of War and State Collapse in Somalia and Somaliland: Local-level Effects, External Interventions and Reconstruction.' *Third World Quarterly* 20(1): 113–27

Alix-Garcia, J., S. Walker, A. Bartlett, H. Onder, H. and A. Sanghi. 2018. 'Do Refugee Camps Help or Hurt Hosts? The Case of Kakuma, Kenya.' *Journal of Development Economics* 130: 66–83

Allan, T., M. Keulertz, S. Sojamo, and J. Warner, eds. 2012. *Handbook of Land and Water Grabs in Africa: Foreign direct investment and food and water security.* London: Routledge

Amanor, K. S. 2010. 'Family Values, Land Sales and Agricultural Commodification in South-Eastern Ghana.' *Africa: Journal of the International African Institute* 80(1): 104–25

Anderson, D. 2014. *Why Mpeketoni Matters: Al-Shabaab and Violence in Kenya.*

Policy Brief, Norwegian Peacebuilding Resource Centre (NOREF), www.files. ethz.ch/isn/183993/cc2dacde481e24ca3ca5eaf60e974ee9.pdf, accessed 1 July 2019

Anderson, D. M. and M. Bollig. 2016. 'Resilience and Collapse: Histories, Ecologies, Conflicts and Identities in the Baringo-Bogoria Basin, Kenya.' *Journal of Eastern African Studies* 10(1): 1–20

Anderson, D. M. and V. Broch-Due. 1999. *The Poor Are Not Us: Poverty and Pastoralism in Eastern Africa.* Oxford: James Currey

Andreff, W. 2016. 'Outward Foreign Direct Investment from BRIC countries: Comparing Strategies of Brazilian, Russian, Indian and Chinese Multinational Companies.' *The European Journal of Comparative Economics* 12(2): 79–131

Andualem Sisay. 2019. 'Kenya, Ethiopia Renew Commitment on Lapsset.' *The East African*, 1 March 2019, www.theeastafrican.co.ke/business/Kenya-and-Ethiopia-renew-commitment-on-Lapsset/2560-5005358-7cvkjf/index.html, accessed 30 July 2019

Antonelli, M., G. Siciliano, M. E. Turvani and M. C. Rulli. 2015. 'Global Investments in Agricultural Land and the Role of the EU: Drivers, Scope and Potential Impacts.' *Land Use Policy* 47: 98–111

Appadurai, A. 2013. *The Future as Cultural Fact.* London: Verso

Asebe Regassa and B. Korf. 2018. 'Post-imperial Statecraft: High-modernism and the Politics of Land Dispossession in Ethiopia's Pastoral Frontier.' *Journal of Eastern African Studies* 12(4): 613–31

Asebe Regassa, Yetebarek Hizekiel and B. Korf. 2018. '"Civilizing" the Pastoral Frontier: Land Grabbing, Dispossession and Coercive Agrarian Development in Ethiopia.' *Journal of Peasant Studies* 46(5): 935–55

Atkins Acuity. 2017. *Lamu Port City Agreed Investment Framework.* London, Nairobi: Atkins Acuity and Atkins Howard Humphreys East Africa

Aukot, E. 2003. 'It Is Better to Be a Refugee than a Turkana in Kakuma: Revisiting the Relationship between Hosts and Refugees in Kenya.' *Refuge* 21(3): 73–83

Auty, R. M. 1993. *Sustaining Development in Mineral Economies: The Resource Curse Thesis.* London, New York: Routledge

Avery, S. 2013. *What future for Lake Turkana?* Oxford: African Studies Centre, University of Oxford

Ayke, A. 2005. 'Challenges and Opportunities of "Salamago Resettlement". The Resettlement of Konso Farmers in the Ethnic Land of the Bodi Agro-Pastoralists, South-West Ethiopia.' Paper submitted to the Forum for Social Studies

Baglioni, E. and P. Gibbon. 2013. 'Land Grabbing, Large-and Small-scale Farming: What Can Evidence and Policy from 20th Century Africa Contribute to the Debate? *Third World Quarterly* 34: 1558–81

Ballard, C. and G. Banks. 2003. 'Resource Wars: The Anthropology of Mining.' *Annual Review of Anthropology* 32: 287–313

Balthasar, D. 2013. 'Somaliland's Best Kept Secret: Shrewd Politics and War Projects as Means of State-making.' *Journal of Eastern African Studies* 7(2): 218–38

Barnes, C. R. 2000. 'The Ethiopian State and its Somalia Periphery, circa 1888–1948.' PhD Thesis, University of Cambridge.

Barry, A. 2006. 'Technological Zones.' *European Journal of Social Theory* 9(2): 239–53

Bear, L., R. Burla and S. S. Puri. 2015. 'Speculation: Futures and Capitalism in India.' *Comparative Studies in of South Asia, Africa and the Middle East* 35(3): 387–91

Beaujard, P. and S. Fee. 2005. 'The Indian Ocean in Eurasian and African World-Systems Before the Sixteenth Century.' *Journal of World History* 16(4): 411–65

Becker, M., M. Alvarez, G. Heller, P. Leparmarai, D. Maina, I. Malombe, M. Bollig and H. J. Vehrs. 2016. 'Land-use Changes and the Invasion Dynamics of Shrubs in Baringo.' *Journal of Eastern African Studies* 10(1): 111–29

BEE. 2017. 'White Paper on the Bagamoyo EcoEnergy Project in Tanzania.' Bagamoyo EcoEnergy Ltd

Behnke, R. and C. Kerven. 2013. 'Counting the Costs: Replacing Pastoralism with Irrigated Agriculture in the Awash Valley.' In A. Catley, J. Lind and I. Scoones, eds, *Pastoralism and Development in Africa: Dynamic Changes at the Margins*. Abingdon: Routledge

Behnke, R. H., I. Scoones and C. Kerven, eds. 1993. *Range Ecology at Disequilibrium*. London: Overseas Development Institute

Behrends, A., S. P. Reyna and G. Schlee. 2011. *Crude Domination: An Anthropology of Oil*. New York and Oxford: Berghahn

Beja, P. 2010. 'Lamu-Shella Sand Dunes' Bewitching Effect.' *Standard Digital*, 6 May, www.standardmedia.co.ke/business/article/2000009083/lamu-shella-sand-dunes-bewitching-effect, accessed 1 July 2019

Beja, P. 2018. 'NLC in a Spot Over Lapsset Land.' *Standard Digital*, 23 February, www.standardmedia.co.ke/article/2000192608/nlc-in-a-spot-over-lapsset-land, accessed 1 July 2019

Benson, P. and S. Kirsch, eds. 2010. 'Entry Points into the Ethnography of Capitalism.' *Dialectical Anthropology* 34 (1): 45–48

Bergius, M. 2014. 'Expanding the Corporate Food Regime: The Southern Agricultural Growth Corridor of Tanzania.' Master's thesis, Noragric, Norwegian University of Life Sciences

Bergius, M., T. A. Benjaminsen and M. Widgren. 2018. 'Green Economy, Scandinavian Investments and Agricultural Modernization in Tanzania.' *Journal of Peasant Studies* 45(4): 825–52

Berry, S. 2002 'Debating the Land Question in Africa.' *Comparative Studies in Society and History* 44(4): 638–68

Betts, A., R. Geervliet, C. MacPherson, N. Omata, C. Rodgers and O. Stercket. 2018. *Self-Reliance in Kalobeyei? Socio-Economic Outcomes for Refugees in North-West Kenya*. Oxford: Refugees Study Centre, Oxford Department of International Development, University of Oxford

Blache, A. 2018. 'Entre "développement" et conservation des aires naturelles: jeux de pouvoir, conflits d'usage et marginalisation dans la vallée du Kilombero en Tanzanie.' *Belgeo* 2, http://journals.openedition.org/belgeo/27419, accessed 22 July 2019

Boamah, F. 2014. 'How and Why Chiefs Formalise Land Use in Recent Times: The Politics of Land Dispossession Through Biofuels Investments in Ghana.' *Review of African Political Economy* 41(141): 406–23

Boas, M. and K. Dunn. 2013. *Politics of Origins in Africa: Autochthony, Citizenship and Conflict*. London, New York: Zed Books.

Bocha, G. 2014. 'Company Used Lamu Land to Get Sh1 Billion Bank Loan.' *Daily Nation*, 2 August, www.nation.co.ke/news/Company-used-Lamu-land-to-get-Sh1-billion-bank-loan/1056-2406700-112io09z/index.html, accessed 1 July 2019

Bollig, M. 1993. 'Intra-and Interethnic Conflict in Northwest Kenya: A Multicausal Analysis of Conflict Behaviour.' *Anthropos* 88(1/3): 176–84

Bollig, M. 2016. 'Adaptive Cycles in the Savannah: Pastoral Specialization and

Diversification in Northern Kenya.' *Journal of Eastern African Studies* 10(1): 21–44

Bollig, M., C. Greiner and M. Österle. 2014. 'Inscribing Identity and Agency on the Landscape: Of Pathways, Places, and the Transition of the Public Sphere in East Pokot, Kenya.' *African Studies Review* 57(3): 55–78

Bondestam, L. 1974. 'People and Capitalism in the North-Eastern Lowlands of Ethiopia.' *Journal of Modern African Studies* 12(3): 423–39

Boone, C. 2012. 'Land Conflict and Distributive Politics in Kenya.' *African Studies Review* 55(1): 75–103

Boone, C. 2014. *Property and Political Order in Africa: Land Rights and the Structure of Politics*. Cambridge: Cambridge University Press

Borras, S. M., Jr and J. Franco. 2013. 'Global Land Grabbing and Political Reactions "From Below"'. *Third World Quarterly* 34(9): 1723–47

Borras S. M., Jr and J. Franco. 2015. 'Global Land Grabbing and Political Reactions "From Below".' In M. Edelman, C. Oya and S. M. Borras Jr., eds, *Global Land Grabs: Historical Processes, Theoretical and Methodological Implications and Current Trajectories*. New York: Routledge

Borras, S. M., Jr, R. Hall, I. Scoones, B. White and W. Wolford. 2011. 'Towards a Better Understanding of Global Land Grabbing: An Editorial Introduction. *Journal of Peasant Studies* 38(2): 209–16

Borras, S. M., Jr, E. N. Mills, P. Seufert, S. Backes, D. Fyfe, R. Herre and L. Michéle. 2019. 'Transnational Land Investment Web: Land Grabs, TNCs, and the Challenge of Global Governance.' *Globalizations*: 1–21

Bose, S. 2009. *A Hundred Horizons: The Indian Ocean in the Age of Global Empire*. Cambridge, MA: Harvard University Press

Boye, S. R. 2007. 'Land Ownership and Conflicts in Isiolo District, Kenya.' Master's thesis, Norwegian University of Life Sciences

Boye, S. R. and R. Kaarhus. 2011. 'Competing Claims and Contested Boundaries: Legitimating Land Rights in Isiolo District, Northern Kenya.' *Africa Spectrum* 46(2): 99–124

Bradbury, M. 2008. *Becoming Somaliland*. African Issues. London: James Currey

Bradbury, M., A. Y. Abokor and H. A. Yusuf. 2003. 'Somaliland: Choosing Politics over Violence.' *Review of African Political Economy* 30(97): 455–78

Branch, D. 2011. *Kenya: Between Hope and Despair, 1963–2011*. New Haven CT: Yale University Press

Bräutigam, D. and H. Zhang. 2013. 'Green Dreams: Myth and Reality in China's Agricultural Investment in Africa.' *Third World Quarterly* 34(9): 1676–96

BRN (Big Results Now). 2013. *Tanzania Development, Vision 2025, Big Results Now: National Key Result Area: Agriculture Lab.* Dar es Salaam: Government of Tanzania

Broch-Due, V. 2000. 'A Proper Cultivation of Peoples: The Colonial Reconfiguration of Pastoral Tribes and Places in Kenya.' In V. Broch-Due and R. A. Schroeder, eds, *Producing Nature and Poverty in Africa*. Uppsala: Nordiska Afrikaininstitutet

Browne, A. J. 2015. *LAPSSET: The History and Politics of an Eastern African Megaproject*. London, Nairobi: Rift Valley Institute

Buffavand, L. 2016. 'The Land Does Not Like Them: Contesting Dispossession in Cosmological Terms in Mela, South-West Ethiopia.' *Journal of Eastern African Studies* 10(3): 476–93

Buffavand, L. 2017. 'Vanishing Stones and the Hovering Giraffe: Identity, Land and the Divine in Mela, South-West Ethiopia.' PhD thesis, Martin Luther University, Wittenberg

Bulley, D. 2014. 'Inside the Tent: Community and Government in Refugee Camps.' *Security Dialogue* 45: 63–80

Cabral, L., A. Shankland, A. Favareto and A. Costa Vaz. 2013. 'Brazil–Africa Agricultural Cooperation Encounters: Drivers, Narratives and Imaginaries of Africa and Development.' *IDS Bulletin* 44(4): 53–68

Cannon, B. and Rossiter, A. 2017. 'Ethiopia, Berbera Port and the Shifting Balance of Power in the Horn of Africa.' *Rising Powers Quarterly* 2(4): 7–29

Caravani, M. 2018. '"De-pastoralisation" in Uganda's Northeast: From Livelihoods Diversification to Social Differentiation.' *Journal of Peasant Studies*: 1–24

Carmody, P. 2013. 'A Global Enclosure: The Geo-logics of Indian Agro-investments in Africa.' *Capitalism Nature Socialism* 24(1): 84–103

Carmody, P. and D. Taylor. 2016. 'Globalization, Land Grabbing, and the Present-day Colonial State in Uganda: Ecolonization and its Impacts.' *The Journal of Environment & Development* 25(1): 100–126

Carrier, N. and H. H. Kochore. 2014. 'Navigating Ethnicity and Electoral Politics in Northern Kenya: The Case of the 2013 Election.' *Journal of Eastern African Studies* 8(1): 135–52

Catley, A. and Yacob Aklilu. 2013. 'Moving Up or Moving Out? Commercialization, Growth and Destitution in Pastoralist Areas.' In A. Catley, J. Lind and I. Scoones, eds, *Pastoralism and Development in Africa: Dynamic Changes at the Margins.* Abingdon: Routledge

Catley, A., J. Lind and I. Scoones. 2013a. 'Development at the Margins: Pastoralism in the Horn of Africa.' In A. Catley, J. Lind and I. Scoones, eds, *Pastoralism and Development in Africa: Dynamic Changes at the Margins.* Abingdon: Routledge

Catley, A., J. Lind and I. Scoones, eds. 2013b. *Pastoralism and Development in Africa: Dynamic Change at the Margins.* Abingdon: Routledge

Chachage, C. 2010. *Land Acquisition and Accumulation in Tanzania: The Case of Morogoro, Iringa and Pwani Regions.* Dar es Salaam: PELUM

Chambers, R. 1986. 'Hidden Losers? The Impact of Rural Refugees and Refugee Programs on Poorer Hosts.' *International Migration Review* 20(74): 245–63

Chimhowu, A. and P. Woodhouse. 2006. 'Customary vs Private Property Rights? Dynamics and Trajectories of Vernacular Land Markets in Sub-Saharan Africa.' *Journal of Agrarian Change* 6(3): 346–71

Chinigo, D. 2014. 'Decentralisation and Agrarian Transformation in Ethiopia: Extending the Power of the Federal State.' *Critical African Studies* 6(1): 40–56

Chinsinga, B. 2017. 'The Green Belt Initiative, Politics and Sugar Production in Malawi.' *Journal of Southern African Studies* 43(3): 501–15

Chome, N. 2020 (Forthcoming). 'Land, Livelihoods and Belonging: Negotiating Change and Anticipating LAPSSET in Kenya's Lamu County.' *Journal of Eastern African Studies* 14(2)

Chome, N., E. Gonçalves, I. Scoones and E. Sulle. 2020 (Forthcoming). 'Demonstration, Anticipation and Contestation: The Political Economy of Development Corridors and Agrarian Change in Eastern Africa.' *Journal of Eastern African Studies* 14(2)

Chung, Y. B. 2017. 'Engendering the New Enclosures: Development, Involuntary Resettlement and the Struggles for Social Reproduction in Coastal Tanzania.' *Development and Change* 48(1), 98–120

Citizen, The. 2009. 'Tanzania: Govt Orders 2000 People Out of Farm.' *The Citizen,*

19 October 2009, https://allafrica.com/stories/200910190372.html, accessed 15 November 2015

Clapp, J. 2014. 'Financialization, Distance and Global Food Politics.' *Journal of Peasant Studies* 41(5): 797–814

Clapp, J. and S. R. Isakson. 2018. *Speculative Harvests*. Black Point, NS: Fernwood

Coleman, C. 2015. 'Letter from Carter Coleman, CEO Agrica Ltd, to Anuradha Mitta, Oakland Institute, and Glen Tyler, Greenpeace Africa.' 26 May 2015, www.oaklandinstitute.org/sites/oaklandinstitute.org/files/Agrica%27s_Response_to_Oakland_Institute_Greenpeace_Africa-May-29-2015.pdf, accessed 4 July 2019

Comaroff, J. L. and J. Comaroff. 2009. *Ethnicity, Inc.* Chicago: University of Chicago Press

Cormack, Z. and A. Kurewa. 2018. 'The Changing Value of Land in Northern Kenya: The Case of Lake Turkana Wind Power.' *Critical African Studies* 10(1): 89–107

Cornwall, A. and C. Nyamu-Musembi, C. 2004. 'Putting the "Rights-Based Approach" to Development into Perspective.' *Third World Quarterly* 25(8): 1415–37

Corson, C. 2011. 'Territorialisation, Enclosure and Neoliberalism: Non-State Influence in Struggles over Madagascar's Forests.' *Journal of Peasant Studies* 38(4): 703–26

Cossins, N. J. 1973. 'Green Heart of a Dying Land: A Study of the New Cotton Wealth of the Old Afar Sultanate of Aussa.' Report for Hunting Technical Services. Addis Ababa

Costagli, R., L. M. Godiah and F. Wanyoike. 2017. 'A Rapid Appraisal of the Yemeni End-Market for Somali Livestock Exporters.' ILRI Discussion Paper 34. Nairobi: International Livestock Research Institute

Côte, M. and B. Korf. 2018. 'Making Concessions: Extractive Enclaves, Entangled Capitalism and Regulative Pluralism at the Gold Mining Frontier in Burkina Faso.' *World Development* 101: 466–76

Cotula, L. 2013. *The Great African Land Grab? Agricultural Investments and the Global Food System*. New York, London: Zed Books

Cotula, L., C. Oya, E. A. Codjoe, A. Eid, M. Kakraba-Ampeh, J. Keeley, A. L. Kidewa, M. Makwarimba, W. M. Seide and W. O. Nasha. 2014. 'Testing Claims about Large Land Deals in Africa: Findings from a Multi-Country Study.' *Journal of Development Studies* 50: 903–25

Coulson, A. 2015. 'Small-scale and Large-scale Agriculture: Tanzanian Experiences.' In M. Ståhl, ed., *Looking Back, Looking Ahead: Land, Agriculture and Society in East Africa. A Festschrift for Kjell Havnevik.* Uppsala: The Nordic Africa Institute, pp. 44–73

Cousins, B., S. M. Borras Jr, S. Sauer and J. Ye. 2018. 'BRICS, Middle-income Countries (MICs), and Global Agrarian Transformations: Internal Dynamics, Regional Trends, and International Implications.' *Globalizations* 15(1):1–11

Cross, J. 2014. *Dream Zones: Anticipating Capitalism and Development in India.* London: Pluto Press

D'Arcy, M. and A. Cornell. 2016. 'Devolution and Corruption in Kenya: Everyone's Turn to Eat?' *African Affairs* 115(459): 246–73

Dahl, G. 1979. *Suffering Grass: Subsistence and Society of Waso Borana.* Stockholm: Department of Social Anthropology, University of Stockholm

Daily Nation, The. 2013a. 'Hunting Ban Fails to End Bloodbath.' 26 August 2013

Daily Nation, The. 2013b. 'Magugu Mastered Art of Political Survival.' 16 September 2013

Daniel, S. 2012. 'Situating Private Equity Capital in the Land Grab Debate.' *Journal of Peasant Studies* 39(3–4): 703–29

De Grassi, A. and J. S. Ovadia. 2017. 'Trajectories of Large-scale Land Acquisition Dynamics in Angola: Diversity, Histories, and Implications for the Political Economy of Development in Africa.' *Land Use Policy* 67: 115–25

De Haan, C., T. S. Van Veen, B. Brandenburg, J. Gauthier, F. Le Gall, R. Mearns and M. Simeon. 2001. *Livestock Development: Implications on Rural Poverty, the Environment, and Global Food Security*. Washington, D.C.:The World Bank

De Lapérouse, P. 2012. *Case Studies on Private Investments in Farmland and Agricultural Infrastructure*. Danvers MA: High Quest Partners

De Montclos, M. A. P. and P. M. Kagwanja. 2000. 'Refugee Camps or Cities? The Socio-economic Dynamics of the Dadaab and Kakuma Camps in Northern Kenya.' *Journal of Refugee Studies* 13(2): 205–22.

Deng, D. K. 2011. '"Land Belongs to the Community": Demystifying the "Global Land Grab" in Southern Sudan.' LDPI Working Paper 4. The Hague: Land Deals Politics Initiative

Dessalegn Rahmato. 2008. *The Peasant and the State: Studies in Agrarian Change in Ethiopia 1950s–2000s*. Addis Ababa: Addis Ababa University Press

Devereux, S. 2006. 'Vulnerable Livelihoods in Somali Region, Ethiopia.' Research Report no. 57. Brighton: Institute of Development Studies

Dolan, C. and D. Rajak, eds. 2016. *The Anthropology of Corporate Social Responsibility*. Oxford, New York: Berghahn Books

Donelli, F. 2017. 'A Hybrid Actor in the Horn of Africa: An Analysis of Turkey's Involvement in Somalia.' In A. Ylönen and J. Záhoŕík, eds, *The Horn of Africa Since the 1960s: Local and International Politics Intertwined*. Abingdon: Taylor & Francis.

Dorward, A., S. Anderson, Y. N. Bernal, E. S. Vera, J. Rushton, J. Pattison and R. Paz. 2009. 'Hanging In, Stepping Up and Stepping Out: Livelihood Aspirations and Strategies of the Poor.' *Development in Practice* 19(2): 240–47

Drew, J. A. 2018. 'Pastoralism in the Shadow of a Windfarm: An Ethnography of People, Places and Belonging in Northern Kenya.' PhD thesis, University of Sussex

Dua, J. 2013. 'A Sea of Trade and a Sea of Fish: Piracy and Protection in the Western Indian Ocean.' *Journal of Eastern African Studies* 7(2): 353–70

Duffy, R. 2000. 'Shadow Players: Ecotourism Development, Corruption and State Politics in Belize.' *Third World Quarterly* 21(3): 549–65

East Africa Business Week. 2019a. 'Bureau to Regulate Livestock Export from Somaliland to UAE.' 29 April 2019, www.busiweek.com/bureau-to-regulate-livestock-export-from-somaliland-to-uae, accessed 9 July 2019

East Africa Business Week. 2019b. 'Works Start on Dual Carriage Linking Somali-land, Ethiopia.' 1 March 2019, www.busiweek.com/works-start-on-dual-carriage-linking-somaliland-ethiopia, accessed 9 July 2019

Economist, The. 2015. 'A Glimpse of Africa's Future: Oil in the Cradle of Mankind.' 11 July 2015Edelman, M., C. Oya and S. M. Borras Jr. 2013. *Global Land Grabs: Historical Processes, Theoretical and Methodological Implications and Current Trajectories*. London: Taylor & Francis

Edelman, M., R. Hall, S. M. Borras Jr, I. Scoones, B. White and W. Wolford, eds. 2017. *Global Land Grabbing and Political Reactions 'from Below'*. London: Routledge

EE (Eco Energy). 2010. *Project Information Memorandum in Respect of Bagamoyo*

Eco Energy Ltd: A Greenfield Agro-Energy Project in Tanzania. Dar es Salaam: Eco Energy

Elliott, H. 2016. 'Planning, Property and Plots at the Gateway to Kenya's "New Frontier".' *Journal of Eastern African Studies* 10(3): 511–29

Elliott, H. 2018. 'Anticipating Plots: (Re)Making Property, Futures and Town at the Gateway to Kenya's "New Frontier".' PhD thesis, University of Copenhagen

Emmenegger, R., K. Sibilo and T. Hagmann. 2011. 'Decentralisation to the Household: Expansion and Limits of State Power in Rural Oromiya.' *Journal of Eastern African Studies* 5(4): 733–54

ENATA (Environmental Association of Tanzania) and R. A. Diaz-Chavez. 2009. 'Report for Environmental Impact Statement: Redevelopment of Rice & Bean Cropping, Mngeta Farm, Kilombero Valley.' Submitted to National Environment Management Council, Dar es Salaam, www.oaklandinstitute.org/sites/oaklandinstitute.org/files/KPL_EIA-Sept.-09.pdf, accessed 22 July 2019

Engström, L. 2018. 'Development Delayed: Exploring the Failure of a Large-scale Agricultural Investment in Tanzania to Deliver Promised Outcomes.' Doctoral thesis, Swedish University for Agricultural Sciences

Engström, L. and F. Hajdu. 2018. 'Conjuring "Win-World": Resilient Development Narratives in a Large-Scale Agro-Investment in Tanzania.' *Journal of Development Studies* 55(6): 1201–20

Enns, C. 2018. 'Mobilizing Research on Africa's Development Corridors.' *Geoforum* 88: 105–108

Enns, C. 2019. 'Infrastructure Projects and Rural Politics in Northern Kenya: The Use of Divergent Expertise to Negotiate the Terms of Land Deals for Transport Infrastructure.' *Journal of Peasant Studies* 46(2): 358–76

Enns, C., B. Bersaglio and A. Sneyd. 2019. 'Fixing Extraction Through Conservation: On Crises, Fixes and the Production of Shared Value and Threat.' *Environment and Planning E: Nature and Space* 2(4): 967–88

Eriksen, S. and J. Lind. 2009. 'Adaptation as a Political Process: Adjusting to Drought and Conflict in Kenya's Drylands.' *Environmental Management* 43(5): 817–35

Escobar, A. 1993. *Encountering Development: The Making and Unmaking of the Third World*, Princeton NJ: Princeton University Press

Fairbairn, M. 2014. '"Like Gold with Yield": Evolving Intersections between Farmland and Finance.' *Journal of Peasant Studies* 41(5–6): 777–96

Fairhead, J., M. Leach and I. Scoones. 2012. 'Green Grabbing: A New Appropriation of Nature?' *Journal of Peasant Studies* 39, 237–61

Falk Moore, S. 1973. 'Law and Social Change: The Semi-Autonomous Social Field as an Appropriate Subject of Study.' *Law & Society Review* 7(4): 719–46

Fana Gebresenbet. 2016. 'Land Acquisitions, the Politics of Dispossession, and State-Remaking in Gambella, Western Ethiopia.' *Africa Spectrum* 51(1): 5–28

Ferguson, J. 2005. 'Seeing Like an Oil Company: Space, Security, and Global Capital in Neoliberal Africa.' *American Anthropologist* 107(3): 377–82

Ferguson, J. 2015. *Give a Man a Fish: Reflections on the New Politics of Distribution.* Durham NC, London: Duke University Press

Ferry, E. E. and M. E. Limbert. 2008. *Timely Assets: The Politics of Resources and their Temporalities.* Santa Fe NM: School for Advanced Research Press

Flintan, F., B. Tache and A. Eid. 2011. *Rangeland Fragmentation in Traditional Grazing Areas and Its Impact on Drought Resilience of Pastoral Communities: Lessons from Borana, Oromia and Harshin, Somali Regional States, Ethiopia.*

Oxford: Oxfam

Fratkin, E. 2013. 'Seeking Alternative Livelihoods in Pastoral Areas.' In A. Catley, J. Lind and I. Scoones, eds, *Pastoralism and Development in Africa: Dynamic Change at the Margins.* Abingdon: Routledge, pp.197–205

Fratkin, E. 2014. 'Ethiopia's Pastoralist Policies: Development, Displacement and Resettlement.' *Nomadic Peoples* 18(1): 94–114

Fratkin, E. and E. A. Roth, eds. 2006. *As Pastoralists Settle: Social, Health, and Economic Consequences of Pastoral Sedentarisation in Marsabit District, Kenya.* New York: Kluwer; Berlin: Springer Science and Business Media

Friedman, J. 2011. 'Oiling the Race to the Bottom.' In A. Behrends, S. P. Reyna and G. Schlee, eds, *Crude Domination: An Anthropology of Oil.* New York and Oxford: Berghahn, pp. 30–45

Gaani, M. X. 2002. *Regulating the Livestock Economy of Somaliland.* Hargeisa: Academy for Peace and Development

Galaty, J. G. 2005. 'Double-voiced Violence in Kenya.' In V. Broch-Due, ed., *Violence and Belonging: The Quest for Identity in Post-colonial Africa.* Abingdon: Routledge, pp. 173–94

Galaty, J. G. 2014. '"Unused" Land and Unfulfilled Promises: Justifications for Displacing Communities in East Africa.' *Nomadic Peoples* 18(1): 80–93

Galaty, J. G. and P. Bonte, eds. 1991. *Herders, Warriors and Traders: Pastoralism in Africa.* Boulder CO: Westview Press.

Gardner, K. 2012. *Discordant Development: Global Capitalism and the Struggle for Connection in Bangladesh.* London: Pluto

Geenen, S. and J. Verweijen. 2017. 'Explaining Fragmented and Fluid Mobilization in Gold Mining Concessions in Eastern Democratic Republic of the Congo.' *Extractive Industries and Society* 4(4): 758–65

Geiger, D. ed. 2008. *Frontier Encounters: Indigenous Communities and Settlers in Asia and Latin America.* Book 120. Copenhagen: International Work Group for Indigenous Affairs

Geiger, D. 2009. *Turner in the Tropics: The Frontier Concept Revisited.* Luzern: Universität Luzern

Goldschmidt, W. 1971. 'Independence as an Element in Pastoral Social Systems.' *Anthropological Quarterly* 3: 132–42

Goldsmith, P. 2012. 'Tana-Delta Clashes Do Not Fit the Farmer-Herder Competition for Resource Narrative.' *The East African*, 15 September, www.theeastafrican.co.ke/oped/comment/Tana-clashes-do-not-fit-farmer-herder-competition/434750-1508556-jo99odz/index.html, accessed 1 July 2019

Goodhand, J. 2018. 'The Centrality of Margins: The Political Economy of Conflict and Development in Borderlands.' Working Paper 2, presented at 'Borderlands, Brokers and Peacebuilding: War to Peace Transitions Viewed from the Margins', 23 May 2018. London: School of Oriental and African Studies

Gravesen, M. 2018. 'Negotiating Access to Land in a Contested Environment: Opposing Claims and Land-use Fragmentation in Western Laikipia, Kenya.' PhD thesis, University of Cologne

Greco, E. 2015. 'Local Politics of Land and the Restructuring of Rice Farming Areas: A Comparative Study of Tanzania and Uganda.' Working Paper 12. Manchester: Leverhulme Centre for the Study of Value, University of Manchester

Greiner, C. 2012. 'Unexpected Consequences: Wildlife Conservation and Territorial Conflict in Northern Kenya.' *Human Ecology* 40(3): 415–25

Greiner, C. 2013. 'Guns, Land and Votes: Cattle Rustling and the Politics of

Boundary (re)making in Northern Kenya.' *African Affairs* 112(447): 216–37

Greiner, C. 2016. 'Land-use Change, Territorial Restructuring, and Economies of Anticipation in Dryland Kenya.' *Journal of Eastern African Studies* 10(3): 530–47

Greiner, C. 2017. 'Pastoralism and Land Tenure Change in Kenya: The Failure of Customary Institutions.' *Development and Change* 48(1): 78–97

Greiner, C. and I. Mwaka. 2016. 'Agricultural Change at the Margins: Adaptation and Intensification in a Kenyan Dryland.' *Journal of Eastern African Studies* 10(1): 130–49

Guyer, J. I., E. F. Lambin, L. Cliggett, P. Walker, K. Amanor, T. Bassett, E. Colson, R. Hay, K. Homewood, O. Linares, O. Pabi, P. Peters, T. Scudder, M. Turner and J. Unruh. 2007. 'Temporal Heterogeneity in the Study of African Land Use: Interdisciplinary Collaboration between Anthropology, Human Geography and Remote Sensing.' *Human Ecology* 35: 3–17

Hagmann, T. and Alemmaya Mulugeta. 2008. 'Pastoral Conflicts and State-Building in the Ethiopian Lowlands.' *Afrika Spectrum* 43(1): 19–37

Hagmann, T. and B. Korf. 2012. 'Agamben in the Ogaden: Violence and Sovereignty in the Ethiopian-Somali Frontier.' *Political Geography* 31(4): 205–14

Hagmann, T. and D. Péclard. 2010. 'Negotiating Statehood: Dynamics of Power and Domination in Africa.' *Development and Change* 41(4): 539–62

Hagmann, T. and F. Stepputat. 2019. 'Politics of Circulation: The Makings of the Berbera Corridor in Somali East Africa.' *Environment and Planning D: Society and Space* 37(5): 794–813

Hall, D. 2012. 'Rethinking Primitive Accumulation: Theoretical Tensions and Rural Southeast Asian Complexities.' *Antipode* 44: 1188–1208

Hall, D. 2013. 'Primitive Accumulation, Accumulation by Dispossession and the Global Land Grab.' *Third World Quarterly* 34: 1582–1604

Hall, R. and B. Cousins. 2018. 'Exporting Contradictions: the Expansion of South African Agrarian Capital within Africa.' *Globalizations* 15(1): 12–31

Hall, R., M. Edelman, S. M. Borras Jr, I. Scoones, B. White and W. Wolford. 2015a. 'Resistance, Acquiescence or Incorporation? An Introduction to Land Grabbing and Political Reactions "from below".' *Journal of Peasant Studies* 42(3–4): 467–88

Hall, R., J. Gausi, P. Matondi, T. Muduva, C. Nhancale, D. Phiri and P. Zamchiya. 2015b. *Large-scale Land Deals in Southern Africa: Voices of the People.* Cape Town: Institute for Poverty, Land and Agrarian Studies, University of the Western Cape

Hall, R., I. Scoones and D. Tsikata. 2015c. *Africa's Land Rush: Rural Livelihoods & Agrarian Change.* Woodbridge: James Currey

Hall, R., I. Scoones and D. Tsikata. 2017. 'Plantations, Outgrowers and Commercial Farming in Africa: Agricultural Commercialisation and Implications for Agrarian Change.' *Journal of Peasant Studies* 44(3): 515–37

Hangoolnews. 2016. 'Magaalada Berbera Oo Maanta Mudaharaad Ku Waabariisatay+Taayiro Lagu Gubay Wadooyinka Dhex Mara Magaalada Iyo Waxa Uu Daarnaa' [demonstration in Berbera against DP World], 20 June 2016, http://hangoolnews.com/2016/06/20/magaalada-berbera-oo-maanta-mudaha-raad-ku-waabariisataytaayiro-lagu-gubay-wadooyinka-dhex-mara-magaalada-iyo-waxa-uu-daarnaa, accessed 9 July 2019

Harrison, E. 2018. 'Engineering change? The Idea of "the Scheme" in African Irrigation.' *World Development* 111 (November): 246–55

Harvey, D. 2003. *The New Imperialism*. Oxford: Oxford University Press

Hetherington, K. 2011. *Guerrilla Auditors: The Politics of Transparency in Neoliberal Paraguay*. Durham NC: Duke University Press

Hjort, A. 1979. *Savanna Town: Rural Ties and Urban Opportunities in Northern Kenya*. Stockholm: Department of Social Anthropology, University of Stockholm

Hodge, G. A. and C. Greve. 2007. 'Public–Private Partnerships: An International Performance Review.' *Public Administration Review* 67, 545–58

Hodgson, D. L. 2000. *Rethinking Pastoralism in Africa*. Oxford: James Currey

Hogg, R. 1983. 'Irrigation Agriculture and Pastoral Development: A Lesson from Kenya.' *Development and Change* 14: 577–91

Hogg, R. 1986. 'The New Pastoralism: Poverty and Dependency in Northern Kenya.' *Africa* 56(3): 319–33

Hogg, R. 1987a. 'Development in Kenya: Drought, Desertification and Food Scarcity.' *African Affairs* 86(342): 47–58

Hogg, R. 1987b. 'Settlement, Pastoralism and the Commons: The Ideology and Practice of Irrigation Development in Northern Kenya.' In D. Anderson and R. Grove, eds, *Conservation in Africa: People, Policies and Practice*. Cambridge: Cambridge University Press

Homewood, K., P. Kristjanson and P. Trench. 2009. *Staying Maasai? Livelihoods, Conservation and Development in East African Rangelands*. New York: Springer

Hopma, J. 2015. '"Planning in the Wind": The Failed Jordanian Agricultural Investments in Sudan.' *Canadian Journal of Development Studies/Revue canadienne d'études du développement* 36(2): 196–207

Hovil, L. 2007. 'Self-settled Refugees in Uganda: An Alternative Approach to Displacement?' *Journal of Refugee Studies* 20: 599–620

Huliaras, A. 2002. 'The Viability of Somaliland: Internal Constraints and Regional Geopolitics.' *Journal of Contemporary African Studies* 20(2): 157–82

Hyndman, J. 2000. *Managing Displacement: Refugees and the Politics of Humanitarianism*. Minneapolis MN: University of Minnesota Press

Hyndman, J. and W. Giles. 2011. 'Waiting for What? The Feminization of Asylum in Protracted Situations.' *Gender, Place and Culture* 18: 361–79

IFC (International Finance Corporation). 2018. *Kakuma as a Marketplace*. Washington DC: IFC

IGIWA (International Work Group for Indigenous Affairs). 2013. 'Forced Evictions of Pastoralists in Kilombero and Ulanga Districts in Morogoro Region in Tanzania.' *IGIWA Brief*, June

Ilado, P. 2014. 'Uhuru Recovers 500,000 Acres of Lamu Land.' *The Star*, 1 August, www.the-star.co.ke/news/2014/08/01/uhuru-recovers-500000-acres-of-lamu-land_c980567, accessed 25 November 2018

International Crisis Group. 2019. 'Intra-Gulf Competition in Africa's Horn: Lessening the Impact.' Middle East Report 206. Brussels: International Crisis Group, www.crisisgroup.org/middle-east-north-africa/gulf-and-arabian-peninsula/206-intra-gulf-competition-africas-horn-lessening-impact, accessed 4 November 2019

ITV Tanzania. 2016. *Zaidi ya hekari za wakulima wa mpunga Kilombero zimeharibiwa na mwekezaji*, www.youtube.com/watch?v=kg6o3XZ5ZO4, 28 February 2016, accessed 8 October 2017

Jacobsen, K. 1997. 'Refugees' Environmental Impact: The Effect of Patterns of Settlement.' *Journal of Refugee Studies* 10: 19–36

Jacobsen, K. 2002. 'Can Refugees Benefit the State? Refugee Resources and African

Statebuilding.' *Journal of Modern African Studies* 40(4): 577–96

James, D. 2011. 'The Return of the Broker: Consensus, Hierarchy and Choice in South African Land Reform.' *Journal of the Royal Anthropological Institute* 17(2): 318–38

Jansen, B. J. 2018. *Kakuma Refugee Camp: Humanitarian Urbanism in Kenya's Accidental City*. London: Zed Books

Jenkins, S. 2012. 'Ethnicity, Violence and the Immigrant Guest-Metaphor in Kenya.' *African Affairs* 111(445): 576–96

Jhazbhay, I. 2008. 'Somaliland's Post-War Reconstruction: Rubble to Rebuilding.' *International Journal of African Renaissance Studies* 3(1): 59–93

Johnson, O. W. and M. Ogeya. 2018. *Risky Business: Developing Geothermal Power in Kenya*. SEI Discussion Brief. Stockholm: Stockholm Environment Institute

Kamski, B. 2016. 'The Kuraz Sugar Development Project (KSDP): Between "Sweet Vision" and Mounting Challenges.' *Journal of Eastern African Studies* 10(3): 568–80

Kanyinga, K. 2009. 'The Legacy of the White Highlands: Land Rights, Ethnicity and the Post-2007 Election Violence in Kenya.' *Journal of Contemporary African Studies* 27(3): 325–44

Kasuku, S. 2013. 'Lamu Port–South Sudan–Ethiopia Transport (LAPSSET) Corridor Project: Building Africa's Transformative and Game Changer Infrastructure to Deliver a Just and Prosperous Kenya.' Presented at Kenya–UK Investment Conference, London, 3 December 2013, http://kenyagreece.com/sites/default/files/lapsset-project-presentation.pdf, accessed 1 July 2019

Kasuku, S. 2015. 'LAPSSET Corridor Program.' PowerPoint Presentation, Africa Infrastructure and Power Forum, Beijing, 15 October 2015, www.energynet.co.uk/webfm_send/1005, accessed 30 July 2019

Kazungu, K. 2018. 'Lamu Fishermen Laud Sh1.7bn Pay Order.' *Daily Nation*, 2 May, https://mobile.nation.co.ke/counties/Fishermen-happy-with-new-Sh1-76bn-award/1950480-4541314-r037ju/index.html, accessed 1 July 2019

Keene, S., M. Walsh-Dilley, W. Wolford and C. Geisler. 2015. 'A View From the Top: Examining Elites in Large-scale Land Deals.' *Canadian Journal of Development Studies/Revue canadienne d'études du développement* 36(2): 131–46

Kenya National Bureau of Statistics. 2018. *Kenya Integrated Household Budget Survey*, March 2018, http://54.213.151.253/nada/index.php/catalog/KIHBS, accessed 25 November 2018

Kenya News Agency. 2017. 'Conflict Looms over Revocation of Titles.' Kenya News Agency, 14 April, http://kenyanewsagency.go.ke/en/conflict-looms-over-revocation-of-lamu-titles, accessed 27 November 2018

Keulertz, M. 2012. 'Drivers and Actors in Large-scale Farmland Acquisitions in Sudan.' LDPI Working Paper 10. The Hague: Land Deals Politics Initiative

Keulertz, M. 2016. 'Inward Investment in Sudan: The Case of Qatar.' In E. Sandstrom, A. Jagerskog and T. Oestigaard, eds, *Land and Hydropolitics in the Nile River Basin*. Abingdon: Routledge, pp. 89–104

Keulertz, M. and E. Woertz. 2016. 'States as Actors in International Agro-Investments.' In C. Gironde, C. Golay and P. Messerli, eds, *Large-Scale Land Acquisitions: Focus on South-East Asia*. Leiden: Brill Nijhoff, pp. 30–52

Keulertz, M. and E. Woertz, eds. 2017. *The Water-Energy-Food Nexus in the Middle East and North Africa*. Abingdon: Routledge

Kibreab, G. 1989. 'Local Settlements in Africa: A Misconceived Option?' *Journal of Refugee Studies* 2: 468–90

Kihara, G. 2013. 'Land Prices Go Up as Investors Scramble to Buy.' *Daily Nation*, 2 March

Kilave D. M. and G. Mlay. 2019. '"SRI" in Kilombero Valley: Potential, Misconception and Reality.' *Future Agricultures*, www.future-agricultures.org/blog/sri-in-kilombero-valley-potential-misconception-and-reality, accessed 30 January 2019

Klein, K. L. 1996. 'Reclaiming the "F" Word, or Being and Becoming Postwestern.' *Pacific Historical Review* 65(2): 179–215

Kloos, H. 1982. 'Development, Drought, and Famine in the Awash Valley of Ethiopia.' *African Studies Review* 15(4): 21–48

Kohler, T. 1987. *Land Use in Transition: Aspects and Problems of Small-Scale Farming in a New Environment: The Example of Laikipia District, Kenya*. Bern: Geographical Society of Berne, Institute of Geography, University of Bern

Kopytoff, I. 1987a. 'The Internal African Frontier: The Making of African Political Culture.' In I. Kopytoff, ed., *The African Frontier: The Reproduction of Traditional African Societies*. Bloomington IN: Indiana University Press

Kopytoff, I. ed. 1987b. *The African Frontier: The Reproduction of Traditional African Societies*. Bloomington IN: Indiana University Press

Korf, B., T. Hagmann and R. Emmenegger. 2015. 'Re-spacing African Drylands: Territorialization, Sedentarization and Indigenous Commodification in the Ethiopian Pastoral Frontier.' *Journal of Peasant Studies* 42(5): 881–901

KPL. 2010. *Resettlement Action Plan: Redevelopment of Rice and Bean Cropping at Mngeta Farm, Kilombero Valley, Kilombero District, Morogoro Region, Tanzania*. Dar es Salaam: Kilombero Plantations Ltd

Kunaka, C. and R. Carruthers. 2014. *Trade and Transport Corridor Management Toolkit*. Washington DC: World Bank

Laher, R. 2011. *Resisting Development in Kenya's Lamu District: A Postcolonial Reading*. Policy Brief 48. Pretoria: Africa Institute of South Africa

Lahr, J., R. Buij, F. Katagira and H. van der Valk. 2016. 'Pesticides in the Southern Agricultural Growth Corridor of Tanzania (SAGCOT): A Scoping Study of Current and Future Use, Associated Risks and Identification of Actions for Risk Mitigation.' Report 2760. Wageningen: Wageningen Environmental Research

Lamphear, J. 1992. *The Scattering Time: Turkana Responses to Colonial Rule*. Oxford: Oxford University Press

Lamu County. 2013. *First County Integrated Development Plan, 2013–2017*, Nairobi: Republic of Kenya

Lane, C. R. 1994. 'Pastures Lost: Alienation of Barabaig Land in the Context of Land Policy and Legislation in Tanzania.' *Nomadic Peoples* 34–35: 81–94

Lane, P. 2004. 'The "Moving Frontier" and the Transition to Food Production in Kenya.' *Azania: Archaeological Research in Africa* 39(1): 243–64

Larmer, M. and V. Laterza. 2017. 'Contested Wealth: Social and Political Mobilisation in Extractive Communities in Africa.' *Extractive Industries and Society* 4(4): 701–06

Larsen, J. and F. Stepputat. 2019. *Gulf State Rivalries in the Horn of Africa: Time for a Red Sea Policy?* DIIS Policy Brief. Copenhagen: Danish Institute for International Studies

Laurance, W.F., S. Sloan, L. Weng and J. A. Sayer. 2015. 'Estimating the Environmental Costs of Africa's Massive "Development Corridors".' *Current Biology* 25(24): 3202–08

Lavers, T. 2012. '"Land Grab" as Development Strategy? The Political Economy of

Agricultural Investment in Ethiopia.' *Journal of Peasant Studies* 39(1): 105–32

Lavers, T. 2016. 'Agricultural Investment in Ethiopia: Undermining National Sovereignty or Tool for State Building?' *Development and Change* 47(5): 1078–1101

Leo, C. 1989. *Land and Class in Kenya*. Harare, Zimbabwe: Nehands

Leonardi, C. 2013. *Dealing with Government in South Sudan: Histories of Chiefship, Community and State*. Woodbridge: James Currey

Letai, J. 2015. 'Land Deals & Pastoralist Livelihoods in Laikipia County, Kenya.' In R. Hall, I. Scoones and D. Tsikata, eds, *Africa's Land Rush: Rural Livelihoods & Agrarian Change*. Woodbridge: James Currey

Letai, J. and J. Lind. 2013. 'Squeezed from All Sides: Changing Resource Tenure and Pastoralist Innovation on the Laikipia Plateau, Kenya.' In A. Catley, J. Lind and I. Scoones, eds, *Pastoralism and Development in Africa: Dynamic Change at the Margins*. London: Routledge

Lewis, I. M. 1961. 'Force and Fission in Northern Somali Lineage Structure'. *American Anthropologist* 63(1): 94–112

Li, T. M. 2000. 'Articulating Indigenous Identity in Indonesia: Resource Politics and the Tribal Slot.' *Comparative Studies in Society and History* 42(1): 149–79

Li, T. M. 2007. *The Will to Improve: Governmentality, Development, and the Practice of Politics*. Durham NC: Duke University Press

Li, T. M. 2010. 'Indigeneity, Capitalism, and the Management of Dispossession.' *Current Anthropology* 51(3): 385–414

Li, T. M. 2014a. *Land's End: Capitalist Relations on an Indigenous Frontier*. Durham NC: Duke University Press

Li, T. M. 2014b. 'What is Land? Assembling a Resource for Global Investment.' *Transactions of the Institute of British Geographers* 39(4): 589–602

Li, T. M. 2018. 'After the Land Grab: Infrastructural Violence and the "Mafia System" in Indonesia's Oil Palm Plantation Zones.' *Geoforum* 96: 328–37

Lind, J. 2017. 'Governing Black Gold: Lessons from Oil Finds in Turkana, Kenya.' *Research Briefing*. Brighton: Institute of Development Studies and Saferworld

Lind, J. 2018. 'Devolution, Shifting Centre–Periphery Relationships and Conflict in Northern Kenya.' *Political Geography* 63: 135–47

Little, M. A. and P. Leslie, eds. 1999. *Turkana Herders of the Dry Savanna: Ecology and Biobehavioral Response of Nomads to an Uncertain Environment*. Oxford: Oxford University Press

Little, P. 2014. *Economic and Political Reforms in Africa: Anthropological Perspectives*. Bloomington IN: Indiana University Press

Little, P. D., J. McPeak, C. B. Barrett and P. Kristjanson. 2008. 'Challenging Orthodoxies: Understanding Poverty in Pastoral Areas of East Africa.' *Development and Change* 39, 587–611

Locher, M. 2015. 'The "Global Land Rush", Local Land Rights and Power Relations: European Forestry Investments in Tanzania.' PhD thesis, University of Zurich

Lonsdale, J. 2008. 'Soil, Work, Civilisation, and Citizenship in Kenya.' *Journal of Eastern African Studies* 2(2): 305–14

Luhmann, N. 1982. 'Trust and Power.' *Studies in Soviet Thought* 23(3): 266–70

Lund, C. 2006. 'Twilight Institutions: Public Authority and Local Politics in Africa.' *Development and Change* 37(4): 685–705

Lund, C. 2008. *Local Politics and the Dynamics of Property in Africa*. Cambridge: Cambridge University Press

Lund, C. 2011. 'Property and Citizenship: Conceptually Connecting Land Rights and Belonging in Africa.' *Africa Spectrum* 46: 71–75

Lund, C. 2012. 'Access to Property and Citizenship: Marginalization in a Context of Legal Pluralism.' In B. Z. Tamanaha, C. M. Sage and M. J. V. Woolcock, eds, *Legal Pluralism and Development: Scholars and Practitioners in Dialogue.* Cambridge: Cambridge University Press

Lund, C. 2016. 'Rule and Rupture: State Formation through the Production of Property and Citizenship.' *Development and Change* 47: 1199–1228

Lund, C. and C. Boone. 2013. 'Introduction: Land Politics in Africa – Constituting Authority Over Territory, Property and Persons.' *Africa* 83 (S1): 1–13

Luning, S. 2018. 'Mining Temporalities: Future Perspectives.' *The Extractive Industries and Society* 5(2): 281–86

Lwanga, C. 2018. 'Sh21 bn Lamu Wind Power Project to Take Off After Suit.' *Daily Nation*, 26 May, www.nation.co.ke/business/Sh21bn-Lamu-wind-power-project-to-take-off/996-4580384-uxtlkk/index.html, accessed 1 July 2019

Lynch, G. 2006. 'Negotiating Ethnicity: Identity Politics in Contemporary Kenya.' *Review of African Political Economy* 33(107): 49–65

Lynch, G. 2011. 'Kenya's New Indigenes: Negotiating Local Identities in a Global Context.' *Nations and Nationalisms* 17(11): 148–67

Maganga, F., K. Askew, R. Odgaard and H. Stein. 2016. 'Dispossession Through Formalization: Tanzania and the G8 Land Agenda in Africa.' *Asian Journal of African Studies* 40: 3–49

Makki, F. 2012. 'Power and Property: Commercialization, Enclosures, and the Transformation of Agrarian Relations in Ethiopia.' *Journal of Peasant Studies* 39(1): 81–104

Makki, F. 2014. 'Development by Dispossession: Terra Nullius and the Social-Ecology of New Enclosures in Ethiopia.' *Rural Sociology* 79(1): 79–103

Maknun Gamaledin. 1987. 'State Policy and Famine in the Awash Valley of Ethiopia: The Lessons for Conservation.' In D. Anderson and R. Grove, eds, *Conservation in Africa.* Cambridge: Cambridge University Press, pp. 327–44

Maknun Gamaledin. 1993. 'The Decline of Afar Pastoralism.' In J. Markakis, ed., *Conflict and the Decline of Pastoralism in the Horn of Africa.* London: Macmillan Press

Manda, S., A. Tallontire and A. J. Dougill. 2019. 'Large-scale Land Acquisitions and Institutions: Patterns, Influence and Barriers in Zambia.' *Geographical Journal* 185(2): 194–208

Margulis, M.E., N. McKeon and S. M. Borras Jr. 2013. 'Land Grabbing and Global Governance: Critical Perspectives.' *Globalizations* 10(1): 1–23

Markakis, J. 2003. 'Anatomy of a Conflict: Afar and Ise Ethiopia.' *Review of African Political Economy* 30(97): 445–53

Markakis, J. 2011. *Ethiopia: The Last Two Frontiers.* Woodbridge: James Currey

Martin, A. 2005. 'Environmental Conflict Between Refugee and Host Communities.' *Journal of Peace Research* 42: 329–46

Maundu, P., S. Kibet, Y. Morimoto, M. Imbumi and R. Adeka. 2009. 'Impact of *Prosopis juliflora* on Kenya's Semi-Arid and Arid Ecosystems and Local Livelihoods.' *Biodiversity* 10(2/3): 33–50

Mburu, J., M. Odhiambo, A. Wachira, N. Kahiro, A. Williams, J. Lodisana and J. Gachigi. 2013. *The Abandoned Lands of Laikipia: Land Use Options Study.* Nairobi: Laikipia Wildlife Forum, Nature Conservancy and Zeitz Foundation

McCabe, J. T. 2004. *Cattle Bring Us to Our Enemies: Turkana Ecology, Politics, and Raiding in a Disequilibrium System.* Ann Arbor MI: University of Michigan Press

McDermott Hughes, D. 2008. *From Enslavement to Environmentalism: Politics on a Southern African Frontier*. Seattle WA: University of Washington Press

McPeak, J.G., C. Doss and P. D. Little. 2011. *Risk and Social Change in an African Rural Economy: Livelihoods in Pastoralist Communities*. London: Routledge

Meester, J., W. Van den Berg and H. Verhoeven. 2018. *Riyal Politik: The Political Economy of Gulf Investments in the Horn of Africa*. The Hague: Clingendael Institute

Mehta, L. 2001. 'The Manufacture of Popular Perceptions of Scarcity: Dams and Water-related Narratives in Gujarat, India.' *World Development* 29(12): 2025–41

Mehta, L., G. J. Veldwisch and J. Franco. 2012. 'Water Grabbing? Focus on the (Re) Appropriation of Finite Water Resources.' *Water Alternatives* 5: 193–207

Meles Zenawi. 2011. Speech at the 13th Annual Pastoralists' Day Celebrations, Jinka, South Omo, 25 January 2011, www.mursi.org/pdf/Meles%20Jinka%20 speech.pdf, accessed 22 January 2019

Melesse Getu. 1995. 'Tsamako Women's Roles and Status in Agro-Pastoral Production.' MA dissertation, Series No. 3., Department of Sociology, Anthropology and Social Administration, Addis Ababa University

Milgroom, J. 2015. 'Policy Processes of a Land Grab: At the Interface of Politics "In the Air" and Politics "On the Ground" in Massingir, Mozambique.' *Journal of Peasant Studies* 42(3–4): 585–606

Ministry of Lands. 2009. Sessional Paper No. 3 of 2009 on National Land Policy. Nairobi: Republic of Kenya, www1.uneca.org/Portals/lpi/CrossArticle/1/ Land%20Policy%20Documents/Sessional-paper-on-Kenya-National-Land-Policy.pdf, accessed 2 July 2019

Mitchell, T. 2002. *Rule of Experts: Egypt, Techno-politics, Modernity*. Berkeley CA: University of California Press

Mkutu, K. 2007. 'Small Arms and Light Weapons among Pastoral Groups in the Kenya–Uganda Border Area.' *African Affairs* 106(422): 47–70

Mkutu, K. 2017. 'Oil and Emerging Conflict Dynamics in the Ateker Cluster: The Case of Turkana, Kenya.' *Nomadic Peoples* 21(1): 34–62

MoFED. 2010. *Growth and Transformation Plan (2010/11–2014/15). Volume I: Main Text*. Ministry of Finance and Economic Development, Federal Democratic Republic of Ethiopia

Mohamed, J. 2004. 'The Political Ecology of Colonial Somaliland.' *Africa* 74(4): 534–66

Mortimore, M. and W. M. Adams. 1999. *Working the Sahel: Environment and Society in Northern Nigeria*. London: Routledge

Mosley, J. and E. E. Watson. 2016. 'Frontier Transformations: Development Visions, Spaces and Processes in Northern Kenya and Southern Ethiopia.' *Journal of Eastern African Studies* 10(3): 452–75

Moyo, S., P. Yeros and P. Jha. 2012. 'Imperialism and Primitive Accumulation: Notes on the New Scramble for Africa.' *Agrarian South: Journal of Political Economy* 1(2): 181–203

Mulenga, G. 2013. *Developing Economic Corridors in Africa: Rationale for the Participation of the African Development Bank*. Regional Integration Brief No. 1. Abidjan: African Development Bank

Müller-Mahn, D., S. Rettberg and G. Getachew. 2010. 'Pathways and Dead Ends of Pastoral Development among the Afar and Karrayu in Ethiopia.' *European Journal of Development Research* 22(5): 660–77

Mung'ong'o, C. G. and J. Kayonko. 2009. 'Kilombero Plantation Ltd: Mngeta

Farm Squatter Survey Report.' Dar es Salaam: Natural Resource Management Consultants

Musa, A. M. and C. Horst. 2019. 'State Formation and Economic Development in Post-War Somaliland: The Impact of the Private Sector in an Unrecognised State.' *Conflict, Security & Development* 19(1): 35–53

Mutambara, S., M. B. K. Darkoh and J. R. Atlhopheng. 2016. 'A Comparative Review of Water Management Sustainability Challenges in Smallholder Irrigation Schemes in Africa and Asia.' *Agricultural Water Management* 171 (June): 63–72.

Mutopo, P. and M. Chiweshe. 2014. 'Large-scale Land Deals, Global Capital and the Politics of Livelihoods: Experiences of Women Small-holder Farmers in Chisumbanje, Zimbabwe.' *International Journal of African Renaissance Studies-Multi-, Inter-and Transdisciplinarity* 9(1): 84–99

Mwakimako, H. and J. Willis. 2014. *Islam, Politics and Violence on the Kenya Coast.* Note 4, Observatoire des Enjeux Politiques et Sécuritaires dans la Corne de l'Afrique, www.lam.sciencespobordeaux.fr/sites/lam/files/note4_observatoire.pdf, accessed 1 July 2019

Mwangi, E. 2007. 'Subdividing the Commons: Distributional Conflict in the Transition from Collective to Individual Property Rights in Kenya's Maasailand.' *World Development* 35(5): 815–34

Mwasumbi, L., C. Mligo and H. Suleiman. 2007. *Baseline Study for Environmental Impact Assessment of proposed SEKAB Biofuel Development Project: Vegetation Survey of Proposed Sugar Cane Plantation on the Former RAZABA Ranch, Bagamoyo District, Tanzania.* Stockholm: ORGUT Consulting

Nalepa, R. A. and D. M. Bauer. 2012. 'Marginal Lands: The Role of Remote Sensing in Constructing Landscapes for Agrofuel Development.' *Journal of Peasant Studies* 39(2): 403–22

Nema, N. 2016. 'County Government Frustrating Investors, Says a Section of Lamu MCAs.' *Baraka FM*, 11 August, http://barakafm.org/2016/08/11/county-government-frustrating-investors-says-a-section-of-lamu-mcas, accessed 1 July 2019

Nema, N. 2017. 'Twaha among Sand Dunes Land "Grabbers" Summoned by NLC.' *Baraka FM,* 24 February, http://barakafm.org/2017/02/24/twaha-among-sand-dunes-land-grabbers-summoned-by-nlc, accessed 1 July 2019

Netting, R. M. and P. M. Stone. 1996. 'Agro-diversity on a Farming Frontier: Kofyar Smallholders on the Benue Plains of Central Nigeria.' *Africa* 66(1): 52–70

Ngilu, C. K. 2014. Statement dated 31 July 2014, from Charity Kaluki Ngilu, Cabinet Secretary, Ministry of Land, Housing and Urban Development to Hon. Uhuru Kenyatta, President of the Republic of Kenya, and Commander in Chief of the Kenya Defence Forces, and others. *Daily Nation*, 9 August, www.nation.co.ke/blob/view/-/2404818/data/800429/-/v84gg9/-/lamu+land+list.pdf, accessed 1 July 2019

Nicol, A. 2015. 'Towards Conflict-sensitive Regional Integration in East Africa.' *IDS Policy Briefing* 100. Brighton: Institute of Development Studies

Nolte, K. 2014. 'Large-scale Agricultural Investments Under Poor Land Governance in Zambia.' *Land Use Policy* 38: 698–706

Nolte, K., W. Chamberlain and M. Giger. 2016. 'International Land Deals for Agriculture. Fresh insights from the Land Matrix.' Analytical Report II. Bern: Centre for Development and Environment, University of Bern, Berne Open Publishing; Montpellier: Centre de coopération internationale en recherche agronomique pour le développement; Hamburg: German Institute of Global and Area Studies; Pretoria: University of Pretoria

Norton, H. 2018. 'Cautious Optimism for Peace in the Horn of Africa.' *Fair Observer*, 6 August 2018, www.fairobserver.com/world-news/ethiopia-eritrea-peace-djibouti-horn-africa-news-81001, accessed 9 July 2019

Nunow, A. A. 2013. 'Land Deals and the Changing Political Economy of Livelihoods in the Tana Delta, Kenya.' In A. Catley, J. Lind and I. Scoones, eds, *Pastoralism and Development in Africa: Dynamic Change at the Margins.* Abingdon: Routledge

Nunow, A. A. 2015. 'Land Deals in the Tana Delta.' In R. Hall, I. Scoones and D. Tsitaka, eds, *Africa's Land Rush: Rural Livelihoods and Agrarian Change.* Woodbridge: James Currey

Nyamnjoh, F. B. 2000. '"For Many are Called but Few are Chosen": Globalisation and Popular Disenchantment in Africa.' *African Sociological Review/Revue africaine de sociologie* 4(2): 1–45

Nyantakyi-Frimpong, H. and R. Bezner Kerr. 2017. 'Land Grabbing, Social Differentiation, Intensified Migration and Food Security in Northern Ghana.' *Journal of Peasant Studies* 44(2): 421–44

Nyerere, J. K. 1966. 'Ujamaa – the Basis of African Socialism'. In J. K. Nyerere, *Freedom and Unity.* Oxford: Oxford University Press

Oakland Institute, GreenPeace Africa and Global Justice Now. 2015. *Irresponsible Investment: Agrica's Broken Development Model in Tanzania.* Oakland CA: Oakland Institute

Oba, G. 2013. 'The Sustainability of Pastoral Production in Africa.' In A. Catley, J. Lind and I. Scoones, eds, *Pastoralism and Development in Africa: Dynamic Change at the Margins.* Abingdon: Routledge

Ocra. 2013. *Opportunities and Threats of Irrigation Development in Kenya's Drylands*, Volume VI, 'Turkana County.' Consultancy Report. Rome: Food and Agriculture Organization

Oğultürk, M.C. 2017. 'Russia's Renewed Interests in the Horn of Africa as a Traditional and Rising Power.' *Rising Powers Quarterly* 2(1): 121–43

Oka, R. 2011. 'Unlikely Cities in the Desert: The Informal Economy as Causal Agent for Permanent 'Urban' Sustainability in Kakuma Refugee Camp, Kenya.' *Urban Anthropology* 40(3/4): 223–62

Okenwa, D. A. 2020. 'Impermanent Development and the Pursuit of Permanence: Mobilising Marginalisation and Uncertainty towards a Rightful Share of Kenya's Oil.' PhD thesis. London School of Economics and Political Science

Oketch, W. 2018. 'Court of Appeal Orders NLC to Submit in Lamu Wind Power Dispute Deal.' *Standard Digital*, 9 October, www.standardmedia.co.ke/business/article/2001298452/court-orders-nlc-to-submit-in-lamu-wind-power-dispute-appeal, accessed 1 July 2019

ORGUT. 2008. *Preliminary Environmental and Social Impact Analysis (ESIA) of BioEthanol Production from Sugar Cane Production on the Former Razaba Ranch, Bagamoyo District.* Stockholm: ORGUT Consulting

Österle, M. 2007. 'Innovation und Transformation bei den pastoralnomadischen Pokot (East Pokot, Kenia).' Inauguraldissertation zur Erlangung der Doktorwürde der Philosophischen Fakultät, Universität zu Köln

Ouma, S. 2016. 'From Financialization to Operations of Capital: Historicizing and Disentangling the Finance–Farmland Nexus.' *Geoforum* 72: 82–93

Ovadia, J. S. 2016. 'Local Content Policies and Petro-development in Sub-Saharan

Africa: A Comparative Analysis.' *Resources Policy* 49: 20–30

Oxfam. 2017. 'Testing Community Consent: Tullow Oil Project in Kenya.' Oxfam Briefing Paper. Oxford: Oxfam, www.oxfamamerica.org/static/media/files/Testing_Community_Consent.pdf, accessed 18 June 2019

Pankhurst, R. 1965. 'The Trade of the Gulf of Aden Ports of Africa in the Nineteenth and Early Twentieth Centuries.' *Journal of Ethiopian Studies* 3(1): 36–81

Pas, A. 2019. *Pastoralists, Mobility and Conservation: Shifting Rules of Access and Control of Grazing Resources in Kenya's Northern Drylands*. Stockholm: Department of Human Geography, Stockholm University

Peck, J. and A. Tickell. 2002. 'Neoliberalizing Space.' *Antipode* 34(3): 380–404

Pedersen, R. H. and L. Buur. 2016. 'Beyond Land Grabbing: Old Morals and New Perspectives on Contemporary Investments.' *Geoforum* 72: 77–81

Peluso, N. L. and C. Lund. 2011. 'New Frontiers of Land Control: Introduction.' *Journal of Peasant Studies* 38(4): 667–81

Phillips, S. 2013. 'Political Settlements and State Formation: the Case of Somaliland.' Research Paper 23. Birmingham: Developmental Leadership Programme

Planel, S. 2014. 'A View of a "Bureaucratic" Developmental State: Local Governance and Agricultural Extension in Rural Ethiopia.' *Journal of Eastern African Studies* 8(3): 420–37

Praxides, C. 2014. 'Swazuri Criticizes LAPSSET Land Deals.' *The Star*, 16 October, https://allafrica.com/stories/201410160855.html, accessed 1 July 2019

Praxides, C. 2017. 'Lamu MP Baffled by Timamy's Backward Rule, Says Investors Fleeing.' *The Star*, 31 July, www.the-star.co.ke/news/2017/07/31/lamu-mp-baffled-by-timamys-backward-rule-says-investors-fleeing_c1607419, accessed 20 November 2018

Prno, J. and D. Slocombe. 2012. 'Exploring the Origins of "Social License to Operate" in the Mining Sector: Perspectives from Governance and Sustainability Theories.' *Resources Policy* 37(3): 346–57

Raeymaekers, T. 2013. *Violence on the Margins: States, Conflict, and Borderlands*. New York: Springer

Rajak, D. 2011. *In Good Company: An Anatomy of Corporate Social Responsibility*. Stanford CA: Stanford University Press

Ram, K. V. 1981. 'British Government, Finance Capitalists and the French Jibuti– Addis Ababa Railway 1898–1913.' *The Journal of Imperial and Commonwealth History* 9(2): 146–68

Rasmussen M. B. and C. Lund. 2018. 'Reconfiguring Frontier Spaces: The Territorialization of Resource Control.' *World Development* 101: 388–99

Rawlence, B. 2016. *City of Thorns: Nine Lives in the World's Largest Refugee Camp*. New York: Picador

Reid, R. S., K. A. Galvin and R. S. Kruska. 2008. 'Global Significance of Extensive Grazing Lands and Pastoral Societies: An Introduction.' In K. A. Galvin, R. S. Reid, R. H. Behnke Jr and N. T. Hobbs, eds, *Fragmentation in Semi-arid and Arid Landscapes*. Dordrecht, The Netherlands: Springer, pp. 1–24

Republic of Kenya. 2018. Petition No. 22 of 2012. Republic of Kenya in the High Court of Kenya at Nairobi, May, https://elaw.org/system/files/attachments/publicresource/ke_LAPSSET_FinalJudgment_No22of2012.pdf, accessed 1 July 2019

Rettberg, S. 2010. 'Contested Narratives of Pastoral Vulnerability and Risk in Ethiopia's Afar Region.' *Pastoralism: Research, Policy and Practice* 1(2): 248–73

Rettberg, S., G. Beckmann, M. Minah and A. Schelchen. 2017. *Ethiopia's Arid and*

Semi-arid Lowlands: Towards Inclusive and Sustainable Rural Transformation. SLE-Discussion Series No. 03. Berlin: Humboldt University

Ribot, J. C. and N. L. Peluso. 2003. 'A Theory of Access.' *Rural Sociology* 68(2): 153–81

Rigby, P. 1988. 'Class Formation among East African Pastoralists: Maasai of Tanzania and Kenya.' *Dialectical Anthropology* 13: 63–81

Rodrigues, C. U. 2017. 'Configuring the Living Environment in Mining Areas in Angola: Contestations between Mining Companies, Workers, Local Communities and the State.' *Extractive Industries and Society* 4(4): 727–34

Romero, P. W. 1986. '"Where Have All the Slaves Gone?" Emancipation and Post-emancipation in Lamu, Kenya.' *Journal of African History* 27(3): 497–512

Rutten, M. 1992. *Selling Wealth to Buy Poverty: The Process of Individualization of Land Ownership among the Maasai Pastoralists of Kajiado District, Kenya, 1890–1990.* Saarbrucken, Germany: Verlag Breitenbach

SAGCOT. 2011. *SAGCOT Investment Blueprint.* Dar es Salaam: Southern Agricultural Growth Corridor of Tanzania

SAGCOT. 2012. 'Investment Partnership Program: Initiatives to Ensure Full Community Involvement and Environmental Safeguards While Putting Underutilised Land to Productive Use.' Presentation by Hon. Minister for Lands, Housing & Human Settlements Development to the Tanzania Agribusiness Investment Showcase Event, Dar es Salaam, 27 November 2012

SAGCOT. 2013. *Applying and Agriculture Green Growth Approach in the SAGCOT Clusters: Challenges and Opportunities in Kilombero, Ihemi and Mbarali.* Dar es Salaam: Southern Agricultural Growth Corridor of Tanzania

Said, E. 1978. *Orientalism.* New York: Vintage

Salih, M., A. M. Salih and J. Baker. 1995. 'Pastoralist Migration to Small Towns in Africa.' In J. Baker and T. A. Aina, eds, *The Migration Experience in Africa.* Uppsala, Sweden: Scandinavian Institute of African Studies, pp. 181–96

Samatar, A., I. Salisbury and J. Bascom. 1988. The Political Economy of Livestock Marketing in Northern Somalia. *African Economic History* 17: 81–97

Sandford, S. 2013. 'Pastoralists and Irrigation in the Horn of Africa: Time for a Rethink?' In A. Catley, J. Lind and I. Scoones, eds, *Pastoralism and Development in Africa: Dynamic Change at the Margins.* Abingdon: Routledge, pp. 72–81

Sanghi, A., H. Onder and V. Vemuru. 2016. '*Yes' in My Backyard? The Economics of Refugees and Their Social Dynamics in Kakuma, Kenya.* Washington DC: World Bank

Sassen, S. 2008. *Territory, Authority, Rights: From Medieval to Global Assemblages.* Princeton NJ: Princeton University Press

Schlee, G. 1989. *Identities on the Move: Clanship and Pastoralism in Northern Kenya.* Manchester: Manchester University Press

Schlee, G. 2010. 'Territorialising Ethnicity: The Political Ecology of Pastoralism in Northern Kenya and Southern Ethiopia.' Working Paper 121. Halle/Saale: Max Planck Institute for Social Anthropology

Schlee, G. and A. Shongolo. 2012. *Pastoralism & Politics in Northern Kenya & Southern Ethiopia.* Woodbridge: James Currey

Schoneveld, G. C. 2017. 'Host Country Governance and the African Land Rush: 7 Reasons Why Large-scale Farmland Investments Fail to Contribute to Sustainable Development.' *Geoforum* 83(July): 119–32

Schritt, J. 2018. 'Contesting the Oil Zone: Local Content Issues in Niger's Oil Industry.' *Energy Research and Social Science* 41: 259–69

Scoones, I. , ed. 1994. *Living with Uncertainty: New Directions in Pastoral Development in Africa*. London: IT Publications.

Scoones, I., R. Hall, S. M. Borras Jr, B. White and W. Wolford. 2013. 'The Politics of Evidence: Methodologies for Understanding the Global Land Rush.' *Journal of Peasant Studies* 40(3): 469–83

Scoones, I., K. Amanor, A. Favareto and G. Qi. 2016. 'A New Politics of Development Cooperation? Chinese and Brazilian Engagements in African Agriculture.' *World Development* 81:1–12

Scoones, I., F. Murimbarimba and J. Mahenehene. 2019a. 'Irrigating Zimbabwe after Land Reform: The Potential of Farmer-Led Systems.' *Water Alternatives* 12(1): 88–106

Scoones, I., R. Smalley, R. Hall and D. Tsikata. 2019b. 'Narratives of Scarcity: Framing the Global Land Rush.' *Geoforum* 101: 231–41

Scott, J. C. 1998. *Seeing Like a State: How Certain Schemes to Improve the Human Condition Have Failed*. New Haven CT: Yale University Press

Scott, J. C. 2009. *The Art of Not Being Governed: An Anarchist History of Upland Southeast Asia*. New Haven CT: Yale University Press

Shipton, P. 2009. *Mortgaging the Ancestors: Ideologies of Attachment in Africa*. New Haven CT: Yale University Press

Sida Helpdesk. 2012. *Review of Project Documentation for the 'Bagamoyo Sugar Project' of Agro EcoEnergy in Tanzania*. Uppsala: Sida Helpdesk for Environment and Climate Change, Swedish University of Agricultural Sciences

Sida. 2014. *Decision for Contribution to Eco Energy Tanzania*. Stockholm: Swedish International Development Cooperation Agency

Sida. 2015. *Granskningsrapport IR 15-04*. Stockholm: Swedish International Development Cooperation Agency

Sida. Undated. 'Collaboration with the Private Sector.' Stockholm: Swedish International Development Cooperation Agency, www.sida.se/globalassets/global/about-sida/private-sector---collected-info.pdf, accessed 7 March 2019

Sikor, T. and C. Lund. 2009. 'Access and Property: A Question of Power and Authority.' *Development and Change* 40(1): 1–22

Slaughter, A. and J. Crisp. 2009. 'A Surrogate State? The Role of UNHCR in Protracted Situations.' New Issues in Refugee Research, Research Paper 168. Geneva: Policy Development and Evaluation Service, Office of the United Nations High Commissioner for Refugees

Smalley, R. 2017. 'Agricultural Growth Corridors on the Eastern Seaboard of Africa: An Overview.' APRA Working Paper 1. Brighton: Agricultural Policy Research in Africa Programme

Soni, R. and M. Essex. 2019. 'Time for A New Narrative on Turkana: Reflections from K-EXPRO's Time Supporting Local Initiatives.' *In Depth* series. Oxford: Oxford Policy Management, www.opml.co.uk/files/Publications/corporate-publications/briefing-notes/in-depth-time-for-a-new-narrative-on-turkana-web.pdf?noredirect=1, 12 May 2019

Spencer, P. 1998. *The Pastoral Continuum: The Marginalization of Tradition in East Africa*. Oxford: Oxford University Press

Standard Digital. 2016. 'President Uhuru Kenyatta Presents over 2,000 Titles to Lamu Residents.' 8 January, www.standardmedia.co.ke/article/2000187383/president-uhuru-kenyatta-presents-over-2-000-titles-to-lamu-residents, accessed 1 July 2019

Star, The. 2017a. 'Is Rebellion the next Phase of Laikipia Violence?' 5 June 2017

Star, The. 2017b. 'I Will Push for Increased Oil Proceeds for Turkana – Governor Nanok.' 14 May, www.the-star.co.ke/news/2017-05-14-i-will-push-for-increased-oil-proceeds-for-turkana-governor-nanok, accessed 27 July 2019

Stave, J., G. Oba, N. C. Stenseth and I. Nordal. 2005. 'Environmental Gradients in the Turkwel Riverine Forest, Kenya: Hypotheses on Dam-Induced Vegetation Change.' *Forest Ecology and Management* 212(1): 184–98

Stein, S. and M. Kalina. 2019. 'Becoming an Agricultural Growth Corridor: African Megaprojects at a Situated Scale.' *Environment and Society* 10(1): 83–100

Stepputat, F. and T. Hagmann. 2019. 'Politics of Circulation: The Makings of the Berbera Corridor in Somali East Africa.' *Environment and Planning D: Society and Space* 37(5): 794–813

Sulieman, H. M. 2015. 'Grabbing of Communal Rangelands in Sudan: The Case of Large-scale Mechanized Rain-fed Agriculture.' *Land Use Policy* 47: 439–47

Sulle, E. and R. Smalley. 2015. 'The State and Foreign Capital in Agricultural Commercialisation: The Case of Tanzania's Kilombero Sugar Company.' In R. Hall, I. Scoones and D. Tsikata, eds, *Africa's Land Rush: Rural Livelihoods & Agrarian Change.* Woodbridge: James Currey, pp. 114–31

Swahilitimeblogspot.com 'Wanavijiji Wafukuzwa Morogoro.' 22 November 2009, http://swahilitime.blogspot.com/2009/10/mashamba-morogoro.html, accessed 15 November 2015

Swazuri, M., T. Chavangi, F. Lukalo and E. Dokhe. 2018. *Experiences in Large-scale Land Acquisition for Mega Projects in Lamu.* Nairobi: National Land Commission

Tache, B. 2013. 'Rangeland Enclosures in Southern Oromia, Ethiopia: An Innovative Response or the Erosion of Common Property Resources?' In A. Catley, J. Lind and I. Scoones, eds, *Pastoralism and Development in Africa: Dynamic Change at the Margins.* Abingdon: Routledge

Tanzania Forest Conservation Group. 2018. 'Terms of Reference: Facilitation of the Design, Establishment and Documentation of a Payment for Ecosystem Services Scheme in Mngeta Valley.' www.tfcg.org/wp-content/uploads/2018/05/ToRMngetaPESFINAL2018.pdf, accessed 4 July 2019

Taylor, E. C. 2013. 'Claiming Kabale: Racial Thought and Urban Governance in Uganda.' *Journal of Eastern African Studies* 7(1): 143–63

Tewolde Woldemariam and Fana Gebresenbet. 2014. 'Socio-political and Conflict Implications of Sugar Development in Salamago Wereda, Ethiopia.' In Gebrehiwot Berhe, ed., *A Delicate Balance: Land Use, Minority Rights and Social Stability in the Horn of Africa.* Addis Ababa: Institute for Peace and Security Studies, Addis Ababa University, pp. 117–43

Throup, D. and C. Hornsby. 1998. *Multi-Party Politics in Kenya: The Kenyatta and Moi States and the Triumph of the System in the 1992 Election.* Oxford: James Currey

Tilly, C. 2008. *Contentious Performances.* New York: Cambridge University Press

Tsing, A. L. 2003. 'Natural Resources and Capitalist Frontiers.' *Economic and Political Weekly* 38(48): 5100–06

Tsing, A. L. 2011. *Friction: An Ethnography of Global Connection.* Princeton NJ: Princeton University Press

Tullow Oil. 2016. 'Human Rights Report.' London: Tullow Oil, www.tullowoil.com/Media/docs/default-source/1_About_us/2018-tullow-oil-code-of-ethical-conduct.pdf?sfvrsn=7, 4 October 2017

Tullow Oil. 2017. 'Stakeholder Engagement Framework South Lokichar Basin,

Turkana Kenya.' London: Tullow Oil, www.tullowoil.com/Media/docs/default-source/operations/kenya-eia/stakeholder-engagement-framework-(sef).pdf?sfvrsn=0, 20 February 2018

Turner, F. J. 2014 [1894]. *The Significance of the Frontier in American History*. Reprint. Marlborough: Martino Fine Books

Turner, M. D. 2011. 'The New Pastoral Development Paradigm: Engaging the Realities of Property Institutions and Livestock Mobility in Dryland Africa.' *Society and Natural Resources* 24(5): 469–84

Turner, M.D. and E. Schlecht. 2019. 'Livestock Mobility in Sub-Saharan Africa: A Critical Review.' *Pastoralism* 9(1): 13

Turton, D. 2011. 'Wilderness, Wasteland or Home? Three Ways of Imagining the Lower Omo Valley.' *Journal of Eastern African Studies* 5(1): 158–76

Turton, D. Forthcoming. 'Breaking Every Rule in the Book: The Story of River Basin Development in Ethiopia's Omo Valley.' in C. E. Gabbert, J. Galaty, Fana Gebresenbet and G. Schlee, eds, *Lands of the Future-Future of the Lands: Anthropological Perspectives on Agro-pastoralist, Investment and Land Use*. New York: Berghahn

Umar, A. and R. Baulch. 2007. *Risk Taking for a Living: Trade and Marketing in the Somali Region of Ethiopia*. Addis Ababa: UN-OCHA Pastoral Community Initiative

UNHCR. 2018. *Kalobeyei Integrated Socio-economic Development Plan in Turkana West: Phase One, 2018–2022*. Nairobi: Office of the United Nations High Commissioner for Refugees

UNHCR. 2019. 'Cash for Shelter in Kenya: A Field Experience.' Nairobi: Office of the United Nations High Commissioner For Refugees, www.cashlearning.org/downloads/user-submitted-resources/2019/02/1549035864.Cash%20for%20Shelter%20in%20Kenya-A%20Field%20Experience_UNHCR.pdf, 25 April 2019

Unruh, J. D. 1990. 'Integration of Transhumant Pastoralism and Irrigated Agriculture in Semi-arid East Africa.' *Human Ecology* 18: 223–46

URT (United Republic of Tanzania). 2013. *2012 Population and Housing Census: Population Distribution by Administrative Areas*, March 2013. Dar es Salaam: National Bureau of Statistics

Van Schendel, W. 2005. 'Spaces of Engagement: How Borderlands, Illegal Flows, and Territorial States Interlock.' In W. van Schendel and I. Abraham, eds, *Illicit Flows and Criminal Things: States, Borders, and the Other Side of Globalization*. Bloomington IN: Indiana University Press

Vandergeest, P. and N. L. Peluso. 1995. 'Territorialization and State Power in Thailand.' *Theory and Society* 24(3): 385–426

Vaughan, C. 2013. 'Violence and Regulation in the Darfur-Chad Borderland c. 1909–1956: Policing a Colonial Boundary.' *Journal of African History* 54(2): 177–98

Vehrs, H. P. 2016. 'Changes in Landscape Vegetation, Forage Plant Composition and Herding Structure in the Pastoralist Livelihoods of East Pokot, Kenya.' *Journal of Eastern African Studies* 10(1): 88–110

Vehrs, H. P. 2018. 'Perceptions and Cultural Appropriations of Landscape-Level Invasions. Environmental Changes and Social Transformations in East Pokot, Kenya.' PhD thesis. Faculty of Arts and Humanities, University of Cologne

Verdirame, G. and B. Harrell-Bond. 2005. *Rights in Exile: Janus-faced Humanitarianism*. New York, Oxford: Berghahn Books

Verhoeven, H. 2016. 'Briefing: African Dam Building as Extraversion: The Case of Sudan's Dam Programme, Nubian resistance, and the Saudi-Iranian Proxy War in Yemen.' *African Affairs* 115(460): 562–73

Verhoeven, H. 2018. 'The Gulf and the Horn: Changing Geographies of Security Interdependence and Competing Visions of Regional Order.' *Civil Wars* 20(3): 333–57

Visser, O., J. Clapp and S. R. Isakson. 2015. 'Introduction to a Symposium on Global Finance and the Agri-food Sector: Risk and Regulation.' *Journal of Agrarian Change* 15(4): 541–48

Voller, L., A. B. Christense, G. Kamadi and H. van der Wiel. 2016. 'A People in the Way of Progress.' Danwatch, 30 May 2016, https://old.danwatch.dk/undersogelse/a-people-in-the-way-of-progress, accessed 19 June 2019

Walwa, J. W. 2017. 'Land Use Plans in Tanzania: Repertoires of Domination or Solutions to Rising Farmer–Herder Conflicts?' *Journal of Eastern African Studies* 11: 408–24

Watts, M. J. 2004. 'Antinomies of Community: Some Thoughts on Geography, Resources and Empire.' *Transactions of the Institute of British Geographers* 29(2): 195–216

Watts, M. J. 2018. 'Frontiers: Authority, Precarity, and Insurgency at the Edge of the State.' *World Development* 101: 477–88

Waweru, P. 2002. 'Frontier Urbanisation: The Rise and Development of Towns in Samburu District, Kenya, 1909–1940.' *Azania: Archaeological Research in Africa* 36–37(1): 84–97

Weng, L., A. K. Boedhihartono, P. H. Dirks, J. Dixon, M. I. Lubis, and J. A. Sayer. 2013. 'Mineral Industries, Growth Corridors and Agricultural Development in Africa.' *Global Food Security* 2(3): 195–202

White, B., S. M. Borras Jr, R. Hall, I. Scoones and W. Wolford. 2013. 'The New Enclosures: Critical Perspectives on Corporate Land Deals.' In B. White, S. M. Borras Jr, R. Hall, I. Scoones and W. Wolford eds, *The New Enclosures: Critical Perspectives on Corporate Land Deals*. London: Routledge, pp. 13–42

Whittaker, H. 2014. *Insurgency and Counterinsurgency in Kenya: A Social History of the Shifta Conflict, c. 1963–1968*. Boston MA: Brill

Willis, J. and N. Chome. 2014. 'Marginalization and Political Participation on the Kenya Coast: The 2013 Elections.' *Journal of Eastern African Studies* 8(1): 115–34

Willis, J., G. Lynch and N. Cheeseman. 2017. 'Kenyan Elections are Much More than Just a Ruthless Game of Thrones.' *The Conversation*, 3 August 2017, http://theconversation.com/kenyas-elections-are-much-more-than-just-a-ruthless-game-of-thrones-81957, accessed 2 July 2019

Wirth, M. K. 1988. *Project Evaluation Food Security Programme III, Nginyang Division/Baringo District, Kenya*. Nairobi: Kenya Freedom from Hunger Council

Woertz, E. 2013a. *Oil for Food: The Global Food Crisis and the Middle East*. Oxford: Oxford University Press

Woertz, E. 2013b. 'The Governance of Gulf Agro-investments.' *Globalizations* 10(1): 87–104

Wolford, W., S. M. Borras Jr, R. Hall, I. Scoones and B White. 2013. 'Governing Global Land Deals: The Role of the State in the Rush for Land.' *Development and Change* 44: 189–210

Woodhouse, P., G. J. Veldwisch, J. P. Venot, D. Brockington, H. Komakech and A. Manjichi. 2017. 'African Farmer-led Irrigation Development: Re-framing

Agricultural Policy and Investment?' *Journal of Peasant Studies* 44(1): 213–33

World Bank. 2014. 'World Bank Boosts Support for Pastoralists in Horn of Africa.' Press release. World Bank, www.worldbank.org/en/news/press-release/2014/03/18/world-bank-pastoralists-horn-africa, accessed 6 June 2019

World Bank. 2015. 'Leveraging Oil and Gas Industry for the Development of a Competitive Private Sector in Uganda.' Kampala: World Bank, http://documents.worldbank.org/curated/en/521361468302082824/pdf/ACS125280REVIS0itive0Private0Sector.pdf, accessed 30 July 2019

World Bank. 2017. 'Horn of Africa Initiative: Corridor Opportunities in the Horn of Africa.' Washington DC: World Bank

World Bank. 2019. 'Ethiopia: Overview.' Washington DC: World Bank, www.worldbank.org/en/country/ethiopia/overview, accessed 26 July 2019

Yacob Arsano and G. Basechler. 2002. 'Transformation of Resource Conflicts and the Case of Woito River Valley in Southern Ethiopia.' In M. Flury and U. Geiser, eds, *Local Environmental Management in a North-South Perspective: Issues of Participation and Knowledge Management*. Zurich: IOS Press, pp: 91–108

Yacob Aklilu and A. Catley. 2009. *Livestock Exports from the Horn of Africa: An Analysis of Benefits by Pastoralist Wealth Group and Policy Implications*. Medford MA: Feinstein International Center, Tufts University

Zoomers, A. 2018. 'Plantations are Everywhere! Between Infrastructural Violence and Inclusive Development.' *Geoforum* 96: 341–44

INDEX

accumulation; by dispossession 10; local opportunities for 6, 25, 27, 157–8, 161, 164–5; new patterns of 19, 27, 29, 31, 116, 118, 120 ; resistance to 132

Afar pastoralists ; conflict with Issa-Somali 168, 170–71, 174; loss of grazing sites 16, 168, 172; impact of dispossession on 172–5

Africa's Land Rush (Hall et al.) 10, 14

African Development Bank 35, 137, 140–41

AgDevCo 78, 84

Agrica Ltd 78, 88; Business Plan 82, 84, 86

agriculture; commercial/large-scale 9, 11–12, 20, 22, 36, 89, 122, 134, 166; small-scale/subsistence 11, 14, 78, 104–5, 174; *see also* Bagamoyo sugar project, Tanzania; South Omo Valley, Ethiopia: sugar plantations in;

agro-pastoralism 4, 11, 31–2, 118, 122, 166; flood cultivation systems 23, 124, 131, 168; Sukuma 80, 87; *see also under* South Omo Valley, Ethiopia

aid dependency 13, 92

Alemmaya Mulugeta 7, 167

Al-Shabaab 37–8

Anderson, Y 5, 37, 104, 157

Arabian Peninsula 3, 112, 118–19

Asebe Regassa 35, 42

Awash Valley, Ethiopia; conflicts/violence in over land control in 167–9*m*, 173, 176 ; large-scale sugar/cotton estates in 16, 30*b*, 170, 172; impact of expropriation/

infrastructural violence on 171–5; state securitisation of 30*b*, 170–73; *see also* Afar pastoralists

Bagamoyo sugar project, Tanzania 99, 136*m*, 138; delays/lack of accountability around implementation of 30*b*, 134–5, 137, 141–3; disregard for environmental complexity 139–40; disregard for socio-political contestations 135, 140–41; ethanol production 134–5, 137; Memorandum of Understanding 134, 137, 139, 143; lack of monitoring 142–3; outgrower programme 135, 137, 139

Barabaig pastoralists 134–5

Baringo County 10, 103, 146, 174

Baringo County, large-scale geothermal investment in 13, 23–4, 26, 30*b*, 101–2*m*, 103–4; land investment/commodification due to 45, 106–9, 151, 153, 165; Pokot-Turkana conflict over access to 108–9; Silali Development Trust 107–8

basic service delivery 5–6, 8, 11, 15–17, 23, 30*b*, 31, 58, 89, 93, 95, 126, 172

belonging *see* politics of belonging

Benna-Tsemay district 11, 122–3*m*, 124, 129–30, 165; Gisma resettlement village 126, 131; local responses to state-building in 11, 124–6, 128–9&*t*, 130, 132–3

Berbera corridor development 18, 23, 25–6, 110–1*m*, 117-21, 143; economic promise of 114–15,

202

14; impact of large-scale investment on 2, 31, 122
state sovereignty 20, 22, 52, 115, 167–8, 173; subversion 3, 32; inclusion by 21–2, 56, 60, 62, 64
Sulle, E. 84–5, 138
Swedish International Development Cooperation Agency (Sida) 137–8, 140, 142–3

Tanzania 11, 29 ; agricultural policy in 137–8; Dar es Salaam 85, 134–5
Tanzania Zambia Railway Authority (TAZARA) 79*m*, 80; *see also* Bagamoyo sugar project, Tanzania; Kilombero rice development scheme, Tanzania; Southern Agricultural Growth Corridor of Tanzania
taxation/tax collection 16, 126
territorial claims *see* land claims
territorialisation; counter- 174; of identity 26, 73, 116, 144; new forms of 3, 8, 25–6, 57, 167–8, 175; of social relations 171–3; state-driven 13, 19–20, 22; *see also* ethnic territoriality
Timamy, Issa 40–41
traditional knowledge systems 29, 38–9
transformation 8; local reshaping of 35, 42–3, 54; national 3, 5, 13, 16, 122; regional 5, 91, 101, 114; 'top down' 10, 25, 43, 80, 103, 155; *see also* livelihoods: transformation of
transport ; improvements 23; services 6
Tsemay agro-pastoralists 127–9*t*, 130–2; dispossession/displacement of 11, 125–6; monetisation of lifestyles 130–1; state efforts to 'civilise' 124–5, 130; *see also* Benna-Tsemay district
Tsing, A. L. 11–12, 103, 114
Tullow Oil 21, 28, 57–8, 60–64
Turkana County ; Government 16, 21, 28, 58, 93, 95, 99; infrastructural expansion in 93–5; land investment in 45; rise of hyper indigeneity in 58, 60; *see also see also* Kakuma refugee camp, Turkana; Kalobeyei Integrated Socio-Economic Development Programme
Turkana County, farmer-led irrigation schemes in 22–3, 155–6*m*; donor support for 155, 157, 164; Nanyee 161–2, 165; Napak

161–5; Napool 161–5; opportunities for accumulation and 161–5; rehabilitation of old infrastructure 155, 157, 159, 161–2
Turkwell Irrigation Scheme Association (TISA) 155, 157–60; water users associations (WUA) 157–160, 162, 164
Turkana County oil politics 20–21, 27; disputes around access to benefits 30*b*, 55–8, 63–4, 108, 173; 2016 blockade 60–2; monetary compensation 64; rise of community brokerage 28, 63–5; *see also* South Lokichar Basin; subversion: inclusion by
Turkana pastoralists 16, 21–3, 45, 48, 91–2, 95–100, 158 *see also* Samburu pastoralists: conflict with Turkana
Turner, Frederick Jackson 12–13, 103, 109
Twaha, Fahim 40–41

Uganda 17, 24, 93
United Arab Emirates (UAE) 18, 110, 118, 120
United Kingdom ; Department for International Development (DFID) 35, 84
United Nations; Educational, Scientific and Cultural Organisation (UNESCO) 38, 155; Free Prior Informed Consent (FPIC) 56–7; High Commissioner for Refugees (UNHCR) 16, 89, 91–6, 99; Cash for Shelter programme 97–8
urban expansion/development *see* urbanisation
urbanisation 6, 8, 23, 91, 94, 138, 157
USAID 78, 84

Watson, E. 2, 13, 16, 35, 37–8, 103–4, 127
Waweru, P. 49–50
wind power 2, 8, 12, 17, 27, 29; LAPSSET farm 33
Wood Group 35
World Bank 5, 17, 93, 119
World Food Programme ; Bamba Chakula 97–8

Zenawi, Meles 127, 171